The Teaching of Science in Primary Schools

Fourth Edition

Wynne Harlen and Anne Qualter

David Fulton Publishers

This edition reprinted 2006 by Routledge
2 Park Square, Milton Park, Abingdon, Oxon, OX14 4RN
Simultaneously published in the USA and Canada
By Routledge
270 Madison Avenue, New York, NY 10016

First published in Great Britain in 2004 by David Fulton Publishers

10 9 8 7 6 5 4
Reprinted 2005, 2006

British Library Cataloguing in Publication Data
A catalogue record for this book is available from the British Library.

ISBN 1 84312 132 8

Typeset by FiSH Books, London.
Printed and bound in Great Britain

Brief Contents

Contents

3   Assessment

4   Practical work and using ICT

5   Planning and managing primary science

Acknowledgements

We are grateful to the following for permission to reproduce figures from their publications:

- The Association for Science Education for permission to reproduce material from various isues of *Primary Science Review* and from *Primary Science*;

- RoutledgeFalmer for permission to reproduce material from *Coordinating Science across the Primary School* by L.D. Newton and D.P. Newton (1998);

- Paul Chapman Publishing for permission to reproduce materials from *Assessing Science in the Primary Classroom: Written Tasks* by M. Schilling, L. Hargreaves, W. Harlen and T. Russell (1990);

- Stuart Naylor and Brenda Keogh for permission to reproduce a concept cartoon from *Concept Cartoons in Science Education* (2000);

- Taylor & Francis for permission to reproduce material from *Making Progress in Primary Science Handbook* (Second Edition) by W. Harlen, C. Macro, K Reed and M. Schilling (2003);

- Liverpool University Press for permission to reproduce various drawings from SPACE Research Reports on *Growth* (1990), *Sound* (1990), *Processes of Life* (1992) and *Evaporation and Condensation* (1990).

Introduction

Four years is quite a long time in primary science, it seems. Although science now has a well-established place in the primary school curriculum it is far from just 'ticking over'. There have been various changes, both favourable and unfavourable, in recent years, which justify a fresh look at some of the ways we deal with science in practice. This is what is attempted in this new edition of *The Teaching of Science in Primary Schools,* the fourth since the first edition was published in 1992. Since then it has been revised every four years.

This edition differs from the previous one in some important respects: in authorship, in structure and in content. Beginning with authorship, I am extremely pleased that Anne Qualter agreed to join me in revising the book, adding to this edition her considerable experience as a researcher, teacher educator, practitioner and author. Anne and I have worked together on several primary science projects since we first met over twenty years ago, when we were both working for the Assessment of Performance Unit in London. Since then Anne has been involved in several projects relating to the National Curriculum in science, based at the University of Liverpool. She is author of *Differentiated Primary Science* (Open University Press 1996).

In terms of structure, this edition retains the form of short chapters that enable the reader to dip straight into topics of interest at a particular time, helped by cross-referencing between chapters. But in this edition the chapters are organised into five parts to make the book more accessible. Part 1, 'Getting started', brings to the front of the book topics regarded as essential for effective primary science teaching. These include using children's ideas, teachers' and children's questions, the importance of talk and dialogue and adapting activities to increase opportunities for learning. While the practices discussed in this first part are all based on a theory of learning and on research, the supporting arguments and evidence are provided later in the book, to leave the initial focus primarily on classroom events.

The theory of learning underpinning the approach to learning and teaching pervading the book is discussed in Part 2, 'Learning and teaching for understanding'. Here we provide a theoretical model of learning that describes how learners use and develop their existing ideas, constructing more scientific ideas by using evidence. The model highlights the role in this process of the mental skills, which are variously described as enquiry or investigative skills and for which we use the term process skills. The model helps to identify the overall direction of progression in the development of ideas, process skills and scientific attitudes and the teacher's role in helping this progress.

Part 3 comprises seven chapters on the subject of assessment, a topic that has grown in significance in all areas of the curriculum. The major focus in these chapters reflects the recent move away from thinking of assessment only in terms of measuring what has been learned, to identifying its role in helping learning. Thus the emphasis is on formative assessment (or assessment for learning) and the content has been updated to reflect recent developments in ways of putting this into practice in the classroom. This work has served to emphasise in particular the role of children in self-assessment and highlights all that this implies for the teacher. The latter includes clarifying and communicating with children the goals of activities, sharing with them the standards of quality in their work that they should be aiming for and providing constructive feedback during discussion and from marking work. The discussion of summative assessment includes references to research on the negative impact of 'high stakes' testing on children's motivation for learning. Despite the greater attention to process skills in recent national tests in England, there is still a need to question the value of external tests in primary school science.

Part 4 comprises chapters focusing on the provision for practical work in science. This part also includes what is perhaps the fastest changing area in education, the use of information and communications technology (ICT). However, although ICT can give children access to a wider range of evidence than from their first-hand enquiries, we have to remember that direct experience – through which children come to realise that they can find answers to their questions by their own actions – remains paramount in early science education. But ICT can also support primary science in ways other than supplementing and aiding practical experience. The use of interactive whiteboards and the digital camera, for instance, can support discussion and sharing of ideas, which are important in helping children to think through their own ideas and develop understanding that is shared with others.

In the final part, we deal with the important topics of planning at the class and school levels. The role of the subject leader has become better defined and more significant in all subjects in recent years, and science is no exception. The benefits of having nationally agreed programmes of study or guidelines depends on how these general statements are translated into provision for the learning of individuals and groups of children. Collaborative planning, coordinated by the subject leader, is essential for achieving the delicate balance between the flexibility that a teacher must have to meet the needs of individual children and the requirement to ensure coherence and continuity in the school programme.

In conclusion, we have endeavoured in revising the book to preserve those parts of the previous edition that have an enduring relevance and remain useful to teachers today, while adding new information and thinking, particularly about developments in the use of ICT, using assessment to help learning, the organisation of science and the role of science subject leaders in this, planning at the classroom level and the emphasis on creativity in science education. As before, the aim is to increase teachers' understanding of underlying reasons and issues in teaching science. We hope this will add to the pleasure of teaching and of helping children to enjoy investigating and developing understanding of the scientific aspects of the world around them.

Wynne Harlen
2004

Part 1 Getting started

1 Primary science in action

In the first part of this book the five chapters focus on what can be described as the key aspects of effective primary science teaching. These are: using children's own ideas; asking and responding to questions; talk, between teacher and child and between child and child; and providing experiences that promote the development of scientific ideas, process skills and attitudes. In later parts we deal with the theory behind these aspects of activities and with matters related to assessment, with the provision of resources and with planning of activities and programmes. These are not less important but, no matter how much theory one knows and planning one does, primary science will not take off without attention to the topics in this first section.

It is no longer necessary, as was the case 20 years ago, to argue for the value of teaching science in the primary school. It is universally accepted that learning science is important for the future lives of all citizens and because of this it is a required part of primary and secondary education in practically all countries. Science is a major area of human mental and practical activity and the knowledge that it generates plays a vital part in our lives and in the lives of future generations. It is essential that the education of the whole population, not just of future scientists, provides them with a broad understanding of the status and nature of scientific knowledge, how it is created and how dependable it is.

That said, we begin by going straight into the classroom to provide a picture of primary science in action in two classes, one of nine- and ten-year-olds and one of six- and seven-year-olds. These provide some real events, which convey something of what happens when primary children are involved in learning science. We return to these examples at several points later in the book. The discussion of certain features of these mini-case studies, in this chapter, starts an analysis of what is going on, the rationale for including these features and what lies behind them in terms of preparation by the teacher.

Two brief case studies

We begin by looking into two classrooms where science is in progress. These case studies, in Boxes 1.1 and 1.2, were created by observing and talking to real teachers in real classrooms. Thus not everything that happens is exemplary; they are not 'model' lessons to be followed. Indeed, they clearly have features specific to the classes, teachers and contexts involved that make them difficult to transfer to other classrooms. But they also have features that are common to good practice in primary science and they provide us with real examples that help to communicate these features both later in this chapter and in the chapters that follow in this book.

Box 1.1	Graham's class investigating soil

Graham was introducing science activities within an overall topic about growing food to his class of nine- and ten-year-olds. He planned that the children should discuss and investigate the differences between types of soil. He had in mind that the children should undertake some investigations of sandy, loamy and clay soil, so he provided samples of each of these, to which some of the children contributed samples that they brought from gardens at home. He wanted the investigations to advance the children's ideas and therefore to start from their ideas and questions. It would have been easy to ask the children to find out, for example, 'Which soil holds most water?' 'Does water drain more quickly through some soils than through others?' and to start the children's investigations from these questions. These are perfectly good questions for children to investigate and likely to be among those the children ended up investigating, but he wanted to hold back his questions to find out what the children would ask and what ideas they had.

The first part of the work was an exploratory phase of looking at the different soils. In groups, the children were given samples of the three main types, some hand lenses, sieves, disposable gloves and some very open instructions:

■ Separate the different parts that each of the soils contains.

■ Find out what is contained in all the soils.

■ Find out what is different in each soil.

■ Think about how these differences might affect how well plants grow in the soils.

This task required children to use their ideas about soil in making their observations. It encouraged them to look closely at the soil and to think about the differences they found. During this activity the teacher visited each group to listen in to what the children were saying about the types of soil. Many of their statements at this stage contained hypotheses and predictions. The children were quick to say which they thought would be best for plants to grow in (the darkest coloured one) and to identify the ability to hold water as a property that was needed.

There was then a whole-class discussion, pooling findings and ideas from different groups. Graham said that they would test their ideas about which was best for growing plants when they had found out more about the soils and the differences that might make one better than another. What would the plants need to grow? Water was the most popular answer. Some mentioned 'fertiliser' and there was a discussion of what this meant in terms of the soils they had looked at. It was eventually identified with the bits of leaves and decayed plant material they had found, particularly in the loam. Graham introduced the word 'humus' to describe this part of the soil.

No one mentioned the presence of air in the soil until the teacher asked them to think about the difference between soil that was compressed and the same soil in a loose heap. He challenged them to think about whether there was the same amount of air between the particles in each soil and whether this was likely to make a difference to how well plants would grow in it.

The discussion identified four main differences to be investigated: the differences in the amount of water held in the soil; how quickly water drained through each one; the amount of humus in each; and the amount of air. Each of the six groups in which the children were working chose one of these and set about planning how they would go about their investigation. Although having different foci, the investigations of all the groups were relevant to developing understanding of the nature and properties of soil so that, when they did the trial of which enabled plants to grow best, they would be able to explain and not just observe the result.

The investigations provided opportunities to help the children to develop their process skills, in order to carry out systematic and 'fair' tests through which they would arrive at findings useful in developing their ideas. He asked them first to plan what they would do and identify what they would need in terms of equipment. He probed their thinking about what variables to control and what to observe or measure by asking questions such as 'How will you be sure that the difference is only caused by the type of soil? How will you be able to show the difference?' He had ideas, gathered from various sources, about useful approaches, but kept these 'up his sleeve' to be introduced only if the children did not produce ideas of their own. Graham encouraged the children to make notes of what they found as they went along and then use these to prepare a report from each group to the whole class. He told them that they should report what they did and what they found, but also say whether it was what they had expected and try to explain the differences they found.

At the end of the practical work and after a period for bringing their ideas together in their groups, each group in turn presented a report, while other children were given the opportunity to question. Graham refrained from making comments at this stage and asked questions only for clarification. When all the reports had been given he listed the findings for each soil and asked the children to decide which might be best for growing some seedlings. The choice was not as obvious as some children had initially thought, so they were very keen to try this next investigation and find out what really would happen.

Graham then turned to the samples of soil that the children had brought from home. In order to compare them with the three soils they had investigated he suggested mixing some of each with enough water to loosen the parts from each other and allow the constituents to separate as they settled to the bottom. They then used these observations on what they had found about soil to predict which might be 'good growing' soils. These samples were then included in the seedling trials.

Before going on to set up the next investigations, Graham asked the children to reflect on which parts of the work just completed they had enjoyed most, which they would do differently if they could start again and what they now felt they could do better than before.

Box 1.2   Chris's class investigating ice

Chris's class of six- and seven-year-olds were working on a broad topic of changing materials. The children had made a collage using natural materials, they had made cakes and animals out of clay, they had developed appropriate language to describe materials and they had experience of making predictions. They were now moving on to look at ice. Chris wanted the children to explore ice, describe it and, by thinking about how to slow down melting, consider fair testing.

In the morning the children were told that there was something different about their classroom. A notice on the door read 'Penguins in Year 2, take care!' The children were encouraged to creep into the classroom, which was in semi-darkness and rather cool. They found some footprints on the floor, a large 'iceberg' in the middle of the room and two penguins sitting on it. The iceberg was constructed from the polystyrene packing materials around a new television, and some tinsel to make it glisten. Ice cubes were found in crevasses in the iceberg, and around it, along with some small pebbles. The children's imagination was fired and they were full of questions about icebergs, ice and the penguins. It transpired that the two penguins (puppets), Flapjack and Waddle, spent much of their time in the freezer department of the local supermarket but had been banned for leaving footprints in the ice cream. They had arrived with plenty of ice borrowed from the supermarket.

The children were given ice cubes on small dishes to explore and asked to look after them for the morning. The literacy lesson that morning involved the children describing their ice, finding lots of 'icy' words and, after much discussion, writing some sentences about 'what I know about ice'.

The afternoon began with Chris calling the register, including Flapjack and Waddle, and some discussions with the two puppets. Chris asked where penguins come from and what sort of temperatures they are used to. The children knew they came from Antarctica and that this was a very cold place where it was difficult to keep warm. They talked about how people generally preferred warmer climates. The teacher showed the children a big book about penguins. They discussed how flocks of penguins keep warm, huddling together and taking turns to be in the centre of the group. Chris emphasised the fact that this meant that all the penguins had an equal chance of keeping warm, that they made it fair.

Chris reviewed with the children what they know about ice, using their sheets from the literacy session. 'Ice melts in the sun', 'There are cold icebergs', 'Ice can build you a house', 'Ice is frozen water', 'Ice is "see-through"', 'Ice can be dangerous'. One child then told how he had swallowed an ice cube once. In discussion it was established that his warm body had melted the cube, although it had felt very cold and hard going down. Chris asked the children to describe their ice cubes,

Chris: Who rubbed it on their forehead? [Many hands went up] How did it feel?
Hannah: Cold and wet.
Chris: What happened to your ice cube?
Scott: It gone watery.
Lianne: Spread over the dish.
Ryan: Runny.
Paula: Melted.

The penguins confided that, having borrowed the ice from the supermarket, they were keen to find the best place to store their ice so that it would not melt too quickly. Chris brought some more ice from the store cupboard. She had kept it in a freezer bag wrapped in layers of paper. Chris pointed out that the ice that was in the 'iceberg' crevasses had not melted away. She wondered why this was.

John: Maybe the penguins cuddled it under their legs.
Chris: But wouldn't that make it warmer?
Paula: There was not just one block, but a lot of blocks together.

The class found this idea extremely difficult and Chris realised that, apart from Paula, they were not yet ready to consider it. She told Paula that they would come back to this 'brilliant' idea later.

The children decided to put ice cubes in different places in the classroom and see how long they took to melt. Flapjack then selected an ice cube from the tray to test, and Waddle selected a large cube made in an ice cream tub. The children could immediately see that this was not fair. They discussed how to make their test fair.

Back at their tables, each group was given four ice cubes on small dishes and asked to think about where they might put them. The teacher gave them a simple worksheet for planning and recording, as in Figure 1.1

Where it was	Prediction	Result
1.	I think	
2.	I think	
3.	I think	
4.	I think	
I think the ice changed because		

Figure 1.1 What happens to ice?

The children began to discuss where they would place their ice cubes. Some children had asked to put their ice cubes in the freezer, some wanted to put them in the school office (as it always seems cold in there). This caused a good deal of discussion about which was the coldest place, but for their investigation they had to stay in the classroom.

Many found the worksheet a challenge. However, they were seen to be moving around the room, and some held out their hands to test the temperature of different locations. Chris circulated among the groups asking them to explain why they had chosen particular places. She was keen to find out their ideas about why the ice melts. 'Why do you think that might be a good place to keep the ice?' One thing that emerged was that a number of children seemed to believe that sunlight was a factor and that putting ice in the dark (as in the store cupboard or in the cardboard (Peter's) house) would slow down melting. However, when one child suggested wrapping the cube in plastic the other children rejected the idea because that would make it warmer.

The children went out for break and on returning looked at their ice cubes. Chris asked them to think about which was the best place to keep the ice cubes for longest.

At the end of the afternoon the children sat on the floor to discuss their findings with Chris, Flapjack and Waddle. It was agreed that the coolest place in the classroom was on the windowsill. The children thought that the cold wind coming in kept the cubes frozen for longer. Yet the cubes in the iceberg were still there. Paula, having thought about the problem, suggested that 'The polystyrene might have kept it cooler than the cups did.' Again other children struggled, finding this emerging idea of insulation a challenge.

The final part of the lesson considered the problem of how to get ice back for Flapjack and Waddle to take back to the supermarket. The children were asked to think about this overnight as the follow-up lesson would look at making ice from water.

In reviewing her lesson Chris felt that the children had enjoyed the lesson and that they had been able to explore ice and were aware that ice melts at different rates in different temperatures. During the practical activity she had focused her observations on a small number of children who, she felt, might struggle with the investigation. As she discussed the work with the children she found that they had not really grasped the purpose of the activity. They were struggling with the notion of fair testing and had difficulty understanding what was meant by a prediction. Many of the children had trouble completing the worksheet. Although individual questioning revealed that they were able to make and support their predictions, their difficulties were in articulating this in writing. She felt that some children were still at the stage of exploring and describing materials, while others were at a point where they understood the idea of a fair test, could make predictions and could describe and compare the properties of materials. However, most were not able to record their ideas clearly in the table provided. She decided that, in the next lesson, she would focus more on fair testing and on prediction and perhaps find less demanding ways to record findings.

Key features of the case studies

As already noted, these examples are not being held up as good lessons to be copied. Both teachers would no doubt see ways of improving their lessons. Chris, in particular, in reviewing her lesson, identified aspects that needed to be changed. The worksheet, particularly, was not as successful as she had hoped.

However, her reflection on this and recognition of the problem is part of good practice. All we want to do here is to pick out for comment certain features that, despite the differences in the two classes, indicate how the teachers provided opportunities for the children's learning in science. A more detailed list is considered in Chapter 5.

Creating links to the children's experience

The overall goal of primary science is to help children to make sense of the phenomena and events in the world around. So it is important for the children (and not just the teacher) to see that what is being investigated helps in understanding their everyday experiences. Graham made the link to the children's experience by inviting them to bring soil samples from home so that even the samples that Graham provided were seen as 'real'. The 'reality' that Chris provided was through the make-believe iceberg and the toy penguins, but this clearly caught the children's imagination and provided the motivation to take the question they were investigating seriously.

Providing first-hand experience

Both teachers provided not only the materials for first-hand experience but also the time to explore them – to look closely at the soils using hand lenses, to feel the ice in their hands and against their foreheads. Although not all primary science can involve first-hand manipulation of the objects being investigated (think of Earth in space topics and some concerning the human body), where this is possible it helps understanding, since young children need to see, feel and experience for themselves. However, the most important thing is that the children have evidence against which to judge the adequacy of their ideas. Sometimes this evidence comes from secondary sources, but where possible children should collect the evidence through their own action. In Chris's class they did this by seeing where the ice cubes melted more quickly. In Graham's class it was by measuring the amount of water draining through the soils, seeing the difference in growth of seedlings in different soils and so on.

Giving children the opportunity to use their own ideas

Although both teachers had in mind the goals they wanted their children to achieve, they provided opportunities for the children to express their own ideas and to investigate them. In Graham's class the children's ideas about the factors that made one soil better than another for growing plants were the starting point, but he also extended their first ideas so that a more complete set of variables, including air, were investigated. Chris used the literacy lesson to gather some of the children's ideas about ice and encouraged the children to express their ideas about what prevented ice from melting, as well as what made it melt. She challenged John's idea that the penguins cuddling ice might keep it from melting, although she could have asked John to try this to see what happened.

Ensuring the development of process skills

The goals of both teachers included the development of investigative skills, and the investigations provided opportunities for thinking about fair tests. In neither class did the teacher dictate to the children what to do: 'put one ice cube here and another there . . . ' or 'put the same amount of each of the soils and the same amount of water . . . '. Instead, both gave the children the opportunity to decide what to do. This not only gave them some ownership of their investigations, but provided the opportunity for them to use and develop process skills, such as planning a fair test, making a prediction and communicating a result.

For Chris's class the development of these skills was only at the starting point and it was clear that in several cases the children needed more opportunities to develop them. Chris built into her planning the penguins' unfair suggestion to start the children thinking about fair testing. She found that the children were not as sure about what making a prediction meant as she had assumed on the basis of their previous experience of doing this. The difficulties the children had in using the worksheet that she provided led to her realising that communication on paper was more difficult for the children than talking about their ideas. Graham's focus was on helping the children to develop their planning skills and their use of notes during the activity to help in producing a final report. He also encouraged their reflection on how they could have improved their investigations. These differences between the two classes reflected the maturity of the children.

Giving children chance to share experiences and ideas

Children's own ideas (as we see in Chapter 2) result from their thinking and individual experience. Finding out what others think is a key factor in developing more widely shared ideas. Douglas Barnes (1978) calls this 'co-constructing' ideas, helping each other to make sense of things. In simple terms it means 'putting our heads together', which we know so often leads to a better understanding than anyone working things out alone. The importance of talk and discussion is a theme throughout this book and cannot be overemphasised. In both Graham's and Chris's classes groups tried different things, so combining the experiences of different groups was important to get an overall result. Reporting to each other had a definite purpose and whether done formally, with preparation, as in Graham's class or less formally as in Chris's it provided the opportunity for children to combine experience and evidence to reach a shared result and understanding.

Behind the events in both these case studies, there was, of course, a great deal of planning – long-term, medium-term and short-term. The topics fitted in to the long-term plans of each school's programme, devised to ensure progression in development of conceptual understanding and skills and meet the requirement of the national guidelines. In his medium-term planning, Graham worked out how the work on soil fitted into the current term's work and built on what the children had done previously about what was needed for plant growth and how it would lead on to ideas about the formation of soil and how its fertility has to be preserved. In his short-term planning, he worked out what both he and the children would do, considered some of the questions he would pose and prepared himself with information about the ideas children might have and with suggestions for activities from sources such as the *Rocks, Soil and Weather* Teachers' Guide of Nuffield Primary Science. Chris's school was following the published scheme of work (DfES 1998) and her lesson fitted into Unit 2D.

Underpinning all of this planning was a view of the learning that the teachers wanted to promote and of the kinds of activities and interactions most likely to bring this about. The teachers' view of these things helps to answer questions such as why Graham decided to start by making sure that the children looked closely at the soil samples and identified for themselves what kind of things they contained, instead of telling them what soil contains (which would certainly have been quicker and much less trouble to organise). Why did he not demonstrate, for example, how to find out how much air is in a certain amount of soil and then let the children do this, rather than asking them to work it out for themselves? Why did he want them to try to explain their findings rather than just know what happened?

The answers lie in an understanding of the meaning of 'learning science', which in turn depends on a view of learning and a view of science. These are matters that we discuss in Part 2 of this book. At this point it is enough to note that both teachers were committed to the view of learning described as 'constructivist', which takes seriously the ideas that children have already formed about the materials and events being investigated. We look at some children's ideas in Chapter 2. It is also clear that the teachers worked out what questions they would ask in order to access the children's ideas or to encourage them to use process skills. There is more about this in Chapter 3. There was also careful planning to ensure the right contexts and time for children to talk about their investigations and share their results and ideas; points that we take up in Chapter 4. In Chapter 5 we look at the activities again in relation to some criteria for evaluating the opportunities for learning that they provided.

Summary

This initial chapter has provided two short case studies showing primary science in action and an initial analysis of some of their key features. The main points highlighted were:

- The importance of links to children's experience.

- The provision of first-hand experience.

- The opportunities for children to use their own ideas.

- The use and development of process skills.

- The importance of facilitating discussion.

- The detailed planning that is necessary and the way in which this planning is influenced by the teachers' views of what it is to learn science.

All these points are taken further in later chapters.

2 Children's own ideas

Introduction

One of the key themes in this book is that developing children's understanding in science has to start from children's existing ideas. It is appropriate, therefore, that in one of the first chapters we look at children's ideas and begin to consider the implications of taking them into account in teaching. In this chapter we refer briefly to reasons for doing this and then look at some examples of children's ideas. The chapter concludes with a list of characteristics of children's ideas that give clues to helping children to develop more scientific ideas. We pick these up later, in Chapter 9.

The significance of children's ideas

One of the points of difference between the teachers in the vignettes in Chapter 1 was in relation to their use of the ideas that the children had about the materials they were investigating. Graham gave opportunities for the children to explore different soils and then held a discussion pooling ideas and observations. He prompted them to extend their ideas about the differences between the soils so that the variables they investigated were ones they thought to be important. He questioned them about their reasons for thinking one soil might be better than the others for growing the seedlings and what were the important factors that made a difference. Chris, dealing with much younger children, asked mainly questions that children answered by reporting their observations rather than their ideas. So she missed the opportunity to find out what they thought had made the ice melt. When she 'wondered aloud' about why the ice cubes encased in polystyrene had not melted, two ideas were suggested. One of these was not something that could be followed up immediately but she promised to return to it. This acknowledged the value of the idea. The other suggestion was something of a surprise and she did not follow up the child's idea behind it.

Finding out children's ideas – and more importantly being serious about taking them into account in teaching – is a relatively recent aspiration in education, although the background in Box 2.1 acknowledges that this is a development with long roots.

Box 2.1   **Developments in understanding and using children's ideas**

Pioneers of elementary science (for example, Susan Isaacs 1930; Evelyn Lawrence 1960) urged this in the earliest years of the twentieth century but, by and large, most educators woke up to the significance of children's ideas through the work of Piaget (1929, 1955, 1956). It was not until the 1960s that the notion of 'starting from where the child is', and so taking their ideas seriously, became part of the thinking that went into curriculum reform and so into (some) classrooms. Where this happened it was due to pioneering projects such as the *Nuffield Junior Science* project and *Science 5–13* (and the *Elementary Science Study* in the USA and the *African Primary Science Project*). The authors of these early curriculum materials used their observation of and experience with children as the basis for their work, for in the 1960s and 1970s there was no systematic research into students' ideas, beyond that of Piaget and those who replicated his studies.

Systematic research into children's ideas in science began in the late 1970s with work mainly at the secondary level. The main work of this kind at the primary level began with ground-breaking studies in New Zealand in the 1980s (Osborne and Freyberg 1985) and the SPACE (Science Processes and Concepts Exploration) project in the UK (1987–92). The SPACE project studied children's ideas across the full range of the curriculum for children aged five to eleven years.

There are several reasons why we should start, in developing children's scientific ideas, from their initial ideas, rather than just 'telling them the correct ideas'. There are theoretical reasons related to how children learn, which will be explored in Chapter 7. There are also practical reasons: the latter method just does not work. If you insist on children 'learning' the correct idea when they still have their own ideas, they will possibly memorise the correct one, but without really believing it, and will hold on to their own ideas in the way they make sense of real phenomena around them.

The strongest reason of all comes from looking at what the children's ideas are. If we do this it reveals that the ideas are the product of thinking about experience (necessarily limited experience) and are not childish fantasy. The children have reasons for what they think and unless they are helped to have even better reasons for thinking differently and more scientifically, they will retain their own ideas. So this is why we now look at some examples of children's ideas, mostly from the SPACE research.

Some examples of children's ideas

Ideas about growth inside eggs

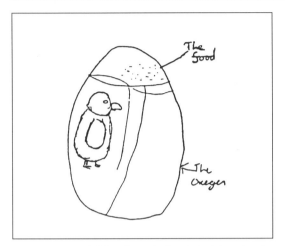

Figure 2.1 A child's idea of what is inside a hen's egg when incubating (from Russell and Watt 1990: 31)

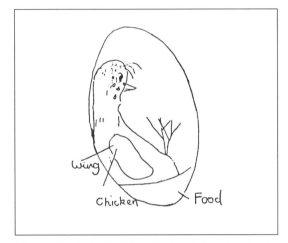

Figure 2.2 A child's idea of what is inside a hen's egg when incubating (from Russell and Watt 1990: 10)

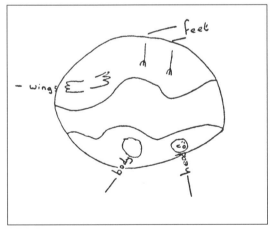

Figure 2.3 A child's idea of what is inside a hen's egg when incubating (from Russell and Watt 1990: 26)

Research in the SPACE project studied the ideas of children about what was happening inside hens' eggs that were being incubated in the classroom. The most popular idea was that there was a miniature but mainly complete animal inside the egg, feeding on what was there. This is evident in the drawings made by the children when asked to depict what they thought was inside an egg while it was incubating. An alternative was that the complete animal was inside simply waiting to hatch. There was also the view that the body parts were complete but needed to come together.

The more scientific view that transformation was going on inside the egg was evident in some children's ideas. It was also clear that the children used knowledge derived from experience of reproduction of pets and observations of human babies when trying to understand what was going on inside the eggs.

Ideas about growth in plants

When asked 'What do you think plants need to help them grow?' infant (Key Stage 1) children generally mentioned one external factor. For example, Figure 2.4 suggests that light is necessary.

Other young children mentioned soil or water or sun, but rarely all three. Characteristically the younger children made no attempt to explain why these conditions were needed or by what mechanism they worked. Junior children, however, made efforts to give explanations, as in Figure 2.5.

Figure 2.4 A young child's idea of what plants need to help them grow (unpublished SPACE research)

Figure 2.5 An older child's idea of what plants need to help them grow (unpublished SPACE research)

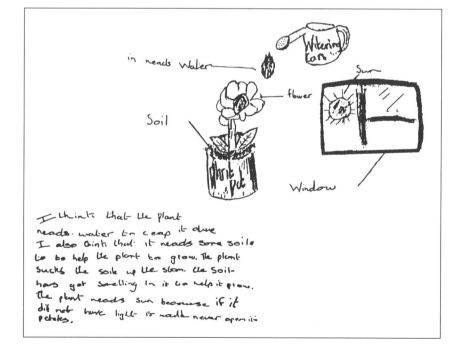

Ideas about how sounds are made and heard

Children's ideas about sound were explored after they had the opportunity to make sound with a variety of instruments. The instance in Figure 2.6 suggests no mechanism for sound being produced by a drum or for it being heard; it is as if being 'very loud' and 'listening hard' are properties that require no explanation.

Figure 2.6 A young child's idea of how a drum makes a sound and how the sound is heard (from Russell and Watt 1990: 36)

The simplest mechanism suggested is that the impact of hitting produces 'sound'. In contrast, Figure 2.7 explains the sound in terms of vibration. But notice that the vibration comes out of the drum through 'the hole'. A very common understanding of children was that sound travelled through air, or at least through holes in solid objects, and not through the solid itself.

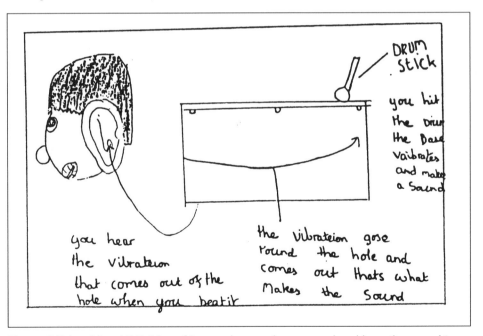

Figure 2.7 An older child's idea of how a drum makes a sound and how the sound is heard (unpublished SPACE research)

The notion of 'vibration' was associated with sound in ambiguous ways, with sound sometimes being the same as vibration and sometimes having some cause and effect relationship to it. Figure 2.8 illustrates this struggle to connect the two.

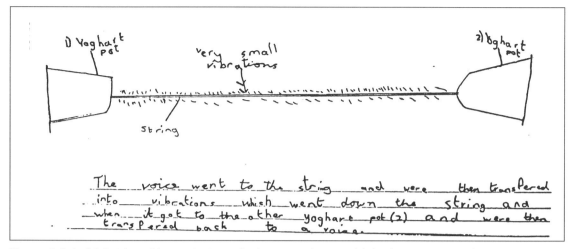

Figure 2.8 A child's idea of how a 'string telephone' works (unpublished SPACE research)

Ideas about forces

Children's ideas about how things are made to move and what makes them stop were explored in various contexts, including the 'cotton reel tank', which is propelled by the energy put into twisting a rubber band. Again the younger children found no need to explain more than 'it works because you're turning it round' and 'it stops because it wants to'. Another six-year-old could see that the pencil (used to twist the rubber band) was important but the idea of why went no further than its presence: 'When we wind it up it goes because of the pencil. When the pencil goes to the tip it stops.' Energy was mentioned in the ideas of older children (Figure 2.9) but the meaning the word was given was not entirely consistent.

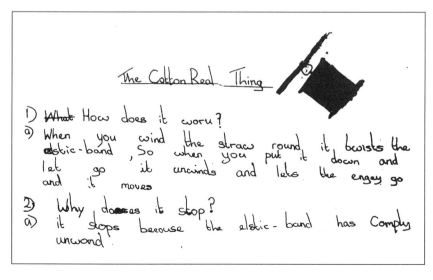

Figure 2.9 A child's idea of how a 'cotton reel tank' works (unpublished SPACE research)

Ideas about solids, liquids and gases

The idea that air is all around, including inside 'empty' containers, was expressed in some way by most junior age children but by a much smaller proportion of five- to seven-year-olds. This statement by an eight-year-old shows a child who has not yet acquired an idea of air as a substance, although its presence is accepted: 'You can't see the air, but sometimes you think there is nothing in there 'cos you can't see anything, but it isn't a matter of seeing, it's a matter of knowing.'

Even young children have relatively little difficulty in identifying something hard, such as steel, as solid, and something watery as a liquid. A five-year-old, after activities with liquids, managed to give a general definition: 'Liquids are all kinds of things that don't stay where you put them. They just run. If you put them on the table it runs along the table.' But where does talcum powder fit? One explanation was:

It's something like a kind of liquid, but it isn't a liquid, it's talcum powder. It goes fast like vinegar and it's not a solid because you can put your finger through it. It's a bit solid, but not like a liquid. A liquid feels wet and this doesn't.'

(Quoted in Russell *et al.* 1991)

Ideas about changes in materials

In relation to changes in materials, too, there is a stage in which there seems to be no need for explanation. Children use their experience of finding rust under bubbles of paint on metal gates or bicycle frames to conclude that rust is already there under the surface of metal. Hence there is no need to explain what causes it to form. For example, an eight-year-old wrote the explanation in Figure 2.10. For other examples of ideas about materials, see Chapter 14, Figures 14.2 and 14.3.

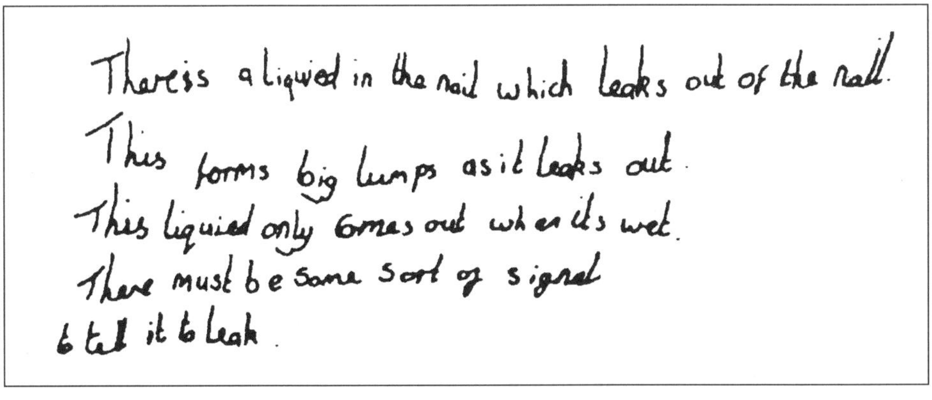

There is a liqued in the nail which leaks out of the nail.
This forms big lumps as it leaks out.
This liquied only comes out when its wet.
There must be some sort of signal
6 tel it to leak.

Figure 2.10 An eight-year-old's idea about rust (from ASE 1998)

Characteristics of children's ideas

It is not difficult to see some reasoning, albeit limited, in these ideas and that they may well make sense to the children themselves. It is precisely because of this that we must take these ideas seriously. If we just ignore them, the children may well hold on to them, since non-scientific explanations often seem more rational to children than the scientific ones. (For instance, it makes more sense to conclude that puddles dry up because water seeps away through the ground than that water particles fly off the surface into the air.)

Looking through these examples, it is evident that the ideas have certain characteristics. In many cases it is easy to see why children might come to hold these ideas. After all, they reflect what the children have experienced and clearly indicate an effort to make sense of their experience. Would anyone know what is inside an incubating egg unless they had seen it? But clearly this doesn't stop children thinking about it and forming their own ideas. Often, however, the ideas seem to result from a limited reasoning that ignores some of the evidence that is available to them. Indeed, there are several general features of the children's ideas, such as those identified in Box 2.2

Box 2.2	Some general characteristics of children's own ideas

- Generally children's ideas *are* based on experience but this is necessarily limited and therefore the evidence is partial. So children may well consider rust to be within metals if they have only noticed it when it appears under paint or flaking chromium plating.

- Children pay attention to what they perceive through their senses rather than the logic that might suggest a different interpretation. So if the sun appears to move around and follow them, then they think it *does* move in this way.

- Younger children particularly focus on one feature as a cause for a particular effect rather than the possibility of several factors. For example, children of six or seven might mention water or light or soil as needed by plants to grow, but not all of these.

- Although it may satisfy them, the reasoning children use may not stand comparison with scientific reasoning. For example, if they were to make genuine predictions based on their ideas, these ideas would be disproved. But instead they may 'predict' what they know to fit their idea.

- They often hold different ideas about the same phenomenon when it is encountered in different contexts. For example, while they may realise that exposure to air helps washing to dry outside, they often consider that puddles on the road dry up only because the water leaks through the ground.

■ Children may use words without a grasp of their meaning. We have seen that this can happen with 'vibration' and 'evaporation' but many more examples could be cited.

■ They may hold on to earlier ideas even though contrary evidence is available because they have no access to an alternative view that makes sense to them. In such cases they may adjust their idea to fit new evidence rather than give it up, as in the examples given later in Chapter 7.

We return to these characteristics in Chapter 9, for they give important clues to how to help children's development of more scientific ideas. When we do so we need to start from their ideas and help them, through scientific reasoning or testing, to change them or replace them with ideas that fit the evidence better than their own.

Summary

This chapter has been concerned with the reasons for taking children's ideas into account in science education. The main points are:

■ The reasons are related to the way we understand children's learning (taken further in Chapter 7), what is found in practice about how to change children's ideas and the characteristics of the ideas.

■ From considering examples of children's ideas we find that they are the product of reasoning, and so make sense to the children. It follows that these ideas have to be taken seriously and addressed in helping children to come to hold more scientific ideas.

■ The characteristics of children's ideas help in indicating how more scientific ideas can be developed (taken further in Chapter 9).

3 Teachers' and children's questions

Introduction

A feature of effective primary science teaching noted in the vignettes in Chapter 1 is the role of the teachers' questions. Changing practice in questioning is one of the most effective ways of improving opportunities for children to develop their understanding. In this chapter we look at the kinds of questions that teachers can ask to encourage children's active enquiry, and at the importance of giving sufficient time for children to answer questions. We also deal with encouraging children to ask questions, since this is an important way of indicating where their understanding has reached. However, when children ask questions, they have to be answered, or at least addressed in some way. This is often a worry to teachers who feel that their knowledge of science is not adequate. So in the final section we look at ways of dealing with children's questions of different kinds.

Teachers' questions

Questioning is frequently mentioned in discussions of the teacher's role and is perhaps the main means of encouraging children's thinking and use of process skills. But what kinds of questions? Teachers ask many questions, but the overwhelming majority are 'closed' and a large proportion of these ask for facts. Occasional questioning of what the children know is expected, but often teachers ask a factual question when they really want children to give their ideas or think things out. The question does not achieve its purpose. The change that is needed is not in the number of questions asked but in their form and content.

The form of questions

In relation to form, the important distinctions are between open and closed questions (Box 3.1) and between person-centred and subject-centred questions (Box 3.2).

Box 3.1	Open and closed questions

Open questions give access to children's views about things, their feelings and their ideas, and promote enquiry by the children. Closed questions, while still inviting thought about the learning task, require the child to respond to ideas or comments of the teacher. For example, the questions

What do you notice about these crystals?
What has happened to your bean since you planted it?

are more likely to lead to answers useful to both teacher and children than their closed versions:

Are all the crystals the same size?
How much has your bean grown since you planted it?

Closed questions suggest that there is a right answer and children may not attempt an answer if they are afraid of being wrong.

Box 3.2	Person-centred and subject-centred questions

A *subject-centred* question asks directly about the subject matter; a *person-centred* question asks for the child's ideas about the subject matter.

Subject-centred questions such as

Why do heavy lorries take longer to stop than lighter ones?
Why did your plant grow more quickly in the cupboard?

cannot be answered unless you know, or at least think you know, the reasons. By contrast, the person-centred versions

Why do you think heavy lorries take longer to stop than lighter ones?
Why do you think you plant grew more quickly when it was in the cupboard?

can be attempted by anyone who has been thinking about these and has some ideas about them, whether or not correct.

When the purpose of the question is to explore children's reasons and the ideas behind them, or to encourage their process-based thinking, person-centred questions are clearly essential. At other times, too, they are a more effective, and a more friendly, way of involving children in discussions that help in making sense of their work.

The content of questions

Elstgeest (2001) distinguished between 'productive' and 'unproductive' teachers' questions. The latter are questions that ask directly for facts or reasons where there is clearly a right answer. The former are far more useful in helping children's investigation and thinking. There are different kinds of productive question, set out in Box 3.3, which serve different purposes in encouraging enquiry.

Box 3.3	Elstgeest's types of productive questions

Attention-focusing questions have the purpose of drawing children's attention to features that might otherwise be missed. 'Have you noticed…?' 'What do you think of that?' These questions are ones that children often supply for themselves and the teacher may have to raise them only if observation is superficial and attention fleeting.

Comparison questions – 'In what ways are these leaves different?' 'What is the same about these two pieces of rock?' – draw attention to patterns and lay the foundation for using keys and categorising objects and events.

Measuring and counting questions – 'How much?' 'How long?' – are particular kinds of comparison questions that take observation into the quantitative sphere.

Action questions – 'What happens if you shine light from a torch on to a worm?' 'What happens when you put an ice cube into warm water?' 'What happens if…?' – are the kinds of question that lead to investigations.

Problem-posing questions give children a challenge and leave them to work out how to meet it. Questions such as 'Can you find a way to make your string telephone sound clearer?' and 'How can you make a coloured shadow?' require children to have experience or knowledge that they can apply in tackling them. Without such knowledge the question may not even make sense to the children.

Questions for different purposes

It is evident from what has just been said that questions should be framed so that their form matches their purpose.

Questions for finding out children's ideas

The following questions were among those designed to be used by teachers to find out children's ideas in the SPACE project. They are the kinds of questions that led to the children's work presented in Chapter 2. These particular questions were used when children had been involved in handling, observing and drawing sprouting and non-sprouting potatoes:

What do you think is coming out of the potato?
What do you think is happening inside the potato?
Why do you think this is happening to the potato?
Do you think the potato plant will go on growing?
Can you think of anything else that this happens to?

(Russell and Watt 1990: A-10)

They can readily be seen to be open, person-centred questions, since there was a need for children to be given every encouragement to express their thoughts at the time before investigations started, so that the teachers would know the children's initial ideas.

Questions for developing ideas

According to the kinds of ideas the children start from, activities to develop them may take various forms, as discussed in Chapter 9. Questions can be used to initiate investigation of children's ideas. For example, questions of the kind 'What evidence would you need to show that your idea works?' 'What would show that ... was better than ... ?' 'What could you do to make it even better?' require children to think through the implications of an idea and extend its application.

When the development of children's ideas seems to require further experience and comparisons between things, then attention-focusing, measuring and counting and comparison questions are the most useful. For applying ideas, the problem-posing questions are appropriate. For discussing the meaning of words, it is best to ask for examples rather than abstract definitions, through questions such as 'Show me what you do to "dissolve" the butter', 'How will you know if the sugar has dissolved?' and other questions discussed in Chapter 4.

Questions for encouraging process skills

Questions can be framed so that children have to use process skills to answer, encouraging process-based thinking and giving the teacher the opportunity to find out how far the skills have been developed. The following examples of questions relating to some of the process skills are set in the context of children investigating a collection of different seeds.

Observing

■ What do you notice that is the same about these seeds?

■ What differences do you notice between seeds of the same kind?

■ Could you tell the difference between them with your eyes closed?

■ What difference do you see when you look at them using the lens?

Predicting

■ What do you think the seeds will grow into?

■ What can we do to them to make them grow faster?

■ What do you think will happen if they have water without soil?

■ What do you think will happen if we give them more (or less) water, light or warmth?

Planning
■ What will you need to do to find out . . . (if the seeds need soil to grow)?

■ How will you make it fair (to be sure that it is the soil and not something else that is making the seeds grow)?

■ What equipment will you need?

■ What will you look for to find out the result?

Interpreting
■ Did you find any connection between . . . (how fast the plant grew and the amount of water, light or warmth it had)?

■ Is there any connection between the size of the seed planted and the size of the plant?

■ What made a difference to how fast the seeds began to grow?

Giving time for answering

Allied to the careful selection and framing of questions to promote thinking and action is the need to allow time for children to answer and to listen to their answers. Questions that ask children to think require time to answer. Teachers often expect an answer too quickly and in doing so deter children from thinking. Research shows that extending the time that a teacher waits for children to answer increases markedly the quality of the answers (Budd-Rowe 1974). This is a case where patience is rewarded and time saved overall by spending a little more in allowing children to think about their answers before turning to someone else, or rephrasing the question. The time given for answering has become known as 'wait time' (see Box 3.4).

Box 3.4	'Wait time'

In 1974 Mary Budd-Rowe published significant research on teachers' questions in elementary science classes in the USA. She reported that teachers waited on average less than one second after asking a question before intervening again if no answer was forthcoming. Teachers tended to rephrase the question or ask a different one that the children could answer more quickly – invariably making the question more closed and fact-related. Research in the UK confirmed that this situation was far from being confined to American classrooms.

Budd-Rowe found that when teachers were advised to increase the 'wait time' after asking questions requiring explanations, the children's answers were longer and more confident. Moreover:

- the failure to answer decreased;

- children challenged, added to or modified each other's answers;

- children offered more alternative explanations.

Recent research with teachers (Black *et al.* 2003) has found that increasing wait time for answering, without feeling the need to 'fill the silence', has led to

more students being involved in question and answer discussions and to an increase in the length of their replies. One particular way to increase participation is to ask students to brainstorm ideas, perhaps in pairs, for two or three minutes before the teacher asks for contributions. This allows the students to voice their ideas, hear other ideas and articulate a considered answer rather than jumping in to utter the first thing that comes into their head in the hope that it is what the teacher is seeking.

(Black *et al.* 2003: 35)

Children's questions

Asking questions is an important means for adults as well as children to try to understand the things around us. When engrossed in the study of something new we use our existing knowledge to make sense of it and try out the ideas we already have to see if they fit. When we find a gap between what we already know and making sense of something new, one way of trying to bridge it is to ask questions. We might do this immediately by asking a question if there is an authority present, as might happen at an exhibition, on a guided tour or in a class or lecture. At other times the question may remain unspoken but guide us to a source of information that is then more efficiently used because we know what ideas or information we are looking for.

Encouraging children's questions

We all, adults and children alike, ask a number of kinds of question as well as those seeking information or ideas. Some questions are rhetorical and some just show interest; neither of these expects an answer. Some questions are asked so as to establish a relationship with someone, or to gain a response; some to attract attention; some even to irritate or harass (as in parliaments). Questions that arise from curiosity and the desire to understand have the main part to play in learning science but it is important not to discourage any questions by implying that only some are worth answering. At the same time, while we recognise the value to children of encouraging the expression of their questions, including the vague and unspoken ones, it is helpful to their learning if they begin to recognise the kinds of questions that can be addressed through scientific activity (see Box 3.5).

Box 3.5	The importance of children raising questions they can investigate

Science is concerned with questions about the 'what, how and why' of objects and relationships in the physical world. The most productive kinds from the point of view of learning science are those that enable children to realise that they can raise questions and answer them for themselves, i.e. investigable questions. These are the questions that keep alive the close interaction between child and environment, between question and answer.

Children who realise that they can find out answers to 'what, how and why' questions by their own interaction with things around have made the best start they can in scientific development. They realise that the answers to 'Why do daisies spread out their leaves?' 'Why do paper tissues have three thin layers rather than one thick one?' 'What happens when you turn a mirror upside down?' are to be found directly from observations and actions on the daisies, the tissues, the mirror.

The importance of stimulating questions means that the classroom should foster the curiosity from which they arise. Here are some ways of doing this:

- provide plenty of interesting materials for children to explore;

- make provision for children to bring materials and objects into the classroom, for these have built-in interest that is likely to be shared by other children;

- set up a 'question corner' or a 'question of the week' activity where there are materials to stimulate enquiry that might be incorporated into class work;

- while introducing new or unusual things to stimulate curiosity, provide familiar materials as well (see Box 3.6);

- encourage children to question as well as to report what they have done and to say what they don't understand;

- more generally, and importantly, regularly extend the invitation 'what question would you like to ask about . . . ' either orally or in writing on work-cards or worksheets;

- resist the temptation, as a teacher, to do all the question raising.

Box 3.6	A stimulating display of familiar things

A display of different tools, nuts and bolts and screws was set up with a 'question box', enabling children to post their questions on small pieces of paper. The apparently sex-biased subject matter produced no bias in the interest and questions when this was put into practice. When the box was opened and each question was considered, girls were as ready as boys to come up with reasons for different sizes and shapes of heads of screws, why screws had threads but nails did not or whether the length of the handle of a screwdriver made any difference. They followed up some suggestions through practical investigations and others were left pinned to the display board awaiting information from an 'expert'. The work added considerably to their experience of materials and their properties, as well as showing that questions were valued.

Handling children's questions

Despite the value to children's learning of encouraging their questions, many teachers are worried about answering children's questions and, perhaps unconsciously, adopt classroom strategies that reduce opportunities for children to ask questions. So if questioning is to be encouraged, being able to handle the questions that children raise has a high priority.

Fortunately, handling questions is a skill that can readily be developed. It requires thought about the kind of question being asked and about the likely motive for asking it, and knowledge of how to turn a question into one that can be a useful starting point for investigation. The word 'handle', rather than 'answer', is used deliberately here. One of the first things to realise – perhaps with some relief – is that it is often better not to answer children's questions directly (even if the teacher does know the answer). But it depends on the question that is asked and so we look now at what is appropriate for different types of question.

Responding to some different types of question that children ask

Most questions children ask in the context of science activities fall into one of five categories, chosen because they group together questions requiring certain kinds of response.

Comments expressed as questions

These are questions that children ask when they are intrigued or excited. The questions don't really need to be answered but there has to be some response that acknowledges the stimulus that gave rise to the question. For example, here is how an infants' teacher handled a question from a six-year-old when she and a group of children were examining a bird's nest:

Child: How do they weave it?
Teacher: They're very clever...
Child: Birds are very clever with their beaks.
Child: Nobody would ever think they were because they're so small.
Teacher: Yes, it's wonderful isn't it? If we turn this right round and let you have a look at this side...

The child's question was used to maintain the close observation of the nest and a sense of wonder. She might have replied 'Look carefully and see if you can tell how it is done?' but perhaps she judged that this was too early a stage in the exploration for focusing on one aspect, and her response leaves open the possibility of returning to the subject in this vein if the children's interest is still there. Another way of putting this is that she judged the question to be a way of expressing wonder rather than a genuine query. The child might just as easily have said 'Look at how it's woven!'

Philosophical questions

This is another category of questions to which the response has to be of the 'yes, isn't it interesting/intriguing' kind, sharing the wondering behind the question. 'Why do we have birds and all different things like that?' is such a question. Taken at face value the only answer is to say that there is no answer. However, we should not read too much into the exact words children use. They often phrase questions as 'why' questions, making them sound philosophical, when the answer they are wanting is much more related to 'what makes it happen' than to 'why does it happen'. When children's questions seem philosophical the initial step is to ask them to explain their question. It may well then turn into a question in a different category, but if not it should be treated as an interesting question but one to which no one can give a definite answer.

Requests for simple facts

These are questions that satisfy the urge to name, to know, to identify. These are questions to which there are simple factual answers, which might help the children to give a context to their experience and their ideas, as, for example, in Box 3.7 about the lives of birds. The teacher may know the answers and if so there is no point in withholding them.

Box 3.7	The lives of birds

The children looking at the bird's nest asked 'Where did it come from?' 'What kind of stuff is this that it's made of?' 'How long do the eggs take to hatch?' In this case the teacher knew where the nest had come from and helped the children to identify the 'stuff' as hair. But for the length of hatching she did not have the knowledge and the conversation ran on as follows:

Teacher: Well, you've asked me a question that I can't answer – how many days it would take – but there's a way that you could find out, do you know how?
Child: Watch it . . .
Child: A bird watcher. . .
Child: A book.
Teacher: Yes, this is something you can look up in a book and when you've found out . . .
Child: [who had rushed to pick up the book by the display of the nest. I've got one here, somewhere.
Child: Here, here's a page about them.
Teacher: There we are . . .

The children were engrossed in the stages of development of a chick inside an egg for some time. The question was answered and more was learned besides. Had the book not been as readily available the teacher could have suggested that either she or the children could look for the information and report back another day.

Requests for names of things fall into this category, as do definitions that arise in questions such as 'Is coal a kind of rock?' While names can be supplied if they are known, undue attention should not be given to them. Often children simply want to know that things do have a name and, knowing this, they are satisfied. If work requires something to be named and no one knows the proper name at that moment then children can be invited to make up a name to use. 'Shiny cracked rock', 'long thin stem with umbrella', 'speedy short brown minibeast' will actually be more useful in talking about things observed in the field than their scientific or common names. Later the 'real' names can be gradually substituted.

Some requests for simple facts cannot be answered. Young children often have a view of their teacher as knowing everything and it is necessary to help them to realise that this is not the case. When the children ask 'Where are the birds now, the ones who built the nest?' they are expecting a simple question to have a simple answer. In this case the teacher judged that the kind of answer they wanted was 'They've probably made their home in another shed, but I really don't know for sure', rather than an account of all the possibilities, including migration and whether or not birds tend to stay in the same neighbourhood. A straight 'I don't know' answer helps children to realise the kinds of questions that cannot have answers, as well as that their teacher is a human and not a superhuman being.

Questions requiring complex answers

Apart from brief requests for facts, most questions children ask can be answered on a variety of levels of complexity. Take 'Why is the sky blue?', for example. There are many levels of 'explanation', from those based on the scattering of light of different wavelength to those relating to the absence of clouds. Questions such as 'Why is soil brown?' 'Why do some birds build nests in trees and others on the ground?' 'How do aeroplanes stay up in the air?' fall into this category.

They seem the most difficult for teachers to answer. The difficulty lies in the fact that many teachers do not know the answers and those who do will realise that children could not understand them. There is no need to be concerned, whichever group you fall into, because the worst thing to do in either case is to attempt to answer these questions!

It is sometimes more difficult for the teacher who does know the scientific explanation to resist the temptation to give it than to persuade the teacher who does not know not to feel guilty about not being able to answer. Giving complex answers to children who cannot understand them is underlining for them that science is a subject of facts to memorise that you don't expect to understand. If their questions are repeatedly met by answers that they do not understand the children will cease to ask questions. This would be damaging, for these questions particularly drive their learning.

So what can be done instead of answering them? A good answer is given by Sheila Jelly in Box 3.8

Box 3.8	'Turning' complex questions to find related investigable ones

The teaching skill involved is the ability to 'turn' the questions. Consider, for example, a situation in which children are exploring the properties of fabrics. They have dropped water on different types and become fascinated by the fact that water stays 'like a little ball' on felt. They tilt the felt, rolling the ball around, and someone asks 'Why is it like a ball?' How might the question be turned by applying the 'doing more to understand' approach? We need to analyse the situation quickly and use what I call a 'variables scan'. The explanation must relate to something 'going on' between the water and the felt surface causing the ball. That being so, ideas for children's activities will come if we consider ways in which the situation could be varied to understand better the making of the ball. We could explore surfaces, keeping the drop the same, and explore drops, keeping the surface the same. These thoughts can prompt others that bring ideas nearer to what children might do.

(Sheila Jelly 2001: 44, 45)

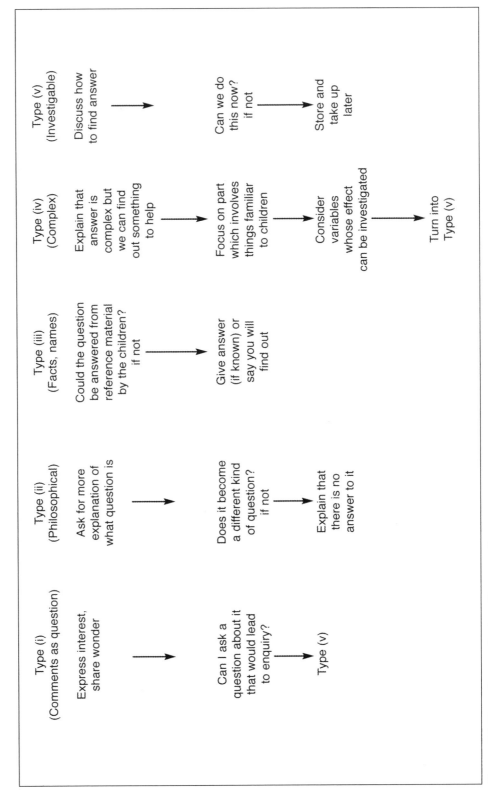

Figure 3.1 Flow diagram for handling questions

Turning questions in this way enables teachers to treat difficult questions seriously but without providing answers beyond children's understanding. It also indicates to children that they can go a long way to finding answers through their own investigation, thus underlining the implicit messages about the nature of scientific activity and their ability to answer questions by enquiry.

Questions that can lead to investigation by children

Teachers looking for opportunities for children to explore and investigate will find these are the easiest questions to deal with. The main problems are resisting the urge to give the answer because it may seem so evident (to the teacher but not the child) and storing questions that pop up at an inconvenient time.

Questions that can be profitably investigated by children will come up at various times, often times that are inconvenient for embarking on investigations. Although they cannot be taken up at that moment, the questions should be discussed enough to turn them into investigations and then, depending on the age of the children, picked up some time later. Some kind of note has to be made and this can usefully be kept publicly as a list of 'things to investigate' on the classroom wall, or just kept privately by the teacher. For younger children the time delay in taking up the investigations has to be kept short – a matter of days – but the investigations are also likely to be short and so can be fitted into a programme more easily. Older children can retain interest over a longer period – a week or two – during which the required time and materials can be built into the planned programme.

The five categories of questions and ways of handling them are summarised in Figure 3.1.

Summary

This chapter has concerned issues relating to questions: questions asked by teachers, ways of encouraging children's questions and ways of handling the questions that children ask. The main points have been:

- The form and content of questions should match their purpose and the kind of response that the teacher is seeking from the child (attention, action, problem-solving etc.).

- Teachers should ensure that enough time is given for children to think about their answers to questions.

- Children's questions are valuable for a number of reasons: they show the gaps that the children feel they need to fill in their understanding; they can provide the basis for children's investigations; and they give children the opportunity to realise that they can find things out for themselves and satisfy their curiosity.

■ Teachers can encourage children to raise questions by providing interesting and thought-provoking materials in the classroom, mechanisms for inviting questions, such as a question box, and an atmosphere that welcomes and does not deter questioning.

■ Children will ask all kinds of questions and not just those that can lead to investigations. In order not to deter questioning, teachers need to be able to handle these different kinds. Some suggestions for how to do this have been given.

4 Talking, listening and using words

Introduction

The spoken word clearly has a central role in children's learning. In this chapter we focus particularly on the talk of children in the classroom and its value in developing their understanding in science. In the first section we consider the role of talk in helping the development of ideas through reflection and in communicating ideas and reporting activities to others. We provide examples to illustrate how teachers can facilitate reflection and productive discussion. In the final section we look at the issues relating to the use of scientific words and address the questions of when and how correct scientific words should be introduced.

The roles of talk in learning

It is useful to draw a distinction, following the ideas of Douglas Barnes, between speech as communication and speech as reflection. Throughout this book there are many references to the value of children discussing with each other, exchanging ideas and developing their own views through the act of trying to express them and explain them to others. This involves both communication and reflection. The reflective part is sorting out their own ideas aloud, indeed 'thinking aloud'. The communication is sharing with others, and involves listening as well as presenting in a way that is coherent and understandable by others. Barnes claims that both are needed and that it does not serve learning to focus only on the more formal communication, since 'if a teacher is too concerned for neat, well-shaped utterances from pupils this may discourage the thinking aloud' (Barnes 1976: 28).

Speech as reflection

We have all probably had an experience where talking to someone has resulted in developing our own understanding, although apparently nothing was taken from the other person in terms of ideas. The effect is even more striking when you are the one against whom ideas are 'bounced' and are thanked for helping in sorting out ideas when all you have done is listen and perhaps question in a neutral manner. The presence of one or more other people is essential in these cases, not only to legitimate thinking aloud but to offer the occasional comment or question for clarification, which has the effect of provoking reflection on what we think as we express it.

The same things happen with children discussing in groups, though often less tidily, since the reflection is going on in several minds at the same time. Box 4.1 provides an example of interaction in a classroom, involving the teacher acting as one of the group rather than as an authority figure.

Box 4.1	Group discussion including the teacher

Deidre and Allyson were investigating the way in which three whole hens' eggs, labelled A, B and C, behaved in tap water and in salty water. They knew that one was hard-boiled, one soft-boiled and one raw. They had to find out which was which.

This is how the eggs landed up just after being placed in the salty water. The transcript begins with the teacher approaching them after they had been working alone for some time.

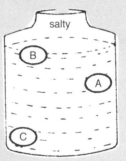

Deidre: . . . hard-boiled.
Allyson: I know.
Teacher: [*coming up to them*] Can you tell me how you're getting on?
Deidre: I think that C is raw.
Allyson: We both think that C is raw.
Teacher: Do you?
Deidre: B is . . .
Teacher: [(*to Allyson*] Why do you think that?
Allyson: Because when you put eggs in water bad ones rise to the top.
Deidre: [*at the same time*] Because it . . . we put them all in . . .
Teacher: Bad?
Allyson: Yes, I think so – or it is the good ones? Well, I don't know.
Teacher: Yes?
Allyson: . . . they rose to the top, so . . .
[*Deidre is putting the eggs into the salty water*]
Deidre: . . . that's the bottom [*pointing to C*].
Allyson: . . . if it's raw it should stay at the bottom.
Teacher: I see.
Deidre: So that's what we think, C is raw and B is medium and A is hard-boiled.

[*Allyson starts speaking before she finishes*]

Allyson: . . . and I think that B is hard-boiled and she thinks that B is medium.

Teacher: Ah, I see. [*to Deidre*] Can you explain, then, why you think that?

Deidre: If we put . . . er . . . take C out, [*takes C out, puts it on the table, then lifts A and B out*] and put these in, one after the other. Put A in – no, B first. That's what . . . Allyson thinks is hard-boiled, I think it's medium. If you put that in . . . [*she puts B into the salty water*]

Allyson: . . . 'cos it comes up quicker.

Deidre: It comes up quick. And if you put that in . . .

[*She puts A into the salty water. It goes to the bottom and rises very slowly*].

Allyson: And that one comes up slower.

Deidre: So, I think that one [*pointing to A*] is hard-boiled because it's . . . well . . .

Allyson: I don't. I think if we work on the principle of that one [*pointing to B*]. Then that one comes up quicker because it's, you know, not really boiled. It's like a bit raw.

Teacher: A little bit raw.

Allyson: So, therefore, it'll come up quicker.

Deidre: Yes, but it's not bad.

Teacher: What'll it be like inside?

Allyson: Runny.

Teacher: It'll be runny still, I see.

Having agreed that C is the raw egg, Deidre and Allyson disagree about the identity of the other two eggs. Allyson has a reason for considering B is hard-boiled on the basis that 'bad ones rise to the top', so she considers that B behaves as if it had had something done to it. But she does not articulate the consequences of this until Deidre attempts to give her reason. Then it is as if Deidre's reason, which she interrupts, sparks off her own thinking.

Although they respond to the teacher's request for an explanation what they do is to continue their interaction and struggle to work out their own reasoning. Deidre's response in particular is hesitant and disjointed, not at all like a straight answer to the question. Barnes call this 'exploratory talk' and he argues that

it is very important whenever we want the learner to take an active part in learning, and to bring what he learns into interaction with that view of the world on which his actions are based. That is, such exploratory talk is one means by which the assimilation and accommodation of new knowledge to the old is carried out.

(Barnes 1976: 28)

We can see from this interchange about the eggs how the girls use evidence to check their ideas. This comes through most clearly in Allyson's 'if we work on the principle that . . .', where she relates what she predicts on the basis of her judgement to the observation of how quickly the egg floats up in the salty water, but it also occurs throughout. It is worth noting in passing that the origin of her idea is previous knowledge about how to distinguish good from bad eggs.

It is difficult to deny that Deidre and Allyson learn from this experience and from their discussion of it. But this does not always happen. For instance, in Box 4.2, we see how June and David, in the absence of the teacher, seem to regard the task as one where giving an answer is more important than having a reason for the answer. June, particularly, seems keen to move to early closure.

Box 4.2	Group discussion in the absence of the teacher

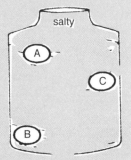

David: Look at that one, this one, look, June.
June: That one's the one that's not boiled.
David: How do you know?
June: Oh, I'm not stupid.
David: Shall I put them in there, or in there? [*On the table or in the container where they were first*]
June: Put them in there.
[*David puts the one he took out in the container and June brings out the other two eggs*]
June: There's B . . . [*as she passes them to David who places them carefully*] Now put them in the salty water.
[*David picks up A and puts it in the jar of salty water*]
David: A floats. A.
June: B [*She puts B in. It sinks*] Sinks.
David: C.
[*He puts it in the salty water. It goes to the bottom and slowly begins to rise again.*]
June: Sinks.
David: Yeah, look . . . no, it doesn't.
June: No . . . that one [*She points to C. Pauses, uncertain for a moment*] No, how are we going to tell . . .
David: That one's . . .
June: Hard-boiled. The one at the bottom's hard-boiled. Put C hard-boiled. [*She instructs David to write. But it isn't C that is at the bottom.*]

Even here there are signs that they are close to becoming more involved. David's 'How do you know?' could have sparked June into explaining her ideas, had she been less defensive. Later on, when an egg that she declares 'sinks' begins to float upwards, there is questioning in the air. The potential seems to be there. The question is then how this potential can be exploited; how, more generally, can we encourage interchanges which involve reflective thinking?

The quality of the discussion – and therefore the quality of the learning – is not determined solely by the ability of the pupils. The nature of the task, their familiarity with the subject matter, their confidence in themselves, their sense of what is expected of them, all these affect the quality of the discussion, and these are all open to influence by the teacher.

(Barnes 1976: 71)

The teacher's role

The role taken by Deidre and Allyson's teacher gives several clues to positive encouragement of reflective thinking:

- joining in as part of the group, without dominating the discussion;

- listening to the children's answers and encouraging them to go on ('I see', 'Yes?');

- asking the children to explain their thinking;

- probing to clarify meaning ('What'll it be like inside?').

Not all aspects of the teacher's role can be illustrated in one short interchange and indeed much of the role involves setting a context and creating a classroom climate that encourages exploratory thinking and talk. Important in this respect are:

- expecting children to explain things, which involves valuing their ideas even if they are unformed and highly conjectural;

- avoiding giving an impression that only the 'right' answer is acceptable and that children should be making a guess at it;

- judging the time to intervene and the time when it is better to allow a children-only discussion to proceed.

The presence of the teacher changes a discussion quite dramatically, for it is difficult for him or her not to be seen as an authority (see also Chapter 14, page 148). Left alone, children are thrown on to their own thinking and use of evidence. But, as we see with June and David, the absence of a teacher does not always lead to productive interchange and it is not difficult to imagine how a question from a teacher could have supported the move towards enquiry that David seemed to be making. The teacher needs to monitor group discussions, listening in without intervening, before deciding whether 'thinking aloud' is going on usefully or whether it needs to be encouraged.

Speech as communication

This is the more formal side of using talk, where shared conventions and expectations have to be observed if others are to be able to make sense of what is said. It is part of socialisation to be able to tell others in a way comprehensible to them about what has been done or thought, and to be able to listen to others, attending not only to the words but also to the implicit messages conveyed by tone of voice and manner. Giving attention in this way is not an automatic response of children, as teachers know all too well; it is a behaviour that has to be taught. Box 4.3 sets out some ways in which the teacher can provide the classroom climate in which children have the opportunity to report orally to others in a setting where they know that others will be listening and where they have to convey their information clearly.

Box 4.3	Creating an atmosphere for productive oral reporting

- Providing guidelines for preparing presentations and a structure for ensuring that each report can be heard and given attention.

- Giving an example, in the teacher's own response, of showing interest, asking questions for clarification, making positive comments etc.

- Making use of children's ideas in comments, thus encouraging children to do the same ('That's an interesting idea you have about...' 'Tell us how you think it explains...').

- Encouraging children to respond to each other and not just to make statements of their own ideas.

- Listening attentively and expecting the children to do so.

- Setting up expectations that children will put effort into their presentations to each other and try to make them interesting, and giving time for and help in preparation with this in mind.

These things have to become part of the general way of working, since expectations that children will respond to what their classmates say are set by the pattern of previous lessons, as well as by the response on a particular occasion. Then the telling and listening can have a role in the development of children's ideas, as well as in their communication skills. It means that they go back over their activities and make sense of them for themselves so that they can make sense of them for others.

Organising class and group discussions

In setting up discussion the (perhaps obvious) point is to ensure the attention of all involved. For a whole-class discussion the location of the children is significant in avoiding distractions. Occasionally it may be necessary to hold a brief discussion during the course of practical activities, for the purpose of bringing together observations that have been made, reporting progress or sharing information that will help everyone (including instructions about safety if unexpected hazards have arisen). On these occasions it may be advisable to move the children away from the materials they are working on in order to ensure their attention. The discussion will only last a few minutes and it will be no hardship for the children if they are cramped in a small space for this time. It is intended to help them with their work when they return to it, otherwise there is no justification for the interruption.

Apart from these infrequent interruptions, whole-class discussion will be at the beginning and end of the group work, with group discussion in between.

Whole-class discussion at the start of a lesson

The initial discussion is the key to setting up group work that is sufficiently clear and motivating to ensure that children begin work promptly and with enthusiasm. Whether the purpose is for children to continue work already begun or to start on a fresh activity the essential function of the initial discussion is to ensure that children know what they have to do, what the goals of the work are (see Chapter 17) and what role is expected of them.

Group discussion during the lesson

Group discussions will often be part of practical work; children should be encouraged to talk freely among themselves. The presence of materials and equipment gives them the opportunity to use evidence to support their points and claims (as Deidre and Allyson did). The noise that this inevitably generates is part of the working atmosphere. If the noise level becomes unacceptable it should be possible to spot the reason:

- too much excitement about certain activities;

- children waiting for equipment and not 'on task';

- 'messing about'.

Once diagnosed, appropriate action can be taken; for example, by diluting the excitement by staggering work on certain activities, organising equipment for easier access, checking the match between the demand of an activity and the children's readiness to respond.

When the teacher is involved in a group's discussion the purpose may be to monitor progress, to encourage exchange of views, to offer suggestions, to assess. Since it is almost impossible for teachers to 'hover' without their presence affecting the children, it is best to make clear what is intended. 'I'm not going to interrupt; just carry on' or 'Tell me what you've been doing up to now'. During a teacher-led group discussion, the teacher should show an example of how to listen and make sure that everyone has a chance to speak. The group might also be left with the expectation that they should continue to discuss: 'Try that idea, then, and see if you can put together some more suggestions.'

Whole-class discussion at the end of the lesson

Holding a whole-class discussion at the end of a practical session, whether or not the work is completed, should be the normal practice. The reasons for this strong recommendation have been well articulated by Barnes (see Box 4.4).

Box 4.4	The value of discussing activities that have been completed

Barnes points out that learning from group activities:

may never progress beyond manual skills accompanied by slippery intuitions, unless the learners themselves have an opportunity to go back over such experiences and represent them to themselves. There seems every reason for group practical work in science, for example, normally to be followed by discussion of the implications of what has been done and observed, since without this what has been half understood may soon slip away.

(Barnes 1976: 30–1)

The teacher should warn the children in good time for them to bring their activity to a stage where equipment can be put away and to allow five or ten minutes for reviewing and reporting ongoing work. At the end of the activities on a particular topic a longer time for whole-class discussion should be organised, with children given time beforehand to prepare to report, perhaps with a demonstration, to others.

Introducing scientific words

The importance of introducing children to scientific vocabulary is made clear in curriculum requirements and guidelines. For example, the National Curriculum (DfEE 1999) states that, at Key Stage 1, pupils should be taught to 'use simple scientific language to communicate ideas and to name and describe living things, materials, phenomena and processes'. At Key Stage 2, the requirement is to 'use appropriate scientific languages and terms, including SI units of measurement, to communicate ideas and explain the behaviour of living things, materials, phenomena and processes'.

Teachers have to decide the answers to the difficult question of when and how new words should be introduced. Should they use the correct word from the moment an idea is involved in an activity and insist on children also using it? Or should they allow children to 'pick up' words as they go along? We know that children pick up and use scientific words quite readily; they often enjoy collecting them and trying them out as if they were new possessions. At first one of these words may have rather a 'loose fit' to the idea it is intended to convey. Does it matter if children use scientific words without knowing their full meaning?

Before we try to answer some of these questions, it will be useful to reflect on the notion of the 'full meaning' of scientific words.

Different levels of meaning

Most scientific words (such as evaporation, dissolving, power, reflection) label concepts that can be understood at varying levels of complexity. A scientist understands energy in a far broader and more abstract way than the 'person in the street'. Even the apparently simple idea of 'melting' is one that can be grasped in different degrees of complexity: a change that happens to certain substances when they are heated or an increase in the energy of molecules to a point that overcomes the binding forces between them. This means that the word melting may evoke quite a different set of ideas and events for one person and for another. Now, to use the word 'melting' in a restricted sense is not 'wrong' and we do not insist that it is only used when its full meaning is implied. Indeed, the restricted meaning is an essential step to greater elaboration of the concept. Therefore, we should accept children's 'loose' use of words as a starting point for the development of a more refined and scientific understanding of the word.

For example, take the child's writing in Figure 2.8 (page 19), where, in describing how the sound is transmitted in a yoghurt pot string telephone, he explains how vibrations go down the string. The word 'vibration' is certainly used here in a manner that suggests that the child understands sound as vibration, until we notice that he writes that the voice is 'transferred into vibrations' at one end and 'transferred back to a voice' at the other. It seems that the sound we hear is not understood as vibration, but only its transmission along the string. It may be that ideas both of sound and of vibration have to be extended, so that vibration is something that can take place in air and occur wherever sound occurs, which will take time and wider experience, but he has made a start. And he is not wrong in using 'vibration' in the way he has done.

When to introduce new words

Teachers seem to be caught between, on the one hand, giving new words too soon (and so encouraging a verbal facility that conceals misunderstanding) and, on the other, withholding a means of adding precision to thinking and communication (and perhaps letting children continue to make use of words that are less than helpful).

The value of introducing the correct word at a particular time will depend on whether

■ the child has had experience of the event or phenomenon that it covers;

■ the word is needed at that time;

■ the word is going to help the child to link related things to each other (since words often give clues to these links).

In other words, *if a word will fill a gap, a clear need to describe something that has been experienced and is real to the children, then the time is right to introduce it.* With young children one of the conditions for the 'right time' is the physical presence or signs of the phenomenon to which the word refers. Only then can we hope to fit the word to an idea, even loosely.

How to introduce new words

The above argument suggests that until the moment for introducing the word is right, the teacher should use the language adopted by the children in discussing their experiences. Then, once the word is introduced the teacher should take care to use it correctly. For example, if children have been exploring vibrations in a string, a drum skin and a tissue paper against a comb, and want to talk about what is happening to all these things, it may well be useful to say 'What all these are doing is called "vibrating".' Before this the children and teacher may have called it by descriptive names: trembling, jumping, moving, going up and down etc. A useful way of ensuring that the new word and the children's words are connected to the same thing, suggested by Feasey (1999), is to use them together ('the thing that's trembling or vibrating') until the new becomes as familiar as the old.

Much more experience of a concept has to follow so that the word becomes attached to the characteristic or property rather than to the actual things present when it was first encountered. But there is no short cut through verbal definitions in abstract terms.

Words describing process skills

It is not only 'concept' words that children need to learn to use correctly. Edmonds (2002: 5) makes the point, in the context of teaching children for whom English is an alternative language, that: 'Children are unsure what is required of them when they are asked to predict, hypothesise or interpret.' This is applicable to all children, however, as are the suggestions she makes (see Box 4.5) for alternatives to giving verbal definitions of processes.

Box 4.5	Suggestions for conveying the meaning of processes

Some of the most effective strategies appear to be:

■ Teacher modelling the procedures with a group or the whole class; demonstrating the whole procedures of planning parts or the whole of an investigation.

■ Providing examples of the kind of procedures the teacher has asked for.

■ Identifying and sharing clear criteria for what the procedure would look like if completed successfully.

■ Looking through pieces of other children's work where they have carried out the procedure or skill and making a running commentary on what the child has done.

■ Detailed feedback and discussion on the child's work.

(Edmonds 2002: 5)

Summary

This chapter has been about oral communication in the classroom. The main points are:

■ Talking has an important function in helping the speaker to sort out his or her ideas, as well as for communicating ideas to others.

■ Teachers can encourage children to reflect on their ideas in groups by giving themselves a low-key role in which they encourage explanations and probe for clarity of meaning.

■ More formal reporting requires a classroom climate in which children listen and respond positively to each other and make an effort to communicate effectively.

■ In general there should be whole-class discussions at the beginning and end of activities aimed at clarifying goals, increasing emerging understanding and the development of enquiry skills.

■ Scientific words for processes as well as concepts are best introduced when the children have experienced the event or phenomenon that they represent.

5 Experiences that promote learning in science

Introduction

The key experiences that promote learning in science are interaction with materials, talk and thought. Interaction with materials provides an opportunity for children to investigate, act upon and observe the scientific aspects of things around them. Talk enables interaction with other pupils and with the teacher. Thought is needed for making sense of these interactions and of information from sources such as books, posters, the media, the Internet, CD-ROMs and other adults. We have discussed the role of talk in Chapter 4 and we look at thinking in Chapter 7, so our focus here is on the interaction with materials and the teacher's role in making this a learning experience.

Since much of the rest of this book is concerned with looking at different aspects of these interactions between child, materials and teacher, what we attempt here is an overview. Throughout there are numerous links to other chapters, where further discussion can be found. We begin with consideration of the key features of experiences that provide genuine opportunities for learning. We illustrate how these can be used as criteria to evaluate activities and to decide how to adapt or elaborate activities to increase their value for learning. Some implications of doing this are discussed and the role of careful planning in providing opportunities for learning is exemplified with reference to the case study in Box 1.1 in Chapter 1.

What kinds of experience promote learning in science?

Knowledge and understanding cannot be passed to children directly. Children do not come to know 'that light passes through some materials and not others, and that when it does not, shadows may be formed' simply by being told this and asked to memorise it. While we deal with learning more thoroughly in Chapter 7, providing theory to support what we know in practice, there is general agreement that to *engage* children in activities, these need to be:

1 Interesting.

2 Linked to their experience.

3 Accessible to all.

But to ensure that activities are opportunities to be engaged in *learning* in science there are other points to add. The activities should enable children:

4 To interact with materials.

5 To develop their scientific ideas.

6 To develop investigative (process) skills.

7 To develop scientific attitudes.

8 To work cooperatively and share ideas in a supportive classroom climate.

We next look at each of these in a little more detail. We then give an example of how they can be used as criteria to evaluate and adapt activities from curriculum materials, or to develop the broad suggestions for activities in the DfEE (1998) scheme of work.

1 *Interesting.* This must be considered in relation to all the children, both boys and girls, and those of different social and ethnic backgrounds. Interest is not always spontaneous and can be encouraged by, for instance, displaying materials in the class prior to a new topic, with questions to stimulate curiosity.

2 *Linked to experience.* For activities to be meaningful and engaging, they should be helping children to understand and find out more about the things that they have encountered directly or indirectly. It should be possible for children to make a link between new experience and previous experience. There can be a dilemma here in relation to whether science activities should be taken from real-life events – often complex and with several ideas involved – or whether they should be 'tidied up' to demonstrate certain relationships or principles. Some degree of extraction from real events is generally necessary, but it should always be possible to see a link between what is learned and real events.

3 *Accessible to all.* This refers not only to the initial interests of different children, already referred to, but also to the provision for children to interact in different ways during the activity. This may mean giving more help, for instance, by explaining words (not just scientific words, but everyday ones used with special meaning in science) to children with special educational needs, or making specific provision for children with more severe learning difficulties.

4 *Interaction with materials.* Although children will learn from secondary sources – books, films, television etc. – the essential understanding of what science is comes from participating in direct investigations with materials (see Box 5.1).

5 *Developing scientific ideas.* This is a central purpose of science education, so the content of activities should involve relevant scientific concepts. Even when

the main aim of an activity is the development of process skills, it can scarcely be described as a 'science activity' unless the process skills are used in relation to content that involves scientific ideas (see Chapter 10).

6 *Use of process skills.* These skills are sometimes referred to as 'investigative' or enquiry skills; here we use the term process skills, since they are involved in the processes of interacting with materials and in the 'processing' of information so gained. Using process skills is central to reasoning and to the development of understanding, and so they should be used in all science activities (see Chapter 7).

7 *Scientific attitudes.* There is a distinction between attitudes towards science and the attitudes that are part of engaging in scientific activity. We are concerned with the latter here, meaning willingness to act in certain ways that promote scientific understanding. These are attitudes such as open-mindedness, willingness to consider evidence and flexibility in taking new evidence into account (see Chapters 6 and 8).

8 *Cooperation and sharing ideas.* The process of learning science involves a development and change in the ideas that individuals hold towards ideas that are more widely shared because they explain a range of phenomena. But sharing and changing ideas can be risky and it is important for teachers to take steps to avoid a classroom atmosphere that would inhibit children from airing and sharing ideas. For example, it is important for teachers to show genuine interest in what the children think, by phrasing questions carefully and allowing time for children to give considered answers (see Chapters 3 and 15 for further discussion).

Box 5.1   Science education begins...

Science education begins for children when they realize that they can find things out for themselves by their own actions: by sifting through a handful of sand, by blowing bubbles, by putting salt in water, by comparing different materials, by regular observation of the moon and stars.

(Harlen 2001: 4)

Using criteria for evaluating and adapting activities

Evaluating activities

From these arguments we can identify criteria that need to be met if activities are to provide real opportunities for learning. A useful approach is to turn the eight points we have discussed into questions to apply to activities. To illustrate, in Box 5.2 we take the lessons that Graham carried out with soil.

Box 5.2	Applying criteria for evaluating activities to Graham's lessons

Were the activities of interest to the children?
Interest was created by the prospect of growing seedlings and using samples from their own gardens.

Were they linked to their experience?
They had experience of seeing plants growing. This might have been provided by a visit to a garden or farm if necessary.

Were they accessible to all?
The activities allowed for a range of different kinds of interaction with the materials. Some children with learning difficulties may have only gone as far as to feel, smell and look at the soils to appreciate their differences.

Could the children interact with materials?
They did this in several ways: through free exploration and more controlled investigation of specific questions.

Could they develop their scientific ideas?
Ideas about important differences between soils were developed, e.g. their ideas advanced from the initial one that dark soils were more fertile.

Could they develop investigative (process) skills?
There were many opportunities to use and develop observational, planning, interpretation and communication skills.

Could they develop scientific attitudes?
They were encouraged to compare their expectations with their findings and to reflect on how to improve their investigations.

Could they work cooperatively and share ideas in a supportive classroom climate?
The reporting to and questioning by each other suggests an atmosphere in which ideas are shared.

Adapting or elaborating activities

The criteria are especially useful in planning activities, particularly in starting from suggestions that are either not well developed in detail or limited in terms of the learning opportunities they provide.

Take the example of the activity presented to children on the workcard in Box 5.3. There are some obvious reasons why this is limited as a learning experience, although it is certainly an activity most children would enjoy.

| **Box 5.3** | **Parachute workcard** |

Parachute

- Cut a 14-inch square from sturdy plastic

- Cut 4 pieces of string 14 inches long

- Securely tape or tie a string to each corner of the plastic

- Tie the free ends of the 4 strings together in a knot. Be sure the strings are all the same length

- Tie a single string about 6 inches long to the knot

- Add a weight, such as a washer, to the free end of the string

- Pull the parachute up in the centre. Squeeze the plastic to make it as flat as possible

- Fold the parachute twice

- Wrap the string loosely around the plastic

- Throw the parachute up into the air

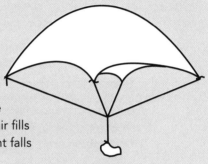

Results The parachute opens and slowly carries the weight to the ground.

Why? The weight falls first, unwinding the string because the parachute, being larger, is held back by the air. The air fills the plastic slowing down the rate of descent, if the weight falls quickly a smaller object needs to be used.

It is perhaps useful to recognise what is valuable about the activity before criticising it. It is capable of relating to children's interests across a broad spectrum, with no obvious gender or cultural bias. Thus it meets the first criterion. It uses simple and safe materials, which are familiar and cheap, and it would be an easy activity for teachers to manage. On the other hand, there are many ways in which the activity could be changed to meet other criteria.

Is the activity linked to the children's experience?

Children's experiences of air resistance are many and not restricted to parachutes. Children could relate it to more everyday events, such as riding a bicycle in a strong wind and the 'helicopter' wings of sycamore seeds seen drifting gently down to the ground. They should be encouraged to think about air resistance in relation to horizontal movement, in yachts and sailing ships and in slowing aircraft landing on short runways and aircraft carriers. They can be challenged to think about the kind of materials and construction needed in each case.

Was the activity accessible to all?

There is no apparent differentiation in the activity. Children could complete it as given or fail to do so, in which case there could be no learning – and possible demotivation. Those who complete it successfully would want to extend it in some way, as suggested below. It is important to build in some opportunities for the children to control the activity, to have some ownership of it and to be able to go as far as they are able in learning from it.

Could the children interact with materials?

They were manipulating the materials according to instructions. This can be a good start when particular techniques have to be learned. They would learn more about what is going on if they were able to interact with the materials more independently. The initial experience would certainly raise question in their minds, which this material could so easily be used to answer: what happens if there is no weight on the string; more weight; a bigger or smaller canopy; a different shape?

Could they develop their scientific ideas?

A main point of the activity is to enable children to recognise the role of air in slowing down the fall of the parachute. With this in mind, it would be useful for children to observe how quickly the parachute falls when it is not allowed to open. Exploration of larger and smaller parachutes might further children's ideas about the effect of the air. The question of why the parachute falls at all could also be discussed, leading to recognition of the main forces acting on the parachute when it is falling. Giving the 'answer' to why the parachute moves slowly is not allowing the children to use and explore their own ideas; so this part should be omitted.

Could they develop process skills?

The provision of precise instructions removes the opportunity for children to investigate and think out for themselves how to make a parachute. Opportunities for children to develop their process skills are further limited by the lack of any investigation once the parachute is constructed. There are many variables that affect the fall of the parachute, such as shape, area and length of strings, that children could explore in a controlled way as they test out various ideas and try to find answers to questions they raise for themselves.

Could they develop scientific attitudes?

The activity might begin with the experience of throwing several parachutes, of different sizes and even shapes, and noticing how they fall. This would provide the context for expressing their initial ideas about what is happening and the opportunity to compare them with evidence. More investigations planned by the children would give the chance for them to review their work critically and to improve their future enquiries.

Could they work cooperatively and share ideas in a supportive classroom climate?

Even within the context of a worksheet, there could be instructions for pooling ideas within a group, planning how to find out 'what happens if...' and preparing a group report to others when they meet together as a class to listen to reports of each other's progress and share ideas. Different groups might investigate different variables and so ideas about explanations could be tested in different ways: does the explanation for the effect of changing the size of the canopy also explain what happens when the shape is changed, or when there is a hole in the canopy?

Implications of creating richer opportunities for learning

There are three main consequences of modifying the activity in these kinds of ways:

■ First, it will depend more on the teacher than on a workcard, although careful wording of worksheets or workcards can go a long way in encouraging children to use their own ideas and think things out for themselves.

■ Second, it will undoubtedly take up more time. This has to be balanced by the much greater learning that takes place. Even if the same time as required for the modified activity was used for several like the original activity there would still be no opportunity for development of real understanding. Fewer activities, with more opportunity for different kinds of learning, for discussion and for developing skills, will make a greater contribution to learning with understanding. Using criteria such as the ones above will help in making this case.

■ Third, it requires a different kind of lesson planning. Planning to allow children to use and develop their own ideas requires more, not less, planning than preparing prescribed activities. It means thinking about the teacher's role and the children's role in the activities. We turn to this in the next section.

Planning for experiences that promote learning

The value of planning cannot be overemphasised and there is more about this in Chapter 23. Among the characteristics of effective teaching in science, widely recognised by inspectors (Ofsted 1998; SEED 1999) and by researchers (Harlen 1999; Monk and Osborne 2000), the following are invariably included:

■ teachers being well prepared and clear about the objective of the lesson and the learning outcomes intended;

■ teachers sharing this information with children in ways appropriate to age and stage, so that the children are clear about expectations;

■ lessons having a clear structure of phases in which different kinds of activity take place, such as introduction, discussion and practical work, ending with whole-class discussion of outcomes and an opportunity to reflect on procedures and learn from mistakes;

■ raising expectations of children and asking questions that require higher levels of thinking;

■ structuring group work to promote collaboration and discussion.

None of these things happens without carefully thinking through the lesson beforehand. To illustrate the nature of the planning that is required, we outline some of the decisions that Graham (see Box 1.1) made in advance of and during his lessons, thinking about his own role and that of the children. As an experienced teacher, not all of this planning would necessarily be on paper; but it would certainly take place in his thinking.

The decisions behind Graham's lessons

Aims and starting activities
Decisions about:

■ the main ideas, skills and attitudes to be developed (see Chapter 6);

■ all the parts of the lesson with these learning goals in mind, including the equipment and materials to provide (see Chapter 20);

■ how to introduce and guide the initial exploration – in this case not by using a workcard but by writing four things for the children to focus on and displaying these on a large sheet of paper during the activity;

■ how to move from the exploring phase to the investigation phase and from the investigations to reporting, discussing and reflecting;

■ what questions to ask at each phase of the lesson (see Chapter 3);

■ which group to observe particularly in order to assess their process skills (see Chapter 15).

In the exploratory stage
The teacher's role:

■ visiting each group, listening and asking carefully phrased questions to find out the children's ideas;

■ keeping them on track by reminding them of the four points but allowing other exploration in addition.

Moving to the investigation phase and preparing a report

The teacher's role:

■ collecting observations from each group, asking for evidence to support their statements;

■ bringing together ideas about what plants need from soil (using a flip chart);

■ scaffolding the addition of any factors not mentioned;

■ agreeing which factors each group will investigate;

■ ensuring that the children know the goals of their work and how they are to report it;

■ during the investigations, making sure that children can find all the equipment they need;

■ asking questions designed to probe their understanding of what they are doing and finding;

■ observing all the groups but with special attention to the planned target group;

■ moving groups into planning their report when their investigations are complete.

Reporting, discussing and reflecting

The teacher's role:

■ arranging the class for reporting to each other so that each group can be heard and seen and that others pay attention;

■ inviting comments from children on each group's results;

■ scaffolding the synthesis of findings from the various groups;

■ inviting reflection on how their investigations could be improved.

After the lessons

Reflecting and recording:

■ annotating lesson plans to record changes, what worked and what didn't work as planned (perhaps evaluating the activities in relation to the eight criteria or similar);

■ recording observations made of the target group and other children;

■ noting strengths and weaknesses in ideas or skills that should be taken into account in planning future lessons;

■ preparing follow-up lessons.

Summary

This chapter has considered the essential features of experiences that promote learning in science at the primary level. The main points have been:

■ If classroom activities are to engage children and provide opportunities for learning there are certain criteria they should meet.

■ Eight criteria have been identified relating to: the interests and experience of the children, relevance to children of both genders and all social and ethnic backgrounds, the opportunity to interact with materials, to develop scientific skills, concepts and attitudes and to work cooperatively and share ideas in a supportive classroom climate.

■ These criteria can be used to evaluate and to adapt activities in respect of opportunities for developing scientific understanding.

■ Some implications of providing such learning opportunities are to emphasise the role of the teacher, to spend a longer time on a smaller number of activities and to underline the importance of planning, particularly in thinking through the role of the teacher at all parts of the activities.

Part 2 Learning and teaching for understanding

6 The goals of learning science

This chapter is concerned with the goals of learning science. What is it that we want our children to know and be able and willing to do as a result of their science education? And what is the contribution that primary science makes to this? Some answers to these questions can readily be found by referring to published curriculum documents, guidelines or standards. But there is a danger of turning too soon to lists of concepts and skills: we may lose sight of the whole. For it is the whole that really gives purpose to teaching. We teach the parts – about particular events or phenomena, such as what makes a simple circuit – not just because they are interesting in themselves, but in order for all children to develop an overall understanding that helps them to make sense of new phenomena and events. Having this overview is what is known as scientific literacy.

So we begin this chapter by considering the notion of scientific literacy, and the foundation for it that primary science provides. We then look at how the 'whole' is broken down into constituents and identify the concept areas, process skills and attitudes that are the way in which the goals of primary science are expressed in this book. The chapter ends by looking at views on the nature of science and the impact that a teacher's view on science can have on his or her decisions about learning experiences.

Scientific literacy: an overall aim

Scientific literacy is the term used for the essential understanding that should be part of everyone's education. Just as the term 'literacy' on its own denotes competence in using language at the level needed for functioning effectively in society, so scientific literacy indicates a competence in relation to science:

- being able to function with confidence in relation to the scientific aspects of the world around;

■ being able to look at something 'in a scientific way', seeing, for example, whether or not evidence has been taken into account in the explanation of an event or phenomenon, whether it makes sense in terms of related events or phenomena and so on;

■ being aware of the nature of (and limitations of) scientific knowledge and the role of values in its generation.

The term 'scientific literacy' is used in statements about the aims of science education in various countries and in statements of international bodies such as UNESCO and the OECD. Box 6.1 gives the definition used in the OECD Programme for International Student Achievement (PISA).

Box 6.1   The PISA definition of scientific literacy

The capacity to use scientific knowledge, to identify questions and to draw evidence-based conclusions in order to understand and help make decisions about the natural world and the changes made to it through human activity.

(OECD 2003: 133).

In the UK, an influential report (*Beyond 2000: Science Education for the Future*) on the aim of the science curriculum for all pupils from age five to 16 recommended that 'The science curriculum for 5 to 16 should be seen primarily as a course to enhance general scientific literacy' (Millar and Osborne 1998: 9). What this means is further set out in Box 6.2.

Box 6.2   A curriculum for developing scientific literacy five to 16

The science curriculum should:

■ sustain and develop the curiosity of young people about the natural world around them, and build up their confidence in their ability to enquire into its behaviour. It should seek to foster a sense of wonder, enthusiasm and interest in science so that young people feel confident and competent to engage with scientific and technical matters.

■ help young people acquire a broad, general understanding of the important ideas and explanatory frameworks of science, and of the procedures of scientific enquiry, which have had a major impact on our material environment and on our culture in general, so that they can:

☐ appreciate why these ideas are valued;

☐ appreciate the underlying rationale for decisions (for example, about diet, or medical treatment, or energy use) which they may wish, or be advised, to take in everyday contexts, both now and in later life;

☐ be able to understand, and respond critically to, media reports of issues with a science component;

☐ feel empowered to hold and express a personal point of view on issues with a science component which enter the arena of public debate, and perhaps to become actively involved in some of these;

☐ acquire further knowledge when required, either for interest or for vocational purposes.

(Millar and Osborne 1998: 12)

The contribution of primary science to scientific literacy

The aims of developing scientific literacy, as described here, may seem remote from primary science, but they are in essence easily identified as developing attitudes ('a sense of wonder, enthusiasm and interest'), developing ideas ('understanding of important ideas and explanatory frameworks') and developing process skills ('the procedures of scientific enquiry'). Primary science has a contribution to make to all of these. We just have to remember that in all cases we are talking about development, starting from the simple foundations that are needed for more abstract ideas and advanced thinking.

Developing ideas

The development of understanding starts from making sense of particular events that we encounter. We might call the ideas found useful for this 'small' ideas, because they are specific to the events studied and have limited application beyond these. As experience extends it becomes possible to link events which are explained in similar ways and so to form ideas that have wider application and so can be described as 'bigger' ideas.

The ultimate aim of developing scientific literacy is to develop the 'big', widely applicable ideas that enable us to grasp what is going on in situations that are new to us. But clearly the 'big' ideas are too abstract and too remote from everyday experience to be a starting point for this learning. Learning has to start from the 'small' ideas and build upwards so that at each point the ideas are understood in terms of real experience. The role of primary science is, therefore, to build a foundation of small ideas that help children to understand things in their immediate environment but, most importantly, at the same time to begin to make links between different experiences and ideas to build bigger ideas.

Development of skills and attitudes

The overall aim of scientific literacy in relation to the development of skills and attitudes is the ability and willingness to recognise and use evidence in making decisions as informed citizens. Again the starting point is to become familiar with the ways of identifying, collecting and interpreting evidence in relation to answering questions about things around. Being able to do this is an essential starting point for reflecting on the kinds of questions that science can, and cannot, answer and the kinds of conclusions that can, and cannot, be drawn from certain kinds of evidence.

Making links with the world around

The achievement of scientific literacy depends on, but is more than, the acquisition of scientific knowledge, skills, values and attitudes. It does not automatically result from learning science; it has to be a conscious goal even at the primary level, by giving attention to linking together ideas from a range of experiences of real phenomena, problems and events both within the classroom and outside it. Indeed, extending first-hand experience beyond what the school can supply, in the way that museums and science centres can do (see Chapter 20), is essential to the development of scientific literacy.

Constituents of scientific literacy

We have already identified three main constituents of scientific literacy:

- concepts or ideas, which help understanding of scientific aspects of the world around and which enable us to make sense of new experiences by linking them to what we already know;

- processes, which are mental and physical skills used in obtaining, interpreting and using evidence about the world around to gain knowledge and build understanding;

- attitudes or dispositions, which indicate willingness and confidence to engage in enquiry, debate and further learning.

To this we add a fourth:

- understanding the nature (and limitations) of scientific knowledge.

We now consider each of these in relation to science education at the primary level.

Scientific ideas at the primary level

Box 6.3 lists scientific ideas that children can begin to develop through learning science at the primary level. We consider the progression in these ideas in Chapters 7 and 9.

Box 6.3	The ideas that primary science begins to develop

Primary science lays the foundation for ideas about:

■ living things and the processes of life (characteristics of living things, how they are made up and the functions of their parts, human health etc.);

■ the interaction of living things and their environment (competition, adaptation, effects of pollution and other human activities etc.);

■ materials (their variety, properties, sources, uses, interactions, conservation, disposal of waste etc.);

■ air, atmosphere and weather (presence of air round the Earth, features of the weather, causes of clouds, rain, frost and snow, freak conditions etc.);

■ rocks, soil and materials from the Earth (nature and origin of soil, maintenance of fertility, fossil fuels, minerals and ores as limited resources);

■ the Earth in space (sun, moon, stars and planets, causes of day and night and seasonal variations);

■ forces and movement (starting and stopping movement, speed and acceleration, simple machines, transportation etc.);

■ energy sources and uses (sources of heat, light, sound, electricity etc.).

In various curriculum statements these are spelled out in more detail so that the content of activities can be selected. For instance, in the National Curriculum for England (DfEE 1999), statements fall under three broad headings: Life processes and living things; Materials and their properties; Physical processes. These are broken down into subheadings and more specific statements of ideas within these for each Key Stage (ages 5–7, 7–11, 11–14, 14–16). This leads to long lists of statements that can be used for selecting the content for learning activities. In the Scottish 5–14 Science Curriculum (SEED 1999) statements are grouped under the headings Earth and space, Energy and forces, Living things and life processes. Greater detail is provided for each of these, indicating what is expected at early stages and later stages of the primary school and at the end of the second year of secondary school.

Process skills of science at the primary level

While content or subject matter being studied determines the ideas that can be developed in science activities, the development of process skills depends on how the learner interacts with the content. However, as we will see in Chapter 7, the development of understanding also depends upon this interaction, so the aims of developing process skills and ideas are interdependent. Nevertheless, the process skills are conventionally identified separately.

The National Curriculum for England identifies key skills and thinking skills intended for implementation across the curriculum, as well as the following process skills as investigative skills within the science curriculum:

■ planning;

■ obtaining and presenting evidence;

■ considering evidence and evaluating.

These are expanded in slightly different terms for Key Stage 1 and Key Stage 2.

In the Scottish 5–14 Curriculum the skills for science are defined in three groups:

■ *Preparing for tasks*. Understanding the task and planning a practical activity. Predicting. Undertaking a fair test.

■ *Carrying out tasks*. Observing and measuring. Recording findings in a variety of ways.

■ *Reviewing and reporting tasks*. Reporting and presenting. Interpreting and evaluating results and processes.

Box 6.4	Process skills and attitudes that primary science begins to develop

Process (enquiry) skills:

■ questioning, predicting and planning;

■ gathering evidence by observing and using information sources;

■ interpreting evidence and drawing conclusions;

■ communicating and reflecting.

Scientific attitudes:

■ willingness to consider evidence and to change ideas;

■ sensitivity to living things and the environment.

Although there are differences in the words used to group the process skills, at a detailed level there is a consensus about the importance of the skills listed in Box 6.4. These are the groups that we use in discussing the development of process skills and how to promote it in Chapters 7 and 10.

Scientific attitudes at the primary level

It is useful to make a distinction between two kinds of attitudes:

■ attitudes towards science as an enterprise;

■ attitudes towards the objects and events that are studied in science and the use of evidence in making sense of them.

To develop an informed attitude towards science it is necessary to have an idea of what 'science' is. Without this, attitudes will be formed on the basis of the many myths about science and about scientists that persist in popular belief and the caricatures that are perpetuated in the media and in some literature. Typically these portray scientists as male, bespectacled, absent-minded and narrowly concerned with nothing but their work (see, for example, Jannikos 1995). Science as a subject may be portrayed as the villain, the origin of devastating weapons and technology that causes environmental damage or as the wonder of the modern world in providing medical advances, expanding human horizons beyond the Earth and being responsible for the discoveries that led to computers and information technology.

At the primary level the concern is to give children experience of scientific activity as a basis for a thorough understanding, which will only come much later, of what science is and is not and of the responsibility we all share for applying it humanely. So the main concern here is with attitudes that we might call the attitudes of science, those that support scientific activity and learning.

Although the development of scientific attitudes is not explicitly identified in all national curricula it is widely acknowledged as an important outcome of science education. The reason for the exclusion from the National Curriculum dates back to the recommendation made in the Report of the Task Group on Assessment and Testing (DES/WO 1989) that 'the assessment of attitudes should not form a prescribed part of the national assessment system' (paragraph 30).

In the Scottish curriculum, which is non-statutory, the development of informed attitudes is an explicit strand of attainment. It states that children should develop:

■ a commitment to learning;

■ respect and care for self and others;

■ social and environmental responsibility.

These fall into the category of attitudes *of* science and would also support learning in several subject areas. The generalised nature of attitudes is such that no clear line can be drawn between 'scientific' and other attitudes and in Chapter 11 we consider what is needed to foster positive attitudes in general as well as the ones particularly relevant to developing ideas through exploration of the world around, listed in Box 6.4.

Understanding the nature (and limitations) of science

Although we have just implied that primary children are unlikely to have sufficient experience of science activity to form opinions and attitudes about science as such (that is, attitudes *to* science), it is important for teachers to have a view of what science is and is not. A teacher's view of science will influence the way (s)he teaches it. For although few primary teachers would regard themselves as scientists, we all have a view of what science is and, like it or not, we convey this through our teaching. So it is necessary to have a 'feel' for the current understanding of science, which may well be different from that we received through our own science education.

In Box 6.5 there are two contrasting view of science and some consequences for teaching of holding these views. These suggest that we view the nature of scientific activity as an important question.

The thinking and experience of scientists and science educators has moved in recent decades from the view on the left of Box 6.5 to the view on the right. The notion of building from earlier ideas and changing them in the light of new evidence is also consistent with modern views of learning in science, as we will see in Chapter 7. This is not surprising since practising scientists are learning science from their experiments and investigations, just as children are from their enquiries and explorations. The link becomes more obvious as we look at what is considered to be 'scientific activity'.

When is an idea scientific and when is it not?

The answer according to modern philosophers of science (e.g. Popper 1988) is 'when it can be disproved'. This is a simple but profound statement that in straightforward language means that:

- if there is no possibility of evidence being used to contradict an idea or theory, then it is not scientific;

- but if the theory or idea can be used to make a prediction that can be checked against evidence, which could either agree or disagree with it, then it is scientific.

Box 6.5	Different views of science and their implications for science education

Science as known facts and principles to be learned about the world around	*Science as development of understanding about the world around*
■ Objective.	■ A human endeavour to understand the physical world.
■ Capable of yielding ultimate truths.	■ Producing knowledge that is tentative, always subject to challenge by further evidence.
■ 'Proving' things.	
■ Having a defined and unique subject matter.	■ Building upon, but not accepting uncritically, previous knowledge and understanding.
■ Having unique methods.	■ Using a wide range of methods of enquiry.
■ Being value-free.	■ A social enterprise whose conclusions are often subject to social acceptability.
	■ Constrained by values.
Leads to:	**Leads to:**
Scientific activity regarded as the application of principles and skills that first have to be learned. Science education is conceived as being primarily to teach these principles and skills, ensuring that the wisdom of the past is received by new generations. The dominant role of class activities is then seen as being to demonstrate the skills and to 'prove' the principles.	Scientific activity seen as developing understanding through testing ideas against evidence, with ideas being accepted as being as good as the evidence which supports them. Classroom or laboratory experiences will enable ideas to be explored rather than accepted and committed to memory, and alternative views will be examined in supporting evidence. Activities involve learners in the process of developing understanding from evidence and in considering accepted scientific principles in this spirit.

This is the test for whether an idea or theory is or is not scientific, not whether the evidence does or does not confirm it. Often, in science, technological developments enable evidence to be found that disproves a theory, for which there had previously only been confirmatory evidence. This is how Newton's theories were overtaken by those of Einstein, but this did not mean that his ideas were unscientific. The very fact that they could be disproved by evidence meant that they *were* scientific. This is because even if the evidence agrees with the prediction, that does not prove the theory to be 'correct', for there is always the possibility of finding further evidence that might not agree with the prediction. This is explained by Stephen Hawking in Box 6.6.

Box 6.6	Science as falsifiable

Any physical theory is always provisional, in the sense that it is only a hypothesis: you can never prove it. No matter how many times the results of experiments agree with some theory, you can never be sure that the next time the result will not contradict the theory. On the other hand, you can disprove theory by finding even a single observation that disagreed with the predictions of the theory.

(Hawking 1988: 10)

Are children's ideas scientific?

This may seem a long way from the primary classroom, but it explains why we want children to express their ideas and questions in terms that are testable. The ideas children create can be scientific if they are testable and falsifiable, and the fact that they are often disproved by the evidence makes them no less scientific. Learning science and doing science proceed in the same way. Indeed, we find many parallels between the development of ideas by the scientific community and the development of children's ideas. For example, both are influenced, and to some extent formed, by the reactions and alternative views of peers. The ideas of both are provisional at any time and may have to be changed to be consistent with new experience or evidence not previously available. Children also have non-scientific ideas, which they hold on to by ignoring contrary evidence or adjusting their ideas to accommodate it bit by bit (see the examples on page 76).

Summary

This chapter has attempted to give an overview of the goals of learning science and a rationale for the identification of particular goals. The main points have been:

- The overall goal of science education for all children is to develop scientific literacy, meaning a level of competence in understanding and using knowledge of science that is needed for functioning effectively as a member of society.

- Primary science has a role in building a foundation for scientific literacy through the development of ideas, skills and attitudes.

■ The view of science that a teacher holds influences his or her teaching. Viewing science as facts leads to transmission of information, while viewing science as the development of a shared understanding leads to providing opportunities for children to investigate and enquire and try to make sense of new experience.

7 A framework for learning in science

Introduction

In this chapter we attempt to describe the process of learning in science in terms of how ideas are modified by experience. In the first section examples are used to suggest a framework, or model, of how different parts of classroom activities come together to help children to develop their understanding. This framework is based on the observation that learners invariably bring ideas from earlier experience to try to make sense of new experience or answer new questions. The framework is used to identify the role of process skills in developing ideas and show how non-scientific ideas may persist if process skills are not developed and used. The notion of progression in process skills is discussed and three dimensions of change are identified. The framework also describes how ideas are developed to become 'bigger'. This is one of the three dimensions of progression in ideas that are suggested.

Analysing learning in Graham's classroom

Looking back at the description of Graham's lessons on soil (pages 4–6) we can identify certain stages in the children's activities and thinking, as set out in Figure 7.1.

The children were given a new experience in the form of the soils to observe and a question about how the differences between the soils might affect how well plants would grow in them. In exploring and making a prediction about which soil would be best they used their existing ideas (dark, damp soils). To find out more about which would be best (and test their prediction) they planned and conducted various tests. The evidence from various groups was collected and interpreted. What they predicted was not supported by the evidence, so the ideas on which the prediction was based were not confirmed. As a result the ideas were modified: dark soil is not necessarily the most fertile. They had not only learned that their initial ideas were limited; they also had reasons for changing them and reached a better understanding of the properties of soil.

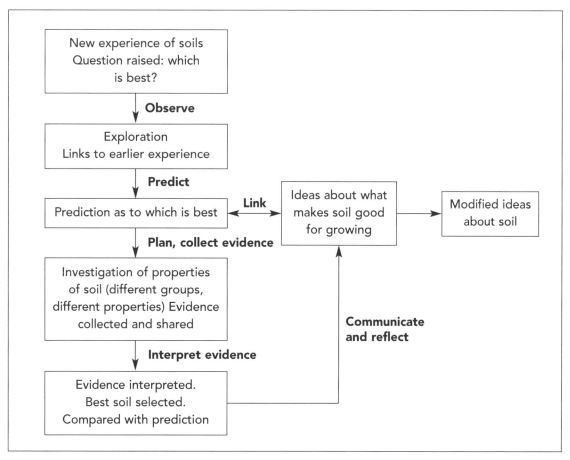

Figure 7.1 Analysis of children's activities in Graham's lesson

In their subsequent work with the soils, they would go through the cycle of thinking again – this time with a more informed idea as a basis for predictions.

A general framework for learning in science

Similar patterns can be seen in other classrooms where investigative science is in action. This suggests a general framework, as in Figure 7.2. Starting with an experience to be explained, or a question that has been raised, the first two stages, (a) and (b), relate to making a link with something similar encountered in previous experience. The link may be made because of some physical property or something else that calls it to mind, such as a word or situation. Creativity and imagination also have a part. Indeed, in the case of the scientist faced with an unexpected phenomenon, it is the ability to try ideas outside the immediately obvious that may be the start of a 'breakthrough'.

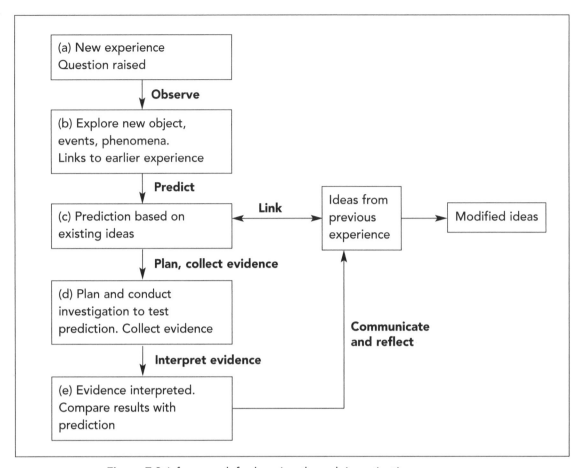

Figure 7.2 A framework for learning through investigation

Stages (c) and (d) are concerned with testing the idea by making a prediction and gathering evidence to see if the idea 'works' in terms of predicting something that actually happens. If when the evidence is interpreted (e) it does not support the prediction it is probably necessary to think of another link that might provide a better idea. If what is predicted is actually found, however, then we might cautiously accept that the idea helps to explain the new experience. The idea is modified by becoming one of wider application than before; just a little 'bigger'.

An example: using alternative ideas

These stages can be seen in the case of some children who were investigating the difference felt in placing their hands on three surfaces in the classroom: one metal, one wooden and one of polystyrene foam.

■ The metal felt considerably colder than the other two surfaces, which raised the question: why? This was stage (a).

■ They immediately said that the metal was at a lower temperature, because that was usually the case when something was felt to be cold, as when touching an object just taken out of the fridge or touching things out of doors on a cold day (b).

■ Their teacher asked them what they would expect to find if they measured the temperature of the surfaces and they predicted that the metal would be lowest, the wood next and the foam about the same as their hands (c).

■ Using a temperature sensor connected to a computer, they tested their prediction (d) and found almost no difference among the three surfaces.

■ They were so surprised by this (e) that they wanted to repeat it and to try it in different places. In particular, they wanted to take the surfaces out of the classroom to where it was colder. The result was the same; no difference in measured temperature, although the metal still felt much cooler than the other surfaces.

■ It was clear that their idea that the metal was at a different temperature from the other surfaces was not explaining what they found. An alternative had to be found.

The teacher helped them to link to a different experience by asking them to think of things that had made their hands cold. Among the suggestions was snowballing. With a little scaffolding (see page 97) the teacher helped them to realise that heat was lost from their hands when they felt cold.

■ Could this account for the hand on the metal getting cold (back to (b))?

■ If so, then the hand would really be colder after touching the metal than after touching the other surfaces (c).

■ A fair test of this was devised by the children (d).

■ This idea seemed to be confirmed (e).

To see whether they could apply this idea, the teacher challenged them to predict what would happen if the surfaces were all warmer than their hands rather than colder. For safety's sake their predictions were not tested, but various experiences were collected that helped to provide supporting evidence: the handles of cooking pans being wooden or plastic rather than metal, the kinds of gloves that keep our hands warm and so on.

What if there are no alternative ideas?

Children may ignore contradictory evidence in interpreting findings and hold on to their initial ideas even though these do not fit the evidence, as in the example in Box 7.1. Here we have an illustration of a common way in which children deal with the situation of lacking experience to give them alternative ideas, so as to modify the idea they do have in order to accommodate the conflicting evidence. It seems characteristic of human beings to try to explain things and if ideas that really fit are not available then less satisfactory ideas will be used. It is more comfortable to modify an idea than to abandon it, especially if it is your only way of making any sense of an observation.

Box 7.1	Children holding on to ideas because there is no alternative accessible to them

Faced with the evidence that varnished cubes of wood stick to each other when wet, several groups of 11-year-olds concluded that the blocks became magnetic when wet (Harlen 2000: 34). The resemblance of a block sticking to the underside of another, without anything to hold them together, to a magnet picking up another magnet or a piece of iron was clearly very strong. An equally good alternative explanation was not available to them and so they held on to their view of magnetism, modifying it to accommodate the observation that the blocks only stuck together when wet by concluding that 'they're magnetic when they're wet'. Had they had experience, say, of 'suction cups' being held to a surface when air is forced out from under the cup they might have used a different linking idea – that air pressure can 'stick' things together.

In such circumstances teachers have to decide what alternative ideas are within the reach of the children and support them in trying out ideas that can explain the phenomenon. This is described as scaffolding and we look more at what it means, with examples, in Chapter 9.

The role of process skills in the development of ideas

Using the framework to reflect on learning enables us to identify the role that process skills play in developing more scientific ideas.

Suppose that the tests that the children in Graham's class carried out were not 'fair', because the soils were not compared equally. Or suppose that the children testing the surfaces did not use the temperature probe correctly and came up with findings that supported their sensations. In such cases the results of their investigations would not lead to a change in ideas. We can see that the development of the children's ideas is dependent on the extent to which scientific process skills have been used.

If the observing, predicting, testing etc. are rigorous and systematic, in the way associated with scientific investigation, then ideas that do not fit the evidence will be rejected and those that do fit will be accepted and strengthened. But it may not be the case that the testing has this quality. The skills of young children – and those of some adults – may not have developed to the appropriate degree.

Young children may base their predictions on unscientific ideas, as in the cases in Box 7.2.

Box 7.2	Children with untestable ideas

Luis had an idea about what made snow melt, which was that it was caused by the presence of air; he did not consider heat. He wanted to preserve some snow and said that it would not melt if it were put in a jar with a lid on to keep out air. His first attempt led to the snow melting when the jar was brought into a warm room. He said that there was still some air there and that if the jar were to be packed with snow it would not melt. But however much snow was put into the jar he still said that there was room for air. He had, therefore, turned his claim into one that was irrefutable, since it would never be possible to have only snow in his jar.

Emma was convinced that something that did not float would do so if the water was deeper. To try to test this, more water was added. But it was never enough and all the time she maintained her claim that it would float in very, very deep water. Again, the idea had become untestable.

Thus the extent to which ideas become more scientific (by fitting more phenomena) depends both on the way ideas from previous experience are linked to new experience and on how the testing of possible explanatory ideas is carried out; that is, on the use of the process skills. *Process skills involved at all stages have a crucial part to play in the development of ideas.* This is one important reason for giving attention to helping children to develop their process skills and to become more conscious of using them with appropriate rigour. The other reason, of course, is that these skills are needed for making sense of new experiences in the future and for learning throughout life.

Progression in process skills

What are the changes in process skills that we take to be 'progression'? By identifying these we find clues to how to help the progression from limited to more rigorous use as needed in scientific investigations.

We can describe changes in how children of different experience and maturity use all the process skills. But rather than going into each skill at this point, we can look for patterns in change across all the skills. We find three types of change, identified in Box 7.3.

Box 7.3	Dimensions of progression in process skills

1 *From simple to more elaborated skills*
This is the most obvious dimension, comprising the development of the ability to perform more aspects of a skill. A parallel in another field is the development from just being able to move round an ice rink on skates to being able to jump, twist and dance and still land on your feet. Both might be called 'ice skating' but one is much simpler and less elaborate than the other. In the case of science process skills it is the difference between observing main features and observing details, between predicting what might happen in vague terms and being more specific, between concluding that a change in one variable does affect another and identifying the direction and nature of the relationship.

2 *From effective use in familiar situations to effective use in unfamiliar situations*
All process skills have to be used in relation to some content and it is not difficult to appreciate that what the content is will influence the way children engage with it. Some children who may be able to make a reasonable prediction or plan an investigation about, say, how far paper darts will fly, may be less likely to do these things effectively in relation to the effect of resistance in an electric circuit. The reason is that some scientific knowledge is always involved in using science processes. Whether or not the required knowledge is the main obstacle in a particular case depends on familiarity with it. A consequence of this is that the extent to which young children can conduct scientific enquiries can only be assessed when they are engaged in enquiries about things familiar to them or ones they have thoroughly explored (we say more about this in Chapter 15).

3 *From unconscious to conscious action*
Unconscious action here means doing something without recognising just what one is doing; for example, noticing something without consciously observing it, or finding an answer to a question by enquiry without recognising the kind of question that is being answered in this way. This dimension of change is connected with the previous one, since becoming aware of one's thinking is necessary for applying certain thinking deliberately to unfamiliar problems.

The kind of thinking that is at the conscious end of this dimension is meta-cognition, being aware of one's thinking and reasoning processes. It is often considered that primary children are not able to stand back from their enquiries or problems and reflect on how they tackled them, so opportunities to do this are not offered. Recent attempts to involve children in such thinking (AKSIS and CASE projects) have, however, provided evidence of some positive effects (see, for example, Robertson 2004; Serret 2004). Giving children more opportunities of this kind may well advance the development of their process skills and thus their ability to make sense of the world around. We return to this in Chapter 10.

The development of 'bigger' ideas

We have noted in Chapter 6 that a major aim of science education is to help children to develop 'big' ideas. These are ideas that help us to make sense of a number of related events or phenomena. They contrast with 'small' ideas that apply only to specific situations. We can see how the model describes the gradual enlargement of ideas.

Using an idea from previous experience immediately links two experiences and if the idea is found to explain both, it becomes 'bigger'. Often several other related events can be linked when a teacher asks children to apply their newly modified ideas to other situations. For instance, in the investigation of the temperature of different surfaces, the teacher took the opportunity to see if the children could extend the idea of metals conducting heat to give a reason for metal pans often having wooden or plastic handles.

Progression in scientific ideas

We can ask the same question about progression in ideas as we have asked in relation to process skills. What are the main differences between the ideas of younger children with less experience and those of older children with more experience? One dimension we have already identified is from 'small' to 'bigger' ideas. Others come from considering the different levels of explanation that we can have for a particular phenomenon.

For instance, consider the ideas which younger and older children might hold about adaptation of living things to their environment:

Younger
There are different kinds of living things in different places and each kind likes a certain kind of place. Some animals would not be able to live where other ones live because they would be too hot or too cold.

Older
In a particular place some things will be able to live and some things will not. The reason for this is that each living thing needs food, water, air, shelter and protection for its offspring, but different ones obtain these in different ways. What suits one will not suit others because of differences in their bodies and structures.

When we look at the difference in these ideas we find the three main changes set out in Box 7.4.

Box 7.4	Dimensions of progression in ideas

From description to explanation

The ideas of the younger children are closely related to gathering information, finding out what is there and what is happening, as opposed to explaining why. There is the beginning of explanation in terms of what the habitat provides for the living things in it. The ideas of the older children are clearly much more related to explanation.

From 'small' to 'big' ideas

Each experience leads to a small idea that helps to make sense of specific observations. 'Worms can live in soil because they can slither through small spaces and can eat things that are in the soil' is an idea that applies to worms only. It is transformed to a bigger idea when it is linked to other ideas, such as 'fish can live in water because they can breathe through their gills and find food there', to form an idea that can apply to all animals. Eventually this idea may be linked to ideas about the habitats of plants, to become an even bigger idea about living organisms in general. This is an important dimension of progress, since the formation of widely applicable ideas, or concepts, is essential if we are to make sense of new experience.

From personal to shared ideas

It is characteristic of young children to look at things from one point of view, their own, and this is reflected in their ideas. These are based on their personal experience and their interpretation of it. As children become older and more willing to share how they see and how they explain things, their ideas are influenced by those of others, including their teacher and other adults and other children. Thus ideas are constructed on the basis of social and educational interactions as well as their own thinking.

Through becoming aware of others' ideas and sharing their own, children negotiate meaning for their experiences and for the words that are used to communicate them (such as 'habitat'). In this way children derive assurance that their understanding is shared by others. It is central to learning in science that children have access to the views of others and to the scientific view, but at the same time retain ownership of their own developing understanding.

These overall dimensions of progress are the kinds of changes that it is helpful to have in mind and to encourage in children, whatever the content of their activities. Ways of encouraging development are the subject of Chapter 9.

Summary

This chapter has provided an overview of learning in science, interpreted as a process in which ideas are developed through the use of process skills. The main ideas have been:

- A model of learning in science helps to identify the role in learning of different parts of classroom activities.

- The model shows the central role that their process skills have in developing children's ideas.

- If skills are not developed to the point of being scientific, then ideas will not be properly tested and may be retained when there is no real evidence to support them.

- Progression in skills can be described in terms of change from simple to more elaborated skills, from effective use in familiar situations to effective use in unfamiliar ones and from unconscious use to conscious use of skills.

- Progression in scientific ideas can be described in terms of change from description to explanation, from 'small' to 'bigger' ideas that explain more phenomena and from personal to shared ideas.

8 Creative learning and creative teaching

Introduction

In this chapter we address the question of the teacher's role in promoting the development of scientific ideas in children, by providing them with the opportunities to make creative leaps of imagination. We first look at what we mean by creativity in science and why it is considered to be such an important characteristic to develop, linking this to the process of learning constructively. We go on to discuss the importance of creative teaching in fostering creativity in learning and some examples of creative teaching. This leads to the question, addressed in the final section, of the role of published schemes of work and programmes of study in primary science teaching. What are the merits and some of the dangers of using such schemes in terms of ensuring the flexibility to teach in a way that promotes children's understanding and enjoyment of science?

Can science be creative?

It is sometimes hard to see that science is creative, and indeed that scientists are creative people. When we look at a painting we can immediately feel the excitement that the artist had in bringing together observations and ideas and using the skills of mixing and teasing the paint on to the canvas. When we read a poem we can see all the skill and originality that went into honing the words to convey the subtlety of the ideas. We do not, on the other hand, think, when taking penicillin, of the beauty of its molecular structure and the pleasure Dorothy Hodkins felt in discovering it. We rarely see scientists running down the street shouting 'Eureka'. Yet 'science is a distinct form of creative human activity which involves one way of seeing, exploring and understanding reality' (Scottish CCC 1996).

What is creativity?

We could think of creativity in two ways. First, we can see it as the province of genius, the Einsteins and Da Vincis of the world. This was an approach adopted by early psychologists who were trying to characterise creativity, to find out what was different about highly creative people. Anne Roe, for example, studied 64 eminent scientists exhaustively in the 1940s and 1950s (Roe 1970). What she found was that scientists vary a great deal, but they tend to be independent people with a fascination with the world and a real thirst to find out more. In a sense Roe seemed to be describing not what creativity is, but what kinds of people fully develop the ability to use their creativity.

This brings us to the second way to look at what it means to be creative: we all have the capacity to be creative. The National Advisory Committee on Creative and Cultural Education report (NACCE 1999) defines creativity as 'Imaginative activity fashioned so as to produce outcomes that are both original and of value'. Its four features are presented in Box 8.1

Box 8.1   **Four features of creativity**

- *Using imagination.* This is not simply fantasy but is the process of generating something original or unexpected; generating new links between ideas, seeing new ways to think about something.

- *Pursuing purposes.* Having an idea, or seeing a possible link, is often only the start of the creative process: exploring the original idea, testing it out and taking it further are all-important in real creativity.

- *Being original.* This can be on a number of levels. Completely new discoveries are rare, but an idea may be original in relation to an individual's peer group, or on the individual level an idea may be entirely new to the person making the connection.

- *Judging value.* The outcome of an activity is judged in relation to the purpose of that activity. Hence sheer whimsy would not count as creative, while a new idea that is valid, useful, tenable, satisfying or effective depending on the circumstances would be a creative idea.

(NACCCE 1999: 31–2)

So what is a creative person? Feasey (2003) presents some of the ideas children had when asked what they think a creative person is. Their ideas included 'free-thinking', with 'lots of ideas', one who 'lets their imagination run wild', is 'brainy', is 'mind-boggling', 'brave' and 'can get ideas out of other ideas'. It is interesting that children recognise that to be creative one needs the freedom to try out new ideas, to think in unconventional ways and to take risks (be brave). These ideas begin to give us some insights into the sort of classroom environment that children believe they need for creativity to blossom.

Why is creativity important?

In recent years businesses have begun to call for a more open-minded, flexible, creative workforce in order to compete in the world market. This has helped to raise awareness of the importance of enabling creativity. At the same time a concern has grown that the more prescriptive curricula can inhibit creative teaching.

We can link creativity, as described in Box 8.1, with the process of constructing understanding we have described in Chapter 7. Learning, as viewed from a constructivist perspective, is a creative act. So promoting creativity goes hand in hand with the development of knowledge and understanding, process skills and scientific attitudes. For instance:

■ *Imagination.* As we saw in Chapter 2, children build their ideas about the world as a result of thinking about their experiences and trying to make sense of them. We have seen how they apply their imagination and use what they know to try to answer the question 'What is inside an incubating hen's egg?' (see Chapter 2, Figure 2.1) and the many other examples of imaginative responses given in Chapter 2. In doing so children are using and developing curiosity, observation skills and questioning.

■ *Pursuing a purpose.* We have emphasised the importance of children and teachers raising questions and seeking answers to these questions. For example, in Chapter 3 a group of children and their teacher were fascinated by a bird's nest: interesting questions ensued that could not be immediately answered, but the children began to look for books that might have answers (see Box 3.7). In Chapter 19 we show a group of children's imaginative responses to how a string telephone works (see Box 19.1). John made the creative connection between the vibrations he felt in the string and those in an empty tin can when a sound is made. He went on to suggest ways to test his ideas. His exploration is not simply musing, but is purposeful. He was seeing the importance of evidence and using his skills of planning and gathering evidence.

■ *Being original.* It is unlikely that children will come up with useful ideas that are completely original, but often they will generate an idea that is completely new to them. This requires a willingness to change ideas. Children faced with the observation that metal feels colder than wood and polystyrene, despite being at the same temperature (see Chapter 7, page 75), led to original connections being made and hence to ideas that were entirely novel for the children. This involves the interpretation of evidence and drawing conclusions. This is the point in a lesson when children are almost heard to shout 'Eureka!'

■ *Judging value*. In the framework for analysing learning presented in Chapter 7 we can see that an important step in the learning process is the interpretation of evidence. It is here that new ideas are tested, asking: does our idea fit the evidence? Have we answered the question we were asking or solved the problem we set out to solve? Does it help us to understand better? This is the essential attitude of critical reflection. Interpreting evidence and communicating our ideas to others is a crucial way to test out the validity of these new ideas.

The teacher's role

The teacher's role in supporting science learning needs to be seen in the light of the notion of what it is to learn in science. Teachers must provide the conditions in which to maximise learning: 'Creative learning requires creative teaching' (NACCCE 1999: 6). Yet Feasey (2003) found that many primary teachers did not believe that the encouragement of creative thinking is central to the process. In Box 8.2 we can see how very young children were encouraged to think creatively by having their ideas challenged.

Box 8.2 Young children thinking creatively in science

Dawn McFall and Chris Macro (2004) report on some exciting work with a nursery class. They were inspired by a visit by the head teacher to the school in Reggio Emilia in Italy where early years education is based on 'a respect for children's natural curiosity and creativity and their ability to produce powerful theories about the world and how it works' (Thornton and Brunton 2003). Having reviewed children's previous work the practitioners decided to focus on colour, camouflage and shadow. They wanted to develop the sense of wonder the children had shown when mixing colours as they painted model birds (after a visit to a local botanic garden) and noticed the shadows that were made.

The whole class sat on the carpet in front of an overhead projector and a blue shadow puppet. They were asked to predict what they would see on the screen when it was placed on the OHP. Most thought it would be blue; some made links with their experience of shadows and suggested grey or black. They tried this out, along with some stiff green foam in the shape of a tree, and one of a house (all part of a story they knew). The children began to modify their ideas as they noticed each time that the shadow was black. Then Mr Red was introduced. He had a shape but no eyes or mouth. The children were asked how these could be produced on the shadow. Initially many suggested drawing a face on the puppet, but this did not work. Finally, after lots of thought some children suggested cutting out eye and mouth shapes. They were given plenty of time and appropriate equipment to try out their ideas. In this way they built up their ideas of light being blocked by a solid shape, and went on to observe that they could change the size and shape of the shadows by moving the puppets closer to and further away from the light. They then went on to explore coloured cellophane, experiencing with their own eyes how light passes through certain materials.

The example in Box 8.2 shows that the key to creative teaching is not simply 'going with the flow' of children's ideas; it is about knowing where the children are, and finding interesting and imaginative ways to build on their initial ideas. Bob Ponchaud, in the primary lecture at the 2004 ASE annual meeting, gave this advice:

- listen to and learn from the children;

- be clear about the reason for learning in terms of purpose;

- allow some unstructured time, but structure it carefully.

Throughout the half term's work the children explored their ideas about light with enthusiasm, developing as they went positive scientific attitudes of curiosity, respect for evidence, willingness to change their ideas and critical reflection. They were also developing their process skills, particularly observation, questioning and planning, gathering evidence, interpreting evidence and drawing conclusions and communicating and reflecting. The children were learning a lot about science within a cross-curricular project.

Feasey (2003) suggests questions that teachers should ask themselves about the science experiences offered to children (see Box 8.3).

Box 8.3	Questions for creative teaching

Will it:

- Be different – scintillating?

- Challenge?

- Remove barriers to risk-taking and failing?

- Offer resources and learning spaces that stimulate creative contributions?

- Allow problem-solving?

- Use up-to-date ICT applications?

- Provide opportunities for children to learn in environments beyond the school that excite and engage interest?
- Allow children to meet and work with different people?
- Offer collaborative ways of working?
- Stretch the imagination?

(Feasey 2003: 23)

The answers to all these questions seem to be yes in the example given in Box 8.2. Yet even the most creative of teaching must meet the requirements of the prescribed curriculum. In the example in Box 8.2 this was the curriculum for the foundation stage (DfEE/QCA 2000).

Where do creative ideas for teaching come from?

It is not always easy to pluck a good idea out of the air. Thus a team approach to planning can be valuable (see Chapter 22), and, in the same way that we aim to encourage children to take risks, there also needs to be a willingness on the part of teachers to take risks and to try out new ideas. Teachers need to be alert to possibilities and be keen to learn from the expertise and experience of others. This is where journals, the Internet, discussion among teachers from different schools and attendance at courses can be most helpful. In addition, many teachers have found published curriculum materials to be a useful way to get practical advice and some really interesting ideas.

In recent years there has been a growing use by schools and teachers of published schemes and resources to support teaching. A heavy reliance on these is being blamed for a lack of creative teaching: 'The use of published resources is also becoming more commonplace: these can be helpful but can also lead to a lack of creative teaching if they are followed rigidly' (Ofsted 2004: 6). The key to ensuring creative teaching is not to rely entirely on inspiration (which would be exhausting), but to take a flexible approach to using all the ideas and opportunities available, including published materials of all sorts. It is for this reason that we now turn to look at the use of published resources.

Using published curriculum materials and schemes

Published curriculum materials and schemes, although not widely taken up before the National Curriculum was introduced, have always been useful for teachers. The best provide ideas for activities, background knowledge for teachers, insights into progression, possibilities for assessment and often interesting materials for children and teachers. Although the distinctions are not always clear it is useful to recognise the difference between published curriculum materials, published schemes and the Programmes of Study that are the required elements in the National Curriculum or other prescribed curricula (DfEE/QCA 2000).

Curriculum materials can have several elements:

- a teacher's guide in which there is a statement about the views of teaching and learning and of primary science on which the materials are based, and explanations as to the how the structure of the materials is intended to support progression, how the materials can be used to meet the learning needs of the children and possibly, the approach taken to assessment and suggested cross-curricular links;

- suggested activities arranged under topics, such as forces, living things or houses and homes, keeping clean;

- indications of resource needs;

- background science knowledge for the teacher;

- pupil materials such as worksheets or pupil books.

Not all curriculum materials have all these elements, but they all include suggested activities around particular topics.

Schemes of work (SOW) present a clear structure and order in which suggested activities might be used to ensure progression and coverage of the prescribed curriculum. They represent one interpretation of a required programme of study. They can include indications of the time that might be allocated for sections of the scheme. They can also include suggestions for differentiation, and for assessment opportunities. They can, because they are so structured, give a clear idea of the resource needs. They tend not to include pupil books.

Programmes of study (POS) are neither schemes nor curriculum materials. They are simply an indication of the concepts and skills that are required by the school, district or country. They tend to be laid out according to the phases of education and to be subject specific.

A scheme published by the DfEE (1998) has been widely taken up in England, perhaps because it has the seal of government approval. Yet in the years following the introduction of the scheme school inspectors reported that not all schools were adapting the science scheme of work to reflect the needs and interests of their pupils. 'SOW can be a crutch for teachers who lack confidence in teaching science; teachers do not have enough time to plan their own curriculum; and schools are unsure of how to adapt SOW to attain Ofsted approval' (Parliamentary Office of Science and Technology 2003).

The DfES report *Excellence and Enjoyment* (2003) states that the Programme of Study in the National Curriculum provides in outline what is to be taught but that schools have freedom to decide how to teach. The report goes on to say that 'Schemes of work are an optional tool – schools can ignore them, adapt them or pick and choose between them...to meet schools' particular needs' (DfES 2003: 14).

If we believe that we need to start from children's ideas and interests, then no scheme can replace the teacher's insights into what will interest and excite the children, what approach is most likely to build on their ideas and help them to develop knowledge and understanding, skills and attitudes. However, there are significant advantages as well as some disadvantages to using published schemes and curriculum materials, some of which are listed in Box 8.4.

Box 8.4   **Some advantages and disadvantages of using published materials**

Advantages of using published materials	Disadvantages of using published materials
■ Helps to ensure coverage.	■ May limit the extent to which teachers use children's initial ideas as a starting point.
■ Saves a lot of planning time.	■ May reduce the use made of the school's own environment and context.
■ Helps to identify resources.	
■ Can offer useful background knowledge for the teacher.	■ May limit the opportunities for cross-curricular links.
■ Can provide useful support as a teacher develops in confidence and knowledge.	■ May limit opportunities to plan for the differing needs of children (by implying that they all move on at the same pace).
■ Curriculum materials can provide exciting resources for children and teachers to use.	■ May become boring for the children.

What we need is to be open-minded about the use of schemes and curriculum materials. In this way schools and teachers can make the most of their advantages, while avoiding the disadvantages. The key is to ensure that, in developing a scheme of work, the needs and interests of the children are central to the planning process on all levels.

Summary

- Creativity involves imagination, purpose, originality and values. We all have the capacity to be creative.

- Science is a creative human endeavour and as such needs to be taught in such a way as to encourage questioning, open-mindedness, risk-taking, enthusiasm and enjoyment.

- Creative learning requires creative teaching that uses children's ideas and enthusiasms as a starting point.

- Published schemes provide useful support and guidance, but the slavish following of any such scheme limits the teacher's ability to teach creatively.

- Making use of appropriate cross-curricular links is an important element in maximising meaningful learning.

9 Ways of helping the development of ideas

This chapter is concerned with the action that teachers can take to help children to make progress in developing scientific ideas. In Chapter 7 we described this progress as: moving from limited 'small' and sometimes unscientific ideas towards 'bigger' ideas that help understanding of the world around; moving from description to explanation; and moving from personal ideas to ones shared by others. We underline the importance of taking children's existing ideas as a starting point for helping this progression. By the time they come to the classroom children have already formed ideas about the things they have encountered. The characteristics of these ideas, identified in Chapter 2, indicate strategies teachers can use to help children to develop more scientific, widely accepted ideas. Two of these strategies are discussed in other chapters, while the others are considered here, with particular emphasis on how to introduce alternative ideas through scaffolding.

The importance of starting from children's ideas

In Chapter 2 we looked at some examples from research into children's ideas. Although these ideas were different from the accepted ways of thinking about the phenomena involved, it was not difficult to see why children come to hold them. They are the result of children trying to make sense of events and phenomena using their own limited experience and thinking. We also referred to research that indicates that these ideas should not be ignored. Ideas that children have worked out for themselves make sense to them and will not be replaced by simply giving them the scientific view. The child has to realise that the scientific ideas are more useful than his or her own for helping understanding of what is going on.

Testing their ideas through the processes represented in the framework for learning, discussed in Chapter 7, is one way of helping children to develop more scientific ideas. But there are other strategies needed to help children along the dimensions of progress identified in Box 7.4. Some of these can be deduced by looking again at the characteristics of children's ideas, which were summarised in Chapter 2 in Box 2.2.

Strategies for helping the development of ideas

Each of the characteristics of children's ideas, briefly identified in the left-hand column of Box 9.1, indicates some action that could help children to change their thinking. Some suggestions for these are made in the right-hand column.

Not surprisingly, given the interdependence of ideas and process skills, some of the strategies involve the development of process skills, linking to Chapter 10.

In the following sections we look at the strategies in Box 9.1 that are not covered in other chapters.

Extending experience

Extending the range of types of material, living things and events in children's experience is a central purpose of primary science activities. Sometimes this new experience is enough in itself to challenge existing ideas and requires children to be more cautious of their generalisations. It can change generalisations to more guarded statements:

- almost all wood floats (not ebony or lignum vitae);

- most conifers are evergreen (but not all);

- sound travels through the air (and through solids and liquids as well).

These are not only matters of definition but also matters of explanation, when used, for example, to 'explain' that something floats because it is made of wood.

Often children's ideas indicate the experience that is lacking. For example, the quite common idea that rust forms inside metals and leaks out on to the surface (see Figure 2.10, p. 20) can be challenged by cutting through a rusty nail. More difficult to provide is more experience of things that cannot be directly seen by the children: the insides of living things and of themselves, for instance. This is where visits outside the classroom can play a really special part in children's learning. More and more industries and commercial organisations have education sections that give children learning opportunities that cannot be provided in the classroom. Ideas about the origins and processing of food can be developed by visits to a farm, dairy or supermarket. (*Primary Science Review*, 62 (2000), describes a number of such opportunities.)

Interactive museums or science centres often have curriculum-related exhibits that are designed to take into account children's ideas and find intriguing ways of

Box 9.1	Strategies matched to the characteristics of children's own ideas

Characteristic	Strategies for development
1 Ideas are based on (inevitably) limited experience	Give experience selected to show that things can behave contrary to the child's idea, e.g. that heavy things can float, seeds can germinate without soil.
2 Children base their ideas on how things appear to change rather than on the whole process	Encourage attention to what happens during a change and not just at the start and end, e.g. to observe closely whether anything has been added or taken away when a quantity appears to change.
3 Younger children, particularly, focus on one feature as an explanation	Ask for observation of other factors that might also explain why something happens, e.g. that plants need light (and possibly heat) as well as water.
4 Their reasoning may not be scientific	Help them to develop the process skills to find and use relevant evidence (see Chapter 10).
5 Their ideas are tied to particular instances and not connected to other contexts where they could apply	Refer to other contexts in which the same idea is applicable, e.g. is there something vibrating in a wind instrument that produces sound in the way that a vibration of a drum skin does?
6 They may use words without a grasp of their meaning	Find out what they mean by a word through asking for examples; give examples and non-examples of what words mean and introduce scientific words along with children's own expressions (see Chapter 4).
7 They may hold on to their ideas despite contrary evidence if they have no access to an alternative view that makes sense to them	Scaffold the introduction of alternative ideas from information sources or other children. Ask children to consider evidence in relation to other ideas than their own. Encourage the wider application of new ideas.

challenging and advancing them. For example, in a science centre for three- to 12-year-olds, the staff designed an exhibit about the human skeleton that takes into account research about young children's ideas of the bones in their body. This shows that children may view their body as a 'bag of bones' or as having strings of many small bones, which could not provide support (see Figure 9.1). The interactive exhibit that was produced enabled a child to sit on and pedal a

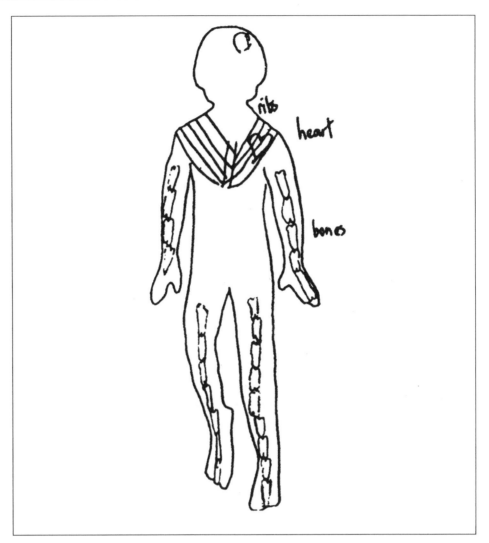

Figure 9.1 An eight-year-old's drawing of the inside of her body
(Osborne *et al.* 1992: 33)

stationary bicycle that was next to a large sheet of glass that acted as a mirror. When the child begins to pedal and looks at the image of his or her legs in the glass, a skeleton is superimposed on this image, showing the moving bones in the legs. This experience was found to have a much greater impact on children's ideas about bones in the body than classroom lessons about the human skeleton (Guichard 1995).

Information from other sources can also be found from the websites that museums and various industries and organisations set up to help education, and from CD-ROMs. The children's ideas about what is inside the egg (page 16) will no doubt be changed by access to photographs of the development of egg embryos and discussion of other evidence of the changes in form and in size that take place in the reproduction of all living things, to be found in books or CD-ROMs.

Developing reasoning about changes in appearance

Some of the well-known, and often replicated, results of Piaget's investigations with children showed that young children may judge by appearance rather than reasoning about when a quantity of a material has changed. A child might claim that, for example, there is more in a lump of Plasticine after it has been squashed out than when it is in a ball. Learning that things are not always what they seem to be is important in science. Reasoning often has to overcome appearance, such as when salt or sugar dissolves in water and appears to have vanished. The action that the teacher can take is to draw attention to the whole process of change, to reverse it where possible (as with the Plasticine) and provide some evidence that will overcome the visual sensation of change.

Encouraging attention to more than one factor

Another feature of young children's thinking, related to the one just discussed, is that it is unidimensional. One view of things, or one factor, is considered when there are others that need to be considered to explain particular phenomena. This shows, for instance, in children saying that plants need water or light to grow, but not both, and rarely adding air or heat. There are very many ideas in science that involve a combination of factors (such as the meaning of something being 'alive'), so it is important to encourage children to think in terms of all possible factors and not just the first that comes to mind. Having children brainstorm in groups about, for example, what we need to maintain good health will not only gather more ideas but help them to realise that a combination of factors is involved.

Creating links between events that have a common explanation

Children develop ideas about events in terms of the particular features of those events. These are 'small' ideas and probably don't apply to other situations that actually share common explanation. For example, children commonly explain the disappearance of water from puddles only in terms of draining away through the ground, while they may explain the drying of damp clothes on a washing line in terms of some action of the air. The children could be helped to link these two: could the air have something to do with the puddle drying up too? Some investigations testing this idea in relation to puddles could make this a useful idea in both situations. Further examples of water disappearing could then be drawn into the range of things explained in this way. The idea has then become one that applies more widely; that is, has become a bigger one.

In other cases the small ideas are ones that refer to different aspects of a phenomenon, and need to be brought together. For instance, understanding why things don't fall off the side of the Earth means bringing together these ideas:

- that things fall downwards;

- that the Earth is spherical;

- that 'down' means towards the centre of the Earth.

Another example is putting together ideas about light and how we see to understand the formation of images in mirrors or lenses. This depends on understanding that:

- we see an object when light enters our eyes from it;

- putting a mirror or lens between the object and our eyes changes the path of the light;

- we interpret the path of the light as a straight line from the object to the eye.

If all these ideas are understood it may be possible to bring them together to realise that the eye does not 'see' the change in direction that the mirror or lens has caused and so interprets it as if it came in a straight line, so the object is interpreted as in a different place from where it really is.

Scaffolding new ideas

While we can often see how to challenge children's unscientific ideas, it is not always clear how they find more scientific ones to replace them. There is an important role for the teacher here, one that has, perhaps, been underplayed in discussions of constructivist approaches to learning. It is also a subtle role, since we must avoid giving the 'right' answer that children have to accept whether or not it makes sense to them. We have to ensure that the new ideas are taken into the children's own thinking. In order to do this, children need:

- access to ideas different from their own;

- support in trying out the new ideas in relation to their existing experience;

- opportunities to apply them to new experiences.

Access to different ideas

New ideas need not necessarily be introduced by the teacher. They can also come from books, CD-ROMs, videos and people who visit the classroom or places that are visited by the children. Other children are often a source of different ideas and these may include ideas that are closer to the scientific view than the ideas of a particular child. Whatever the source, children are likely to need encouragement and support while trying out new ideas.

Analogies may provide the new idea that children need in order to understand something. Analogies can provide a link between one situation (A, which a child wants to understand) and another (B, more familiar) that is thought to illustrate the idea or process in action in A. For instance it is common to illustrate the water cycle (A) using a boiling kettle and condensing the water vapour on a cold surface (B). The problem for the children is making the link between the pieces of equipment in A and B. As consequence, the kettle often ends up in a child's representation of how rain is formed from clouds in the sky.

Often the models that adults think up to represent difficult concepts, such as water flow in pipes as an analogy of flow of electricity in a circuit, can cause more problems of understanding the analogous situation in the first place. Small-scale research (Jabin and Smith 1994) that involved trying different analogies for electric circuits seemed to show that it was the effort made to create a link with something already familiar to the children that had an effect, rather than the nature of any particular analogy. Asoko and de Boo (2001), presenting a collection of analogies used in primary science, warn that analogies can introduce irrelevant or misleading features and may be as difficult to understand as the phenomenon they are supposed to explain.

Support in trying new ideas

This is where the teacher's role in 'scaffolding' new ideas comes in. Box 9.2 explains the meaning of this term.

Box 9.2	Scaffolding children's ideas and skills

Scaffolding means supporting children in considering an idea or a way of testing an idea that they have not proposed themselves but are capable of making 'their own'. The judgement of when this is likely to be possible has to be made by the teacher, taking into account the existing ideas or skills of the children and how far they are from taking the next step. It often means the teacher making links for the children between experiences and understanding they already have but have not linked up for themselves.

In theoretical terms, it means finding what Vygotsky (1962) introduced as the 'zone of proximal development'. This is the point just beyond existing ideas, where the learner is likely to be able to use new ideas with help. What the teacher does in scaffolding is to suggest the new idea and provide support for the children while they use it and, finding it helps to make sense, begin to incorporate it into their thinking.

The teacher might ask children to 'Try this idea' or 'Try looking at it this way' or 'Suppose...' An example might be 'Suppose the water that disappears from the puddle goes into the air' or 'Suppose the sun is not moving but the Earth is turning around.' Each of the 'supposed' ideas can be used to make a prediction that can be tested, and as a result children can see that they do help to explain experience.

Scaffolding can be used to develop skills, too. It is familiar in the teaching of new skills such as using a microscope or a calculator. In these cases the learner needs to be told what to do at first, may need a reminder later and eventually uses the skill confidently.

It is important to underline that scaffolding ideas is not the same as telling children the 'right answer'. It is essentially enabling children to take a further step in progress that is within their reach. It depends on teachers having a good knowledge of their children's ideas and skills and using this in deciding the next steps and helping children to advance their thinking.

Scaffolding is particularly important in relation to ideas that cannot be tested out in practice. It is difficult, for example, for children to understand that if a moving object stops, there must be a force acting to stop it. Many children accept or offer the reason as being 'friction' but don't go as far as realising that without friction the object would not stop moving. Scaffolding is necessary here, just as it is in relation to ideas about the Earth in space, the causes of day and night, the seasons and phases of the Moon. These are cases where the teacher may have to lead children to take a few steps without realising why until they can look back. For example, children are unlikely to decide on their own to make a model of the Sun, Moon and Earth to explain why we see the Moon in different phases. So the teacher takes the initiative and sets up a situation that enables the children to 'see' a spherical object looking like a half-Moon, and then they can make the connection.

Opportunities to try out new ideas in different situations

Given that the new idea is a scientific one, it should help children to make sense of further experience. Helping children to do this will secure the new idea in their thinking, as well as expanding their understanding of things around. It also gives the teacher the opportunity to see how secure the new idea really is. It may be necessary to stop and return to familiar ground if the signs are that the new idea is still a little wobbly. However, if new ideas can be successfully applied this brings a feeling of enjoyment and satisfaction in learning. For example:

■ Can eclipses be explained in terms of the movement of the Moon around the Earth and the Earth around the Sun?

■ Can the idea of friction be used to explain why ice skates have knife-edged blades?

Selecting strategies for helping progression in ideas

It is not until a teacher takes steps to find out children's ideas (as discussed in Chapter 14) that (s)he can decide what is the appropriate action to take. The appropriate action can be decided by diagnosing the shortcomings of the children's ideas and selecting from the kinds of strategies that we have discussed. This requires, of course, that we pay attention to children's ideas and take them seriously.

Summary

This chapter has suggested some strategies for helping children to develop scientific ideas, matched to the particular shortcomings of the ideas that children initially hold. The main points have been:

■ It is important to start from the ideas that children have in trying to help their progress towards more scientific ones.

■ A range of different strategies can be used, the selection depending on the nature of the ideas that children hold.

■ When alternative ideas need to be introduced, their use should be scaffolded by the teacher, with opportunities being given for application in other contexts.

10 Ways of helping the development of process skills

Introduction

In Chapter 7 we showed that process skills have a central role in the development of scientific understanding. We noted that if these skills are not well developed, relevant evidence may not be gathered, or some evidence may be disregarded. As a result, preconceptions may be confirmed when they should be challenged. So the question of how to help development of skills, which we take up in this chapter, is an important one. Four groups of skills were identified in Chapter 6 (Box 6.4). Here we consider the action that teachers can take to help children to make progress in developing these skills, in the directions indicated in Box 7.4. This enables us to identify some common strategies that can apply to all process skills.

Developing skills in the context of science activities

Before outlining the actions that can help children to develop process skills, we should answer the question: what makes these skills *science* process skills? Many of the same processes – observing, predicting, planning, interpreting etc. – are used in learning other subjects, such as geography, history and economics. However, it is only when skills are well advanced (at the level of 'experts') that they are readily transferred across subjects. One of the differences between experts and novices in any field is that experts are able to 'function at a more general level than novices. Indeed, some have argued that educationally assisted development is the process by which thought becomes increasingly disembedded from situational contexts' (Hodson 1998: 117).

Children at the primary level are functioning as novices, who learn particular skills in particular contexts and are not able to transfer skills from one subject to another. This can happen even within science subjects, much to the frustration of secondary science teachers. This is why we have identified, as one dimension of progression in process skills, the ability to use them effectively in unfamiliar as well as in familiar contexts.

The implication of this is that, certainly at the primary level, if we want children to be able to *use* process skills in science, then they must develop them in *science*. In particular, 'content-free' exercises ('black box' activities), where no understanding is involved, have little value for developing science process skills. Consequently, all the strategies suggested here are intended to be used within regular science activities.

Ways of developing particular process skills

Skills of gathering information by observing and using information sources

Box 10.1 summarises some actions that teachers can take to encourage these skills. The first essential is having something to observe. As children will spend most time in the classroom it is important for this to be rich in opportunities for observation: displays of objects related to a theme, posters, photographs, living things etc., with sources of further information nearby, should be regular features.

Box 10.1 | **Developing skills of gathering information by observing and using sources of information**

Action that teachers can take:

- Provide informal opportunities for using the senses for gathering information by
  - (a) regular display of objects and phenomena for children to explore, with relevant information books or CD-ROMs accessible nearby;
  - (b) a collection of objects relating to a new topic two or three weeks ahead of starting it to create interest;
  - (c) time for observing.

- Encourage observation through 'invitations to observe': cards placed next to objects or equipment displayed, encouraging observation and attention to detail.

- Teach the correct use of instruments that
  - (a) extend the senses, including time-lapse photography and the digital microscope;
  - (b) can measure change or differences, such as sensors and probes (see Chapter 21).

- Teach the techniques for using information sources such as reference books and the Internet/intranet.

- Set up situations where observations are shared.

- Organise visits to observe events and objects outside the classroom (see Chapter 20).

Providing time

Time is significant for encouraging observation, perhaps more than for other process skills. Children need time to go back to things they may have observed only superficially or when a question has occurred to them that suggests something they want to check. A display enables children to use odd moments as well as science activity time for observing and so increases an important commodity in the development of this skill.

Encouragement

Some children need encouragement to observe and to do this carefully, with attention to detail. Question cards can be placed by displayed objects: 'Try to make this bottle make a high and a low sound' placed next to a bottle three-quarters full of water encourages interaction. 'How many different kinds of grass are there here?' placed next to a bunch of dried grasses encourages careful observation. Next to a 'cartesian diver', made from a dropper floating in water inside a large plastic bottle (Figure 10.1), a card might ask 'What happens when you squeeze the sides of the bottle?' In this case there are several things to observe, including how the level of the water inside the dropper's tube rises when the bottle is squeezed, which helps to explain why the dropper sinks. So the card could ask 'What do you notice that could explain what happens?'

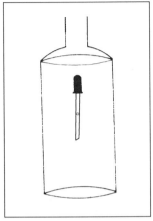

Figure 10.1 A Cartesian diver

Using aids to observation

Observing is the basis of all means of collecting data in a practical situation. Where attention to detail or to small differences is necessary it will be appropriate to extend senses by using an instrument such as a hand lens or stethoscope and to use measuring instruments to quantify observations. Data can also be obtained from secondary sources, of course, such as books, displays, film, television and computer-based sources. Children will need to know how to use these things properly. Some, such as the use of a hand lens, can be taught using a card with a drawing on it, placed next to selected objects in the classroom display. Older children with the required manipulative skill can learn to use a microscope through similar informal opportunities. Other techniques, particularly those involving computers, need more formal instruction.

Reporting and discussing observations

Sharing observations helps children to become aware of what can be found by careful observation. Making a point of spending a few minutes, as a whole class, discussing what has been noticed about things on display, for example, may draw the attention of some children to things they have missed. Asking questions about details during this discussion will help children to pay attention to them in further observation.

Making visits

Not all observations are made in the classroom, of course, and careful preparation for expeditions outside is important if things are not to be missed. There is less opportunity to revisit objects and so it is essential for the teacher to explore in advance the place to be visited, keeping the capabilities and knowledge of the children in mind.

Skills of questioning, predicting and planning

Box 10.2 sets out some key ways of helping children to develop these skills.

Box 10.2	Developing skills of questioning, predicting and planning

Action that teachers can take:

■ Stimulate curiosity through classroom displays, posters, and inviting questions through a question board or box.
■ Help children to refine their questions and put them into investigable form.
■ Ask children to use their suggested explanations for something to make predictions: 'What do you think will happen if your idea is correct?'
■ Provide opportunities for planning by starting with a question to be answered by investigation without instructions.
■ Scaffold planning a fair test using a planning board (see Figure 10.2).
■ Talk through an investigation that has been completed to identify how it could have been better planned.

We discussed in Chapter 3 the importance of encouraging children to raise questions. The ways in which questioning can be promoted through a supportive class climate and by positive reinforcement were included there and need not be repeated here. There is, though, a further point to add.

Identifying investigable questions

The significance in science of being able to put questions in an investigable form (see Chapter 6) means that it is worthwhile taking time to discuss with children explicitly what this means and how to do it, using some examples. The AKSIS project (Goldsworthy *et al*. 2000) has produced lists of questions for discussion with children in structured activities designed to make children aware of the need to clarify questions. The idea is to help children to realise that questions such as 'Does toothpaste make a difference to your teeth?' and 'Is margarine better for you than butter?' can only be answered when the meanings of 'making a difference' and 'better for you' have been clarified. There has to be some indication of the kind of evidence that could be collected to answer the question (even if, in these cases, the children might not be able to collect it themselves). One of the AKSIS activities is to ask children to decide whether, in certain questions, it is clear what would have to be changed and what measured to answer the question. The children can then be asked to reflect on their own questions and reword them to make clear how they could be investigated.

Using ideas to make predictions

Children's predictions are often implicit and helping to make them explicit and conscious enables the children to see the connection between an idea and the prediction from it that is tested. For example, children may explain the moisture on the outside of a can of drink just taken out of the fridge as having come from the drink inside the can. Asking 'What do you think will happen if you put an empty can in the fridge and then take it out?' will make them use this idea to predict something that can be tested. If children are helped to make predictions in simple cases and to think about the way in which they do this, the process will become more conscious and more easily applied in other contexts.

Opportunities to plan how to answer a question by investigation

Too often children's experience of what is required in planning an investigation is by-passed because they are given written instructions to follow, as in the parachute activity on page 52. It also happens when their teachers guide their activities too strongly, as in the following classroom observation of a teacher introducing an activity to find out if ice melts more quickly in air or in water at room temperature:

You'll need to use the same sized ice cubes. Make sure you have everything ready before you take the ice cubes out of the tray. Put one cube in the water and one close to it in the air. Then start the clock.

Here the children will have no problem in doing what is required, but they will have no idea of why they are doing it. If they did, they might challenge the need for a clock in this activity.

If children are to develop the ability to plan there must be opportunities for them to start from a question and work out how to answer it, or to make a prediction and to think out and carry out their own procedures for testing it. To ask them to take these steps by themselves is to ask a great deal of young children and of older ones unused to devising investigations, and they will need help that subsequently can gradually be withdrawn.

Supporting (scaffolding) planning

In the early years, children's experience should include simple problems that they can easily respond to, such as 'How will you do this?' For example, 'How can you find out if the light from the torch will shine through this fabric, this piece of plastic, this jar of water, this coat sleeve?' Often young children will respond by showing rather than describing what to do. With greater experience and the ability to 'think through actions' before doing them they can be encouraged to think ahead more and more, which is one of the values of planning. Involving children in planning is part of setting an expectation that they will think through what they are going to do as far as possible.

The planning of a fair test can be scaffolded (see Box 9.2) by using a planning board. The original planning board was developed in 1972 as part of a *Science 5/13* unit on working with wood. Several variants of it have been devised since, but the main features remain much as in the original description shown in Figure 10.2.

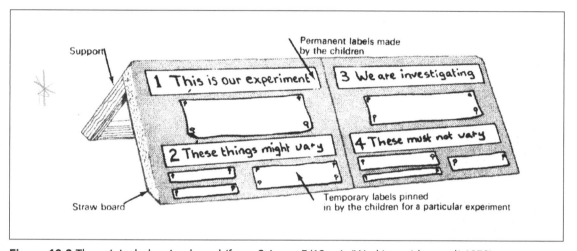

Figure 10.2 The original planning board (from *Science 5/13* unit 'Working with wood' 1972)

Reviewing a complete investigation

For older children, help in planning can begin, paradoxically, from reviewing an investigation that has been completed (whether or not the children planned it themselves), helping them to go through what was done and identifying the structure of the activity through questions such as:

■ What were they trying to find out?

■ What things did they compare (identifying the independent variable)?

■ How did they make sure that it was fair (identifying the variables that should be kept the same)?

■ How did they find the result (identifying the dependent variable)?

Planning continues throughout an investigation and the initial plan may change as the work progresses and unforeseen practical obstacles emerge. However, it is important for children to recognise when they make a change to their plans and to review the whole plan when a change is made. Writing plans down is a useful activity because it requires forward thinking, actions carried out in the mind.

Skills of interpreting information and drawing conclusions

| **Box 10.3** | **Developing skills of interpreting information and drawing conclusions** |

Action that teachers can take:

■ Make sure that the thinking does not stop when data have been collected or observations made and recorded.

■ Provide time and opportunities for children to identify simple patterns or relationships that bring their results together.

■ Ensure that results are used to decide whether a prediction was confirmed or whether a question was answered.

■ Talk about what has been learned about the phenomenon investigated, not just the observed effects.

■ Encourage identification of overall statements that bring all observations together.

Interpreting results means going further than collecting individual observations and recording them. It means trying to find patterns and to relate various pieces of information to each other and to the ideas being tested. As with other process skills, children have to be given the opportunity and encouragement to do these things if they are to develop these abilities. Some of the ways in which teachers can help are summarised in Box 10.3.

Linking results to the question under investigation

The main thrust is to ensure that children use the results of their investigations to advance their ideas. Asking 'Is that what you expected/predicted?' 'What did you find out about...?' (e.g. how the colour of our clothes affects how warm we become, as in the investigation in Figure 16.1, p. 166 brings the children back to the reason for their enquiry and to thinking about the ideas they were testing.

As an example, consider children measuring the length of the shadow of a stick at different times of the day. They must go beyond just collecting the measurements if the activity is to have value for developing ideas. Important outcomes from this activity include:

■ seeing that there is pattern in the decreasing and then increasing length of the shadow;

- realising the possibility of using this pattern to make predictions about the length at times when it was not measured, or the time of day from the measurement of the shadow;

- the development of ideas about how shadows are formed.

All depend on using the results the children obtain, so the development of the skills required is important. The central part of the teacher's role is to ensure that results are used and children don't rush from one activity to another without talking about and thinking through what their results mean.

Identifying patterns in results or observations

Sometimes children implicitly use patterns in their findings without recognising that they in fact do so. Teachers can help to foster greater consciousness of the process by discussing simple patterns, such as the relationship between the position of the sun and the length of the shadow (or the equivalent in a classroom simulation using a torch and a stick). The starting point must be the various ways in which children express their conclusions. For instance, there are several ways of describing the relationship between the length of the shadow and the position of the sun: 'the shadow is shortest when the sun is highest', 'the shortest one is when the sun is high and the longest when it is low', 'its length depends on where the sun is', 'the higher the sun the shorter the shadow'. All of these actually require thinking about the set of information about the position of the sun, or other source of light, and the length of the shadow, but the first three are incomplete expressions of it. The last one refers to all the data in one statement and says not just that there is a relationship, but what this is. Discussion will help children to realise this but it is quite an advanced skill and should not be short-circuited by teaching a formula for 'the great/small-er X, the short/long-er Y'.

Skills of communication and reflection

Communication by children plays an important part in their learning. Actions that teachers can take to encourage communication and reflection are summarised in Box 10.4. In Chapter 4 we noted how thinking and speaking are connected: how we 'talk ourselves into our own understanding'. This points to the importance of regular class discussion of what children have found in group activities. Such exchanges are particularly useful if they are conducted so that children question each other, ask for explanations as well as descriptions and suggest improvements in what was done.

Using a notebook

The same arguments apply to writing as to talking, but children need more help to develop the skills of using personal writing to support their thinking. Providing children with a personal notebook is a start. However, they also need to recognise its function not just as an aid to memory, but also as a means of organising their thinking, through writing rough notes and recording observations.

It is important for personal notebooks to be seen as informal, a place where words do not have to be marshalled into sentences. This can liberate children from seeing writing as a chore – one that often deters some from activities, even ones they enjoy, 'because we will have to write about it afterwards'. Just as informal talk helps reflection (as noted in Chapter 4, page 37), so does informal writing. Teachers can help this benefit by suggesting making notes – 'You might want to think about this and write down some ideas in your notebook before starting' – and by showing an example of using a notebook themselves. Children should begin using notebooks as soon as writing becomes fluent. It is probably best to introduce them to the whole class, encouraging those less able to write to draw and use what words they can.

Box 10.4	Developing skills of communication and reflection

Actions that teachers can take:

■ Provide opportunities for oral reporting and time for preparing, so that procedures and ideas are shared.

■ Provide children with a personal notebook for recording and reflection.

■ Discuss with children how they might use their notebook and set aside time for them to use it.

■ Provide ideas about how to record certain kinds of information, using tables, drawings with labels and symbols.

■ Discuss criteria for evaluating reports and provide time for peer and self-assessment (see Chapter 17).

■ Give time to review activities and reflect on, for instance, whether questions could have been better expressed, other variables controlled, measurements repeated.

■ Discuss ways of communicating particular information to particular audiences.

Time for discussing what and how to report

Children will need to draw upon their notes in preparing for reporting on what they have done when the class gets together at the end of an activity or topic. This is an opportunity for them to realise the value of making notes. It is also the occasion for thinking about what is needed for formal reporting. Different occasions may require different forms of report. Not every activity needs to be written up formally and displayed, but the occasional preparation of a report that could be displayed to other classes or parents or at a science fair is an opportunity for children to think about the audience when deciding what words, diagrams or other illustrations to use for effective communication.

Some general strategies for developing process skills

When we look across the action suggested for helping the development of these groups of skills it is evident that there are common themes. Frequent mention has been made of certain points that appear to be key strategies that can be applied to all process skills. These are:

■ providing the opportunity to use process skills in the exploration of materials and phenomena first hand;

■ providing the opportunity for discussion in small groups and as a whole class;

■ encouraging critical review of how activities have been carried out;

■ providing access to the techniques needed for advancing skills;

■ involving children in communicating in various forms and reflecting on their thinking.

Summary

This chapter has discussed the role that teachers can take in helping children to develop their process skills. The main points have been:

■ Science process skills have to be developed within the context of science activities.

■ There are particular actions that teachers can take to provide opportunities for children to develop particular process skills.

■ These actions include strategies that can be applied to all process skills.

11 Ways of helping the development of attitudes

Introduction

This chapter is concerned with the teacher's role in relation to the affective outcomes of learning: the feelings and emotions attached to learning in general and learning science in particular. Attitudes, meaning readiness or willingness to act in a certain way in particular circumstances, fall into this category. In Chapter 6 (Box 6.4) we identified two attitudes that seem to be particularly important in learning science. They are not, however, the only relevant attitudes, since attitudes that influence learning in general also need to be taken into account. Moreover, the extent to which children are motivated to learn will have an overarching influence on all learning. In this chapter we consider how children's learning can be motivated and how positive attitudes that help learning can be fostered. We begin by looking at the broad context of motivation, then suggest some general strategies for developing positive attitudes that help learning in general and finally some specific actions for developing scientific attitudes.

Encouraging motivation for learning

One of the key aspects of a teacher's role is to encourage motivation for learning; since positive attitudes are encouraged within an ethos that promotes motivation. But all behaviour and learning is motivated in some way so it is necessary to distinguish different kinds of motivation. The idea of motivating learning through rewards and punishments is the basis for the approach to learning known as 'behaviourism' (Skinner 1974). The underlying theory is that behaviours that are regularly rewarded will be reinforced and those that are repeatedly punished will disappear. However, this is completely contrary to the view of learning as being constructed through the mental activity of learners, linking new and previous experience, as we have attempted to convey it in this book. We do not find support for motivating learning with understanding by rewards and punishment, so we have to conceive of motivation in different ways.

Intrinsic and extrinsic motivation

The two main kinds of motivation for learning identified by psychologists are intrinsic motivation and extrinsic motivation. Some (e.g. McMeniman 1989) also add achievement motivation to these, but it is generally agreed that the chief distinctions to be made are between intrinsic and extrinsic. Intrinsic motivation means that someone engages in an activity because of the satisfaction that is derived from doing it. When there is extrinsic motivation the satisfaction comes from a result that has little to do with the activity: a new bicycle for passing an examination or an ice cream for finishing homework. Some main characteristics of extrinsically and intrinsically motivated learners are given in Box 11.1. From this we can see that intrinsic motivation in clearly desirable, since it leads to self-motivated and sustained learning. It is particularly relevant to learning to make sense of things and not being satisfied until they are understood.

Box 11.1	Intrinsic and extrinsic motivation for learning

Learners who are intrinsically motivated:

■ find interest and satisfaction in what they learn and in the learning process;

■ are 'motivated from within' and do not need external incentives to engage with learning;

■ recognise their own role in the learning and so take responsibility for it;

■ seek out information, identify their learning goals and persevere;

■ know that what they achieve depends on their effort.

Learners who are extrinsically motivated:

■ engage in learning mainly because of external incentives such as gold stars and high marks;

■ may cease to learn, or at least decrease effort, in the absence of these external factors, learning only what is closely related to the behaviour that is rewarded;

■ put effort into learning the things not because they have value for developing understanding, but in order to gain praise, reward or privilege.

An important part of the emotional context of learning is how children see themselves as learners and how they attribute their success or failure. Those who attribute their successes to their ability and hard work recognise that their learning is within their own control. When they are challenged by difficulty they try hard and when they fail they consider that they could succeed if they try hard enough. So failure does not damage their self-esteem. The reverse is the case for those who attribute their success to circumstances outside themselves, to chance, to luck or to their teachers. For these learners, experience of failure leads to loss of confidence, for they do not feel they are in control of whether they succeed or fail. Such learners try to protect their self-esteem by avoiding the risk of failure through selecting tasks well within their grasp.

Encouraging intrinsic motivation

Intrinsic motivation is implicit in positive attitudes towards learning. But how is it to be encouraged? Experience from a range of studies of learning across the curriculum suggests that there are things that a teacher can do and things to avoid in creating the climate to foster intrinsic motivation.

Positive action
This includes:

- Providing some choice of activities. This does not mean a free choice to do anything but a choice from among carefully devised alternatives, all seen by the children as having some relevance to them. The act of choosing gives the children some ownership of the activity and transfers some responsibility to them to undertake it seriously and complete it to the best of their ability.

- Involving children in identifying some reasonable objectives for the activity and some ways of achieving these objectives.

- Helping them to assess their own progress, using approaches such as the ones suggested in Chapter 17.

- Setting up activities in a way that requires genuine collaboration in pairs or small groups, so that the effort of all those involved matters and all are obliged to pull their weight.

- Showing confidence that children will do well; having high expectations.

- Encouraging pride in having tried and made a good effort.

This sets up a 'virtuous' circle, where children try harder and as result succeed, which raises their self-esteem. By the same reasoning, it is important to avoid the vicious circle or self-fulfilling prophecy whereby children see themselves as failing even before they begin a task and therefore make little effort, leading to failure that confirms their judgement of themselves. Again, we can identify actions that should be avoided.

Things to avoid
These include:

- Labelling children either as groups or as individuals. This can happen con- sciously, as when children are streamed or grouped by ability and are referred to by a label, or unconsciously. It is difficult to imagine that being labelled 'the B stream', reinforced by the uniformly low level of work expected, does not transfer to the children's self-image. Children are acutely sensitive to being treated in different ways and are not deceived by being described as the 'green' group when this means that they are the 'slow' ones.

■ Making comparisons between children. This encourages competition and detracts from each child working towards his or her own objectives.

Caring for children's feelings about their work

Children have well-formed views about the work they are given, about their teacher and those around them. For example, many children, like eight-year-old Christopher, find school 'boring':

When the book says 'write the answer', I have to write the whole sum because Mrs X says it will help my writing . . . but it takes so long.

It's so boring going over things on the board until all the class knows it. She just goes on and on.

When you write a word and you know it's wrong, you cross it out and try again. Then you have to copy it out because it's messy. You have to copy out all the work, not just the bit where you made a mistake.

They are also sensitive to remarks about their work which seem to be public ridicule. 'When she sees a bit of my writing, she says "Look at that i. It's not like an i, it's like a funny little man." She tells all the class and they laugh.'

So, given that children do have clear ideas about their work, *one important thing that a teacher can do is to find out what these are*. Just showing interest in how the children feel about their work is in itself significant in signalling the importance the teacher attaches to providing work that children will put effort into. Christopher's remarks were made to a sympathetic outsider to the school and it may be difficult for the teacher to obtain such frank statements in discussion with an individual, although this may be possible in some cases. The idea of a regular 'review' involving children in discussions with teachers about their work, proposed as part of some schemes of records of achievement at the secondary level, has been suggested at the primary level (Conner 1991).

Interest in children's feelings and views on their learning has to be sincere. Children are not taken in by the superficial interest of their teacher, for it will be betrayed by manner and tone of voice as well as by whether anything happens as a result. A genuine interest creates an atmosphere in which children's own ideas are encouraged and taken as a starting point, where effort is praised rather than only achievement, where value is attached to each child's endeavours. In this atmosphere, a child who does not achieve as well as others will not be ridiculed. The range of activities available makes allowances for differences in the ability of children and the teacher's interest and approach results in the involvement of children in their work and their own learning.

General approaches to the development of attitudes

Attitudes and learning

Attitudes show not in what children can do or know but in their willingness to use their knowledge or skills where appropriate. They are outcomes of learning that result from a range of experiences across which there is some pattern. For instance, an attitude of willingness to take account of evidence does not result from a single activity or even several activities around a topic. Instead it may result from extended experience in which the value of using evidence has been clear or from the example over a period of time of someone who showed this attitude in their behaviour. In other words, attitudes are picked up from across a range of experience; they are 'caught' rather than 'taught', particularly from influential adults. Thus showing an example of the behaviour is a key action that teachers can take. Others are providing opportunities for children to make the choices that enable them to develop attitudes, reinforcing positive attitudes and discussing attitude-related behaviour.

Showing an example

Given that attitudes are 'caught', showing an example is probably the most important of the positive things that teachers can do. For a teacher to make a point of revealing that his or her own ideas have changed, for instance, can have a significant impact on children's willingness to change their ideas. 'I used to think that trees died after dropping their leaves, until . . . ', 'I didn't realise that there were different kinds of woodlice', 'I thought that it was easier to float in deep water than in shallow water but the investigations showed that it didn't make any difference.' The old adage that 'actions speak louder than words' means that such comments will not be convincing by themselves. It is important for teachers to show attitudes in what they do, not just what they say, by, for example:

- showing interest in new things (which the children may have brought in) by giving them attention, if not immediately, then at some planned time later, and displaying them for others to see, if appropriate;

- helping to find out about new or unusual things by searching books, the Internet or other information sources with the children;

- being self-critical, admitting mistakes and taking steps to make amends.

In a classroom where useful ideas are pursued as they arise and activities extend beyond well-beaten tracks, there are bound to be opportunities for these teacher behaviours to be displayed. Situations in which the teacher just doesn't know, or that bring surprises or something completely new, should be looked upon not as problems, but as opportunities for transmitting attitudes through example.

Providing opportunity

Since attitudes show in willingness to act in certain ways, there have to be opportunities for children to have the choice of doing so. If their actions are closely controlled by rules or highly structured lesson procedures, then there is little opportunity to develop and show certain attitudes (except perhaps willingness to conform). Providing new and unusual objects in the classroom gives children the opportunity to show and satisfy – and so develop – curiosity. Discussing activities while they are in progress or after they have been completed gives encouragement to reflect critically, but unless such occasions are provided, the attitudes cannot be fostered.

Reinforcing positive attitudes

Children pick up attitudes not only from examples but also from how others respond to their own behaviour. When children show indications of positive attitudes, it is important to reinforce these behaviours by approval *of the behaviour*. There is an important distinction here between praising the individual and reinforcing the behaviour. It is important not to adopt a behaviourist approach of giving general praise as a reward for behaving in a certain way, which can reinforce the behaviour without an understanding of why it is desirable. As in the case of feedback to children about their work (see Chapter 16), feedback about attitude-related behaviour should avoid judgement of the person.

For example, if critical reflection leads to children realising that they did not make fair comparisons in their experiment, the teacher's reaction could be 'well you should have thought of that before' or, alternatively, 'you've learned something important about this kind of investigation'. The latter is clearly more likely to encourage reflection and the admission of fault on future occasions. Moreover, if this approval is consistent it eventually becomes part of the classroom climate and children will begin to reinforce the attitudes for themselves and for each other. Those who have not developed positive attitudes will be able to recognise what these are from the approval given to others.

Discussing attitude-related behaviour

Attitudes can only be said to exist when they are aspects of a wide range of behaviour. In this regard they are highly abstract and intangible. Identifying them involves a degree of abstract thinking, which makes them difficult to discuss, particularly with young children. However, as children become more mature they are more able to reflect on their own behaviour and motivations. It then becomes possible to discuss examples of attitudes in action and to help them to identify the way they affect behaviour explicitly. When some ten-year-olds read in a book that snails eat strawberries, they tested this out and came to the conclusion that 'as far as our snails are concerned, the book is wrong'. Their teacher discussed with them how the author of the book might have come to a different conclusion from them and whether both the author and the children might gather more evidence before arriving at their conclusions. The children not only recognised that what was concluded depended on the attitudes to evidence but also that the conclusions were open to challenge from further evidence, thus developing their own 'respect for evidence'.

Ways of developing scientific attitudes

The attitudes of science that we have identified are a subset of attitudes that apply to learning more widely (such as curiosity, perseverance, flexibility). The general points discussed above can readily be applied to the specifically scientific attitudes that we have identified, leading to the action suggested in Boxes 11.2 and 11.3.

Box 11.2	Developing willingness to consider evidence and change ideas

Actions that the teacher can take:

■ protect time for discussing and interpreting evidence, thus conveying how important this is;

■ pay attention to the evidence children gather and make sure that none is ignored, thus setting the expectation of taking note of evidence;

■ provide an example, by talking about how the teacher's own ideas have been changed by evidence;

■ acknowledge when evidence does require a change of ideas ('we need to think again about this');

■ reinforce the importance of not rushing to conclusions with inadequate evidence by approval when children suggest that more evidence is needed before they can come to a conclusion.

Box 11.3	Developing sensitivity to living things and the environment

Actions that the teacher can take:

- provide an example of responsibility for living things by checking on the health of animals and plants in the classroom, even if children have been assigned to look after them;

- give opportunities for children to care for living things, temporarily brought into the classroom (but check on their welfare, as just suggested above);

- discuss the care that should be taken when exploring the natural environment, such as replacing stones to preserve habitats;

- show approval of thoughtful behaviour to living things;

- ensure that living things taken into the classroom for study are replaced afterwards, where possible;

- provide bins for recycling that are used by staff and children.

Summary

In this chapter we have considered how teachers can help the development of motivation towards learning and positive attitudes that promote learning in general and science learning in particular. The main points have been:

- Attitudes are ways of describing a willingness or preference to behave in certain ways. They reflect ways in which people are motivated to learn.

- Attitudes that help learning in science imply motivation that comes from interest and satisfaction in making sense of the world around; that is, intrinsic motivation.

- Teachers can encourage this type of motivation by providing some choice in activities, leading to ownership, involving children in identifying and working towards clear goals and assessing their own progress, setting up situations for genuinely collaborative work and raising children's expectations of themselves.

- It is important that teachers show real interest in how children feel about their work and set up a supportive classroom atmosphere.

- Attitudes in general and scientific attitudes in particular can be encouraged by showing examples in teachers' own behaviour, ensuring opportunities for children to make decisions and form their own ideas, reinforcing relevant behaviours and discussing the value of behaviours that lead to self-motivated learning.

Part 3 Assessment

12 Assessment: what, how and why

Introduction

Over the past 25 years or so, we have recognised assessment as something that is part of everyday life in classrooms. In science, where in the 1980s it was not assessed in the primary school and hardly any records were kept, assessment has now become part of every teacher's responsibility, and seems set to remain so. It is, therefore, essential to be clear about

- what assessment means;

- why we do it (for what purposes?);

- how we do it (who is involved and what do they do?).

This chapter deals with these matters in general terms and the following six chapters we look at them in more detail.

The meaning of assessment

Consider the vignette in Box 12.1. Suppose you were asked to identify assessment taking place, would you say:

- only when the children were writing their individual answers to the questions at the end;

- during the investigation;

- before the investigation?

In its broadest meaning, assessment would cover all of these. Put formally it is a process of *deciding, collecting and making inferences or judgements* about evidence of children's learning and skills. There is always a purpose to the assessment relating to the use to which it is put and the action taken as a result.

- Deciding: the evidence that is required should be related to the goals of learning and should cover all the ideas, skills and attitudes that are important in learning science.

■ Collecting: there is a wide range of ways of gathering evidence. Which is chosen depends on the purposes of the assessment.

■ Making judgements: this involves considering the evidence of achievement of the goals in relation to some standards, or criteria or expectations.

Combining various ways in which evidence is collected and the various bases for judging it creates different methods of assessment. These range from standardised tests where information is gathered while children are tackling carefully devised tasks, under controlled conditions, to assessment carried out almost imperceptibly during normal interchange between teacher and children.

Box 12.1   Dissolving sugar

As part of an overall topic on materials a class of ten-year-olds had mixed different substances with water and looked at the results, describing them in terms of how well they dissolved. The teacher planned to go on to look at different forms of the same substance, and introduced the lesson by showing them some sugar cubes, some loose brown sugar and some icing sugar. He asked them first to discuss in groups of three what they thought would happen when these were put in water. While they were talking he visited each group, listening to their conversations. Several were using the word 'melting' instead of 'dissolving', even though in the previous activities they had appeared to use the correct word.

After a whole-class discussion of their ideas in which the teacher reinforced the difference between dissolving and melting, he then set them to find out which dissolved most quickly. During the investigation he noticed that one group was careful to use the same amount of sugar and to stir each in the same way, but they used different volumes of water. As they were clearly aware of having to control some variables he asked them if they thought it mattered that there were different amounts of water. They said it didn't as long as they were all stirred at the same rate. So he asked them to add just a drop of water to a teaspoonful of sugar, stir and see what happened. He then told them to add water until all the sugar would dissolve. They realised that the amount of water did make a difference and that this was a variable that they had to control in their investigation.

At the end of the dissolving activities, the teacher asked them to work individually to write down answers to several questions such as:

Say whether these mixtures could be separated by adding water and filtering. Explain your reason.

Mixture	Can it be separated by adding water and filtering?	Reason
sand and salt		
sand and gravel		
brown sugar and white sugar		

Assessment, tests etc.: is there a difference?

The distinction between 'tests' and 'assessment' is not at all clear. Some use of the term 'assessment' excludes tests and refers only to various forms of informal assessment usually devised by, and conducted by, the teacher. However, this distinction is not necessarily agreed and here we use assessment as a broad term, covering all ways of collecting and judging evidence and including tests. Tests are specially devised activities designed to assess knowledge and/or skills by giving precisely the same task to children who have to respond to it under similar conditions. Tests are not necessarily externally devised: teachers prepare tests (of spelling, arithmetic, for example) and some 'tests' can be absorbed into classroom work and look very much like normal classroom work as far as the children are concerned. It is therefore not at all helpful to characterise assessment differences in terms of methods but rather in terms of purposes. Other words used in this context are 'examinations' and 'evaluation'. Examinations are commonly combinations of tests or tasks and other forms of assessment used for qualifications, or entry into certain kinds of education or professions. Educational evaluation is the term used in some countries interchangeably with assessment to refer to the achievements of individuals, while in the UK it is normally used in relation to teaching and materials for teaching and, in the context of accountability, to teachers, schools and systems.

The purposes of assessment

Consideration of the purpose of an assessment is a key factor in who and what is involved and how it is carried out. Box 12.2 summarises the main purposes of the assessment that children might experience in their school career. Not all of these are intended to help their learning and for some purposes (national and international monitoring) the children who are assessed are simply representatives of a particular group.

Box 12.2	The main purposes of assessment

1 To help children's learning (finding the aspects in which they are and are not making progress, what particular difficulties they are having).

2 To summarise achievement at certain times (for keeping records, reporting to parents, other teachers and the children themselves).

3 To group or select children (both within a class and where there is streaming or setting, and, at later stages, for certification and progress to higher levels of education).

4 To monitor the performance of children across a region or nation (as in national and international surveys of children's performance, where only a sample of children is assessed).

5 To assist in research or evaluation of new classroom materials or educational reforms.

In this book we are concerned with assessment for the first two purposes only: to help learning, described as formative assessment or assessment *for* learning; to summarise achievement, described as summative assessment of assessment *of* learning.

How the purpose affects the process of assessment

Since purpose is the key to the 'what', 'who' and 'how' of assessment it is important to consider what difference it makes to the process. As mentioned earlier, assessment involves deciding what evidence is required, collecting it, making judgements about it and using it for a purpose.

Deciding and collecting evidence

The decision about the evidence of learning is determined by the goals: the skills and ideas that the learner is trying to achieve. So the starting point is for children to be engaged in an activity relating to the goals. Evidence can then be gathered about their skills and ideas. The main methods for doing this are:

- observing children (this includes listening, questioning and discussing with them);

- studying the products of their regular work (including writing, drawings, artefacts and actions);

- introducing special activities into the class work (such as concept-mapping, diagnostic tasks);

- giving tests (teacher-made or externally produced).

Interpreting the evidence: making a judgement

Once the information is gathered it is interpreted in terms of what it means in relation to progress or achievement to date. This can be done in three main ways:

■ by reference to a description of what it means to be able to do something or to explain something that indicates ideas at a certain level (criterion-referenced);

■ by reference to what is usual for children of the same age and/or ability (norm-referenced);

■ by reference to what each child was previously able to do (child-referenced or ipsative).

Box 12.3. illustrates what these mean in an example that is unlikely in practice but illustrates the principles.

Box 12.3	The bases of judgements in assessment

Suppose that a teacher wants to assess a child's ability in knocking nails into wood. This can be described in different ways:

■ The teacher may have some expectation of the level of performance (knocking the nail in straight, using the hammer correctly, taking necessary safety precautions) and judge the child's performance in relation to these. The judgement is made in terms of the extent to which the child's performance meets the criteria; that is, it is criterion-referenced.

■ Alternatively, the teacher may judge in terms of how the child performs at knocking in nails compared with other children of the same age and stage. If this is the case there will be a norm or average performance known for the age/stage group and any child can be described in relation to this as average, above average or below average, or more precisely identified if some quantitative measure has been obtained. (The result could be expressed as a 'knocking nails age' or a 'hammer manipulation' quotient!) The judgement arrived at in this way is called a norm-referenced assessment.

■ A third possibility is that the teacher compares the child's present performance with what the same child could do on a previous occasion, in which case the assessment is child-referenced, or ipsative.

The steps of deciding, gathering and judging evidence are represented in Figure 12.1.

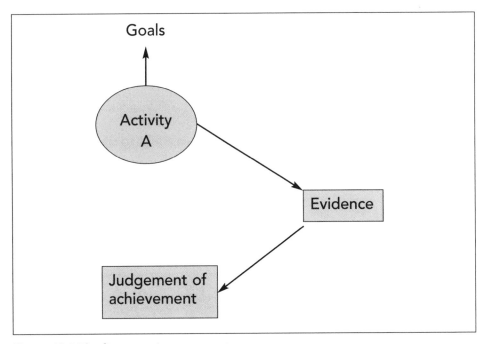

Figure 12.1 The first steps in assessment

Using the judgement

What happens next depends on the purpose of the assessment and will influence the way in which the steps in Figure 12.1 are carried out.

If the purpose is summative (to summarise learning), then the judgement of what has been achieved will be used for reporting this to those who need the information: in addition to the child and his or her teacher, this means other teachers, including the head teacher, the parents and others with an interest in the progress of the children. This use of the information is represented in Figure 12.2, which also indicates that, for this use, the judgements should be made in relation to criteria or norms that are the same for all children. In addition, the evidence used should bring together all the information that is relevant to the achievement of a goal, perhaps gathered over a period of time and perhaps including performance in tests.

If the purpose of the assessment is not to summarise, but to help learning – that is, to be used formatively – then the judgement will be used by those involved in the learning (the teacher and the child) to decide the next steps to take and how to take them. In this case the evidence is likely to come from how the child has been tackling activities as part of regular work and the judgement could be in terms of progress made (child-referenced), as well as in relation to criteria. There would be little value in using norm-referencing in this case. Figure 12.3 shows how this turns the process of assessment into a cycle that leads to decisions about teaching.

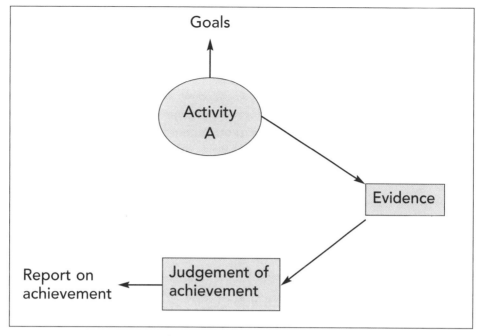

Figure 12.2 Representation of summative assessment

Considerations of reliability and validity

There are some other important differences between summative assessment and formative assessment, which involve the concepts of reliability and validity of assessment. Box 12.4 summarises some points about these concepts.

Box 12.4	The concepts of reliability and validity

Reliability and validity

Reliability refers to how much you can depend on the result of an assessment; that is, how likely it would be that the same result would be obtained if the assessment were to be repeated. Reliability depends on the procedure that is used. Thus tests where children choose between fixed alternative answers, that can be machine marked, are more reliable than ones that ask children to provide answers that then require some judgement in the marking. However, the latter may be a more valid test if the purpose is to find out what answers children can construct. *Validity* refers to the match between what is actually assessed and what it is intended should be assessed.

The interaction between reliability and validity

These aspects of an assessment are not independent of one another, since if reliability is low this means that various unintended factors are influencing the result and therefore what is being assessed is uncertain. However there is a limit to the extent that both reliability and validity can be high. To raise the reliability it is necessary to reduce the error by increasing the control of what is assessed and how. This often means focusing on outcomes that can be more accurately assessed, such as factual knowledge, where there is a clear right answer. But if the purpose is to assess skills and understanding, where we need children to generate rather than select answers, this focussing would reduce the validity. There has to be a compromise and what this is depends on the purpose of the assessment.

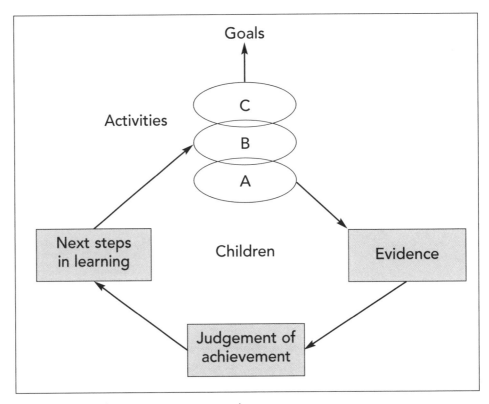

Figure 12.3 The formative assessment cycle

For formative assessment validity is paramount; for summative assessment reliability has to be maintained at the highest level without compromising validity to too great an extent. The reason for reliability being less important for formative assessment than for summative assessment rests on the cyclic nature of the formative assessment process, as shown in Figure 12.3. The information is used to inform teaching in the situations in which it is gathered. Thus there is always quick feedback for the teacher and any misjudged intervention can be corrected.

This is not to say that teachers do not need help with this important part of their work, but the help required is not to be found in examples of work judged to be at different levels. This is needed for summative teacher assessment, but formative assessment is concerned with the future, not with judgements about the past.

Summative assessment, on the other hand, has to provide information about where children have reached in their learning that parents and other teachers can depend upon, so attention has to be given to increasing reliability as far as possible without endangering validity.

The characteristics of formative and summative assessment

We now bring these general points about assessment to bear on the characteristics of assessment for the two purposes being discussed.

Formative assessment

Formative assessment helps the process of learning. This statement is supported by both theories of learning and research into practice, as we will see in Chapter 13.

Formative assessment has to take account of all the aspects of children's behaviour that affect their learning – not only the progress being made in knowledge and skills, but also the effort put in and the other aspects of learning that are unspecified in the curriculum. It must be positive, indicating the next steps to take, not pointing out what is missing. This means that formative assessment is not a pure criterion-referenced assessment. It is more ipsative or child-referenced. The teacher will have in mind the progression that he or she intends for the child, and this will be the basis of the action taken. The teacher will be looking across several instances in which a particular skill or idea is being used and will see variations and possibly patterns in behaviour. It is these variations (which would be seen as sources of 'error' if the purpose of the assessment were summative) that, in the formative context, provide diagnostic information.

A further characteristic of formative assessment, which is increasingly recognised as central to it, is the involvement of children. For this reason children feature at the centre of the cycle in Figure 12.3. The developing theory of educational assessment and various models within it emphasise the important role that children have to play in their own assessment, as they come to understand the process, to learn to work towards explicit standards or targets and to modify their performance in relation to constructive task-related feedback from teachers (Gipps 1994). We pick up these matters in Chapter 17.

To summarise, the characteristics of formative assessment are that:

- it takes place as an integral part of teaching;

- it relates to progression in learning;

- it depends on judgements, which can be child-referenced or criterion-referenced;

- it leads to action supporting further learning;

- it uses methods that protect validity rather than reliability;

- it uses information from children's performance in a variety of contexts;

- it involves children in assessing their performance and deciding their next steps.

Summative assessment

Summative assessment has an important but different role in children's education. Its purpose is to give a summary of achievement at various times, as required. As noted in Chapter 18, it can be achieved by summing up (summarising evidence already used for formative purposes), checking up (giving a test or special task) or a combination of these. Since its purpose is to report achievement to parents, other teachers, children, school governors etc., the reliability of the judgements is important and the criteria have to be used uniformly. Thus, if the summary is based on a review of evidence gathered during teaching, some form of moderation, or procedure for quality assurance, is required. So the characteristics of summative assessment are that:

- it takes place at certain intervals when achievement has to be reported;

- it relates to progression in learning against public criteria;

- it enables results for different children to be combined for various purposes because they are based on the same criteria;

- it requires methods that are as reliable as possible without endangering validity;

- it involves some quality assurance procedures;

- it should be based on evidence relating to the full range of learning goals.

The difference between these two purposes of assessment should be kept very clearly in mind, especially when both are carried out by teachers. It is too often assumed that assessment that is carried out frequently is formative, or that all assessment by teachers is formative. Unless the assessment is used to help the ongoing learning, this is not the case. Where this happens the true value of formative assessment will not be realised. We now turn to explain why formative assessment is so important, particularly in science.

Summary

This chapter has provided an introduction to Part 3 of the book and to some of the concepts involved in assessment. The main points have been:

- Assessment involves judgements about evidence of children's achievement. How it is carried out depends on its purpose.

- The purposes considered in this book are assessment for a formative purpose (assessment *for* learning) and assessment for a summative purpose (assessment *of* learning).

- The process of assessment involves deciding on relevant evidence, collecting it and making inferences or judgements by comparing it against expectations.

- Judgements can be made by comparing against norms, criteria of performance or the child's previous achievement.

- Depending on the purpose of the assessment, different emphasis is laid on reliability (dependability of the judgement) and validity (how well it reflects what it is intended to assess).

- The characteristics of formative and summative assessment differ more in timing and use of the judgements than in the methods used for collecting information.

13 Using assessment to help learning in science

Introduction

There are three sets of reasons for making the effort to take the steps that enable assessment to be used to help learning in science. These relate to the value of formative assessment for learning through enquiry, the benefit of involving children in decisions about their learning and the evidence that it works – that standards of achievement are raised when it is in operation (see Box 13.1). The last of these points applies to all learning and so do the others when there is a constructivist approach to learning, but they apply particularly in science. We expand on each of these points in this chapter.

Box 13.1	Reasons for using assessment to help learning

Three good reasons for implementing formative assessment in primary science:

1 Knowing what ideas learners bring to new experiences and how these ideas develop during their activities is central to learning through enquiry. Using assessment as part of teaching means that information can be collected about progress towards all the goals. If activities provide opportunities for skills, understanding and attitudes to be developed, then they also provide opportunities for these to be assessed and for the information to be used to help learning.

2 Widely accepted theories of learning emphasise the role of learners in constructing their own understanding. Formative assessment involves children in recognising where they are in progress towards goals and in the decisions about what their next steps are and how to take them.

3 There is firmly established evidence that when the key components of formative assessment are practised, levels of achievement are raised.

How formative assessment helps enquiry learning in science

In Chapter 7 we described learning in science as a process in which learners develop their understanding of things around them by using and developing process skills. The process is represented by the diagram reproduced in Figure 13.1. The starting point is some new experience – or a new observation of a familiar one. It raises questions for the learner, for there is something that is not understood that needs to be explained. (Why does the size of the shadow change when you move the torch? Why does clay hold more water than sandy soil? What is happening when a bulb is lit from a battery?) The observation or event engages the attention, stimulates curiosity and motivates the action and effort needed to make sense of it. It may be that there is a mismatch between what is observed and what was expected. (A large object floating when it was expected to sink on account of its weight. The shadow formed by red light being black, not red. A rubber balloon sticking to the wall after being rubbed on a piece of woollen material.)

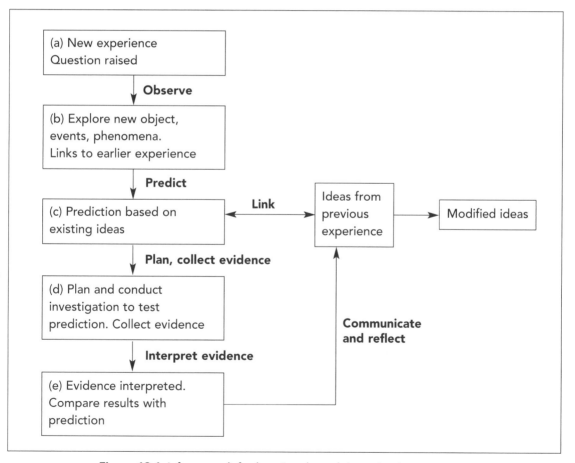

Figure 13.1 A framework for learning through investigation

Many questions and observations occur in children's everyday experience; others are stimulated by the activities teachers provide in the classroom. We are talking here about advancing skills and ideas rather than using already familiar ones if there is to be learning. While we do not deny that this advance can happen when children investigate and develop their ideas in their unguided exploration of chance observations, it is more likely to happen in a situation set up for the child to answer a question or reconcile an observation with his or her understanding of what is going on.

In Chapters 9 and 10 we discussed ways of helping children to develop their understanding and process skills. There it was noted that children learn best when new experiences are within the reach of their existing ideas and skills: experiences that are novel but not too familiar, so that they call for some extension or enlargement of these ideas and skills.

How is this to happen unless the teacher knows what the children's existing ideas and skills are? Finding out where children are in relation to the intended learning goals – the first steps in formative assessment – is a necessary prerequisite for advancing their ideas and skills. The need for the teacher to have opportunities to gather this information has important implications for classroom planning and management. It means ensuring that the children have:

■ experiences within reach of their existing ways of thinking and investigating;

■ opportunities to explore these experiences and to make their ideas explicit to themselves and to other children, as well as to the teacher;

■ encouragement to link the new experience or observations to previous ones;

■ opportunities to question and reflect on their understanding of the events or situation.

All these things are among the most important of the conditions required for learning through enquiry to take place (for a more complete list see Chapter 5). Thus the requirements for using assessment to help learning are central to those for the opportunity to learn science through enquiry.

The teacher's view of learning

The second good reason for using assessment as part of teaching relates to theories of how learning takes place. The view that a teacher has of what is involved in learning has a significant impact on teaching and the role of the teacher, learner and learning materials.

The following extracts from conversations with two teachers indicate how a view of learning implicitly lay behind their decisions about the way to organise their classrooms and to interact with the children. Both were teachers in junior schools in a large city; both schools were of similar, early twentieth-century, architecture; both teachers taught classes of about 32 ten- and eleven-year-olds. The interviews were originally part of the *Match and Mismatch* materials (Harlen *et al.* 1977).

The teacher as responsible for learning

The first teacher arranged the desks in straight rows, all facing the front, where the teacher's desk and blackboard occupied prominent positions. She explained her reasons for this formality in arrangement, which echoed the formality of her teaching, as follows:

Well, you see the main thing – I can't stand any noise. I don't allow them to talk in the classroom ... I just can't stand noise and I can't stand children walking about ... in the classroom I like them sitting in their places where I can see them all. And I mean I teach from lesson to lesson. There's no children all doing different things at different times ... And of course I like it that way, I believe in it that way.

When asked why the desks were all facing the front, she replied:

if they're all facing me, and I – well, I can see them and I can see what they're doing. Because quite honestly I don't think that – when they're in groups, I mean all right they might be discussing their work. But, I mean, how do you know?

As well as her own preference for quietness, she was convinced that it was from the blackboard and from herself that the children would learn. She worked hard to make her method work, setting work on the blackboard and marking books every evening. She did not think that children handling things or talking to each other had any role in learning.

The learners as responsible for learning

The second teacher arranged the desks in blocks of four but in no particular pattern. There was no discernible 'front' or 'back' of the class. The children moved about freely and chatted during their work. She explained:

I hate to see children in rows and I hate to see them regimented. At the same time, you know, often I get annoyed when people think that absolute chaos reigns, because it doesn't. Every child knows exactly what they have to do ... And, it's much more – you could say informal – but it's a much more friendly, less pressing way of working and ... it's nice for them to be able to chat with a friend about what they're doing.

Asked if she worried that the chat might not be about work, she replied:

Oh no. I mean, obviously adults do that when they work. As long as I get the end result that's suited to that particular child I don't mind... I'm not against formal education I'm not against informal, there are advantages to both methods – but I think the great danger of very formal teaching is that the teacher's seen as a tin god figure. And very often the children aren't given the opportunity to think for themselves.

The role of learners

The point here is not to suggest that either teacher is 'right' but to show that both have a clear rationale for the decisions they make about the organisation and methods they use in the classroom, and that this is related to their views of how children learn. Both show consistency between what they do and what they want to achieve through it and so both are at ease in their classrooms.

It is worth noting in passing that to change the practice of either of these teachers would require far more than different teaching materials or an insistence on rearranging the desks. There are masses of examples of teachers who have been asked to make organisational changes that simply result in children sitting in groups but being taught as a class and having to twist their necks to see the blackboard. To make real changes requires a change in teachers that is far more than adopting different ways of working; it means changing their views of how children learn and of their own role and the role of materials in fostering learning.

The chief point of relevance here, however, concerns the role of the children in their own learning. The first teacher implicitly embraces a view of learning that is called 'behaviourist' because it focuses on the external behaviour of the learner rather than what is going on inside the mind. In this view learning is dependent on the teacher providing instruction in the form of information and exercises in a sequence that is the same for all children. The role of the learner is essentially a passive one, as a receiver of knowledge created by others. The second teacher implicitly embraces a constructivist view of learning in which the focus is on thinking and how the learner is making sense of the learning activities. This view of learning is supported by modern psychology, which explains learning in terms of links made to existing mental frameworks, requiring the active participation of the learner. Box 13.2 summarises these two views and the relevance of formative assessment for each.

Box 13.2 How formative assessment relates to the teacher's view of learning

The passive learner
If learning is viewed as the construction of knowledge by the teacher, rather as a builder constructs a building, piece by piece, the teacher will regard all that

children learn as coming from the teacher or other authority. The learning is dependent on how well the teacher sets out the pieces to be learned and the children's role will not be highly valued. Thus there will be no need to find out what the children's ideas are, since the learning experiences do not depend on them. This is the end of the story as far as formative assessment is concerned.

The active learner

If learning is viewed as the construction of knowledge by the learner, the teacher is concerned to adapt learning experiences to match the learner's developing understanding. The teacher therefore needs to know about the children's skills and ideas and to use this information in adapting teaching. Formative assessment has a key role in the teaching and learning.

There is a great deal of evidence, some of which we have presented in Chapters 7–11, to support the notion that the constructivist view of learning leads to understanding, whereas the behaviourist view, which ignores the learners' existing ideas, often means that what is presented is not understood and has to be memorised. For the learners this is not an enjoyable state of affairs and they are likely to lack motivation for further learning. On the other hand, understanding creates motivation and the enjoyment of learning. Thus the use of formative assessment to enable children to arrive at ideas that make sense to them is an important factor in motivation for learning as well as in learning with understanding. Formative assessment enables children to have an active part in their own learning – for they are at the centre of the formative assessment cycle (see Figure 12.3).

The impact on learning

The third point in Box 13.1 refers to the research evidence that using formative assessment raises the levels of children's achievement. The initial evidence came from a review by Black and Wiliam (1998a) of research studies, which were generally carried out in experimental conditions. Since then there have been studies to show that implementing the essential features of formative assessment in normal classrooms leads to gains in achievement that are greater than those of equivalent groups where formative assessment is not practised.

From their review of evidence from over 250 reports of research into assessment and classroom practice, Black and Wiliam (1998a) concluded that improvement of formative assessment could lead to considerable gains in levels of achievement. The outcome of the review was unequivocal evidence that improving formative assessment raises standards by substantial amounts, 'larger than most of those found for educational interventions' (Black and Wiliam 1998b: 4). The main points emerging from the review are given in Box 13.3. One of the key results was that while all children's learning benefited, children with mild learning difficulties gained most, thus reducing the spread of attainment.

However, improving formative assessment requires teachers to make considerable efforts and to have the confidence 'that they can make anyone learn as long as they go about it the right way' (Black 1993: 79). What this means includes sharing learning goals with children, feeding back the teacher's assessment to children in particular ways, involving children in self-assessment and using effective methods of helping children to take the next steps in their learning. We deal in some detail in Chapters 16 and 17 with what changes are required in these practices.

Box 13.3   Formative assessment and changes in teaching

The main points about formative assessment from *Inside the Black Box*

■ All such work involves new ways to enhance feedback between those taught and the teacher, ways that require new modes of pedagogy — which will require significant changes in classroom practice.

■ Underlying the various approaches are assumptions about what makes for effective learning — in particular that pupils have to be actively involved.

■ For assessment to function formatively, the results have to be used to adjust teaching and learning — so a significant aspect of any programme will be the ways in which teachers do this.

■ The ways in which assessment can affect the motivation and self-esteem of pupils, and the benefits of engaging pupils in self-assessment, both deserve careful attention.

(Black and Wiliam 1998b: 4, 5)

Work carried out in England since the publication of the Black and Wiliam review has shown that when teachers changed their practices to implement aspects of formative assessment, there were substantial and significant gains in their pupils' achievement over a period of two years. Although the work so far published has been carried out in secondary schools, the findings have implications for all teachers, since the changes introduced by the teachers were not dependent on their being subject specialists, although most of the work was with teachers of science and mathematics. Indeed, the opportunity for a considerable impact on pupils could be greater in primary schools, since teachers would have more sustained contact with the children.

The teachers involved in what was called the KMOFAP (Kings–Medway–Oxfordshire Formative Assessment Project) decided on particular aspects of their practice that they wished to change in order to implement formative assessment, the main ones being questioning, feedback through marking, peer and self-assessment and the formative use of summative tests. After two years of collaborative working with the researchers, the results for each class were compared with those for an equivalent class in the same school. The differences found could be expressed in terms of National Curriculum levels: just under half a level at Key Stage 2 and just over half a level at Key Stage 3. The researchers pointed out:

Such improvements, produced across a school, would raise a school in the lower quartile of the national performance tables to well above the average. It is clear, therefore, that, far from having to choose between teaching well and getting good national curriculum test and examination results, teachers can actually improve their pupils' results by working with the ideas we present here.

(Black *et al.* 2002: 4)

Summary

This chapter has provided some empirical evidence and some theoretical arguments relating to how learning takes place, to argue that formative assessment has an important role to play in children's learning, particularly in science. The key points are:

■ Formative assessment has particular value in the context of learning science through enquiry, where teachers need to know what ideas and skills children have in order to provide opportunities for their development.

■ Related to this is the role that formative assessment has when practice is derived from a constructivist view of learning. When the children's role in learning is recognised as an active, not a passive, one it follows that they should understand the goals of their work, and take part in decisions about where they are in relation to these goals and about what next steps they need to take.

■ Implementing formative assessment in practice is likely to require some effort to make changes, particularly in relation to questioning, marking and giving feedback, and in involving children in the process of assessing their work. However, the impact on learning is considerable for all children and especially for the previously lower achieving ones, making the effort well worthwhile.

14 Finding out children's ideas

Introduction

This chapter and the next one are concerned with the process of gathering information about children's existing ideas and skills. In Chapter 13 we presented arguments for the importance of this first stage in the cycle of formative assessment, enabling teachers (and children) to use this information in judging progress towards goals and how to make further progress. We describe here various methods that can be used as part of children's activities, for it is in this context that evidence is both gathered and used in formative assessment. It is for convenience only that we separate the discussion of methods relating to ideas and to skills and attitudes, beginning in this chapter with ways of accessing children's ideas and continuing in the next with gathering evidence about process skills and attitudes. In practice both take place in the same activities, and ideas for planning how to do this in practice are taken up at the end of Chapter 15. The interpretation of the information so that it can be used to identify next steps is discussed in Chapter 16.

Having the goals in mind

It may seem too obvious to start with the point that teachers need to know what ideas the children should be developing before they can find out what existing ideas are held. But sometimes activities become an end in themselves and the intended learning is left a little hazy. 'Party pieces', repeated year after year because they 'work' and are fun, can fall into this trap. The danger of this is less since the DfEE/QCA Scheme of Work was produced (DfEE/QCA 1998). Even if teachers do not follow the scheme systematically, they have been made aware of the importance of identifying expectations or outcomes of activities ('small' ideas) and of recognising where an activity fits into the development of 'bigger' ideas. Nevertheless, being clear about the goals is particularly important in the context of using assessment to help learning, for both the teacher and the children (as we see in Chapter 16). How the goals can be communicated to children is something taken up in Chapter 16.

Gaining access to children's ideas

The learning environment

Everything that happens in the classroom takes place within the ethos or social climate created by the teacher. Children have to feel free to express their own ideas and ways of thinking, without fear that they will be giving the 'wrong' answer. So before a teacher can have any chance of gaining access to children's ideas, it is necessary to establish a classroom climate in which children feel that is it 'safe' to express the ideas they have and in which these ideas are valued and taken seriously, not disregarded or ridiculed.

The point is well made by Keogh and Naylor (2004: 18):

As adults we realize how close the connection is between self-esteem and having our ideas accepted and valued. Children are no different. If we want children to 'think out loud', to be creative in their thinking and to argue about alternative possibilities, then we need to provide the kind of learning environment in which they feel comfortable to do that. They need to know that they can make mistakes or give wrong answers and still feel good about themselves.

Such an atmosphere cannot be created overnight. It results from teachers showing by example how to respect others' ideas, how to be sensitive to others' feelings and how to value effort and attitudes of perseverance, responsibility and openness. Box 14.1 sets out some actions by the teacher that foster this climate.

Box 14.1   **Creating a classroom climate in which children can express their ideas**

A supportive classroom climate can be encouraged by teachers:

■ finding out about the children's attitudes and feelings through discussion and conversation with them but, importantly, listening to them;

■ showing real interest in what they feel as well as what they think;

■ using knowledge of their attitudes and feelings to set realistic expectations; not expecting more cooperation or responsibility than is appropriate to their maturity;

■ providing a classroom organisation that supports responsibility and enables them to achieve their best (e.g. by enabling children to have access to and look after materials, giving enough time for them to finish their work);

■ encouraging effort and socially desirable behaviours, not just achievement;

■ setting an example by being patient, sympathetic, encouraging and fair;

■ fostering curiosity and the persistence and creativity to satisfy it.

An environment that lays the foundation for continued learning should not only accept but also motivate change in ideas and ways of thinking. Above all we need to create a desire to learn, to understand things around us, and make this enjoyable. As we noted in Chapter 13, enjoyment in learning comes from understanding at the level that satisfies the learner's curiosity at a particular time.

Classroom strategies

Against this general background of a supporting classroom climate, there are various strategies that teachers can use to eliciteg children's ideas. These are listed in Box 14.2 and each is illustrated in the following sections.

Box 14.2	Ways of gaining access to children's ideas

- Questioning – using open and person-centred questions.

- Asking for writing or drawings that communicate what children think (predictions with reasons, explanations, annotated drawings, strip cartoons).

- Concept maps.

- Concept cartoons.

- Children-only discussions.

- Discussing words.

- Discussing with children digital photographs of themselves engaged in activities.

Questioning

We discussed different ways of phrasing questions in Chapter 3. Here we are interested in the form that is particularly valuable for accessing children's ideas. Consider, for instance, the situation in which a teacher has provided lots of home-made and other musical instruments for children to explore as a preliminary to more structured activities aimed at the idea that sound is caused by objects vibrating. To find out the ideas the children already have the teacher might ask questions such as:

1   Explain to me what is happening when you hear the sound.

2   Why does the sound change when you shorten the string?

3   What causes the guitar to make a sound?

4   Explain why you are able to make the bottle make a sound by blowing across the top.

Or he or she might ask:

5 What do you think makes the sound when you pluck the string?

6 What are your ideas about how the guitar makes a sound?

7 What do you think is the reason for the bottle making a sound when you blow across the top?

8 What do you think is going on when the drum makes a sound?

9 What are your ideas about why you get different sounds when you shorten the string?

Or, again, he or she might ask:

10 What would you do to make the drum make a sound?

11 What do you see happening when the drum makes a sound?

12 What do you think will happen if you make the string even shorter?

13 Can you show me how to make a different note by blowing across the top of the bottle?

14 What could you do to find out if how you pluck the string makes a difference?

The first four questions are open questions, but they ask directly for *the* answer, not the children's ideas about what is happening. These are subject-centred questions and do not lead to the children expressing their ideas. By contrast, questions 5 to 9 are expressed so as to ask for the children's own ideas, with no suggestion that there is a right answer. They are person-centred questions. All the children should be able to answer the second set, while only those who feel that they can give the right answer will attempt to answer the first set. Thus the open, person-centred questions are preferred for eliciting children's ideas.

Questions 10 to 14 are also expressed as open, person-centred questions, but they do not ask for children's ideas directly. They are more likely to lead to action and to the use of process skills. Although the actions taken would imply some ideas about the cause of the effects, these questions are more useful for finding out about children's ways of observing or investigating than for eliciting their ideas. We return to them in Chapter 15.

A further point about questioning that should be recalled in this context is the importance of giving children time to answer. The 'wait' time (see page 27) is necessary not only to allow for the children to think and to formulate their answer but also to convey the message that the teacher is really interested in their ideas and will listen to them carefully. It also slows down the discussion, giving the teacher time to phrase thoughtful questions and the children time to think before answering. The whole exchange is then more productive in terms of giving teachers access to children's real understanding and not just their first superficial thoughts.

Children's writing and drawings

In the discussion above it is implicit that the questioning and answering were oral. In some circumstances it may be best for the children to write down their ideas or produce a drawing, or set of drawings, to express their ideas. This can give the teacher a view of the full range of ideas in the class and a permanent record for each child which can be perused at a later time. The same points made about oral questions apply, however, to questions that the teacher asks in setting children's written work and drawings in order to find out their ideas: open-person-centred questions are preferred.

Examples of children's drawings that reveal their ideas have been given in Chapter 2. It is not easy for anyone to draw abstract things such as ideas about melting, force or evaporation. The use of labels and annotation as a commentary on what is happening is necessary, but the drawing is essential for conveying the image that the child has in mind. For example, the drawing in Figure 14.1 by a seven-year-old shows very clearly that the child considered the direct action of the sun as important in causing the disappearance (by evaporation) of water from a tank.

(Age 7 years)

"The sun is hot and the water is cold and the water sticks to the sun and then it goes down"

Figure 14.1 A seven-year-old's ideas about evaporation of water (from Russell and Watt 1990: 29)

It is important to note that the value of opening access to children's ideas depends on how the drawing task is set. Merely asking for a drawing to show the water levels in the tank would not necessarily be useful in this respect. A request for a drawing of 'what you think makes the water level change' is more fruitful.

Another kind of drawing that helps children to show their ideas is a *'strip cartoon'* or a series of drawings across time, as in the example of the representation of the stages in the manufacture of a spoon in Figure 14.2 and in the production of a rubber in Figure 14.3. In both these cases the teacher asked the children to draw what they thought the object was like just before it was in its present form, then what it was like just before that, and so on.

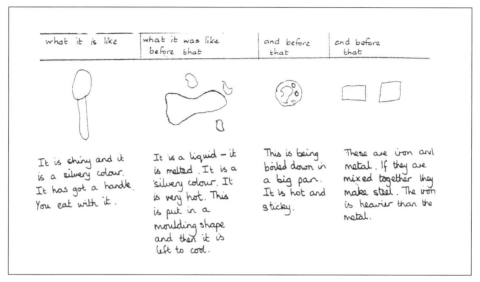

Figure 14.2 A child's idea of the origin of a spoon (unpublished SPACE research)

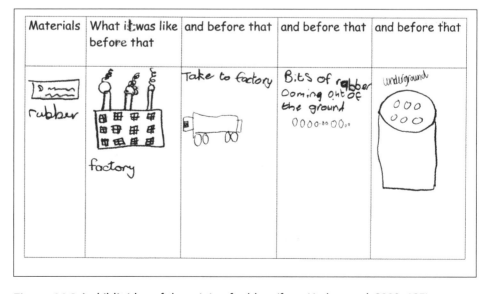

Figure 14.3 A child's idea of the origin of rubber (from Harlen *et al.* 2003: 125)

While drawings can usually be made by even the youngest children, writing is most helpful when children become at ease in doing it. Figure 14.3 was written by a six-year-old to explain why the condensation from her breath on a cold window went away.

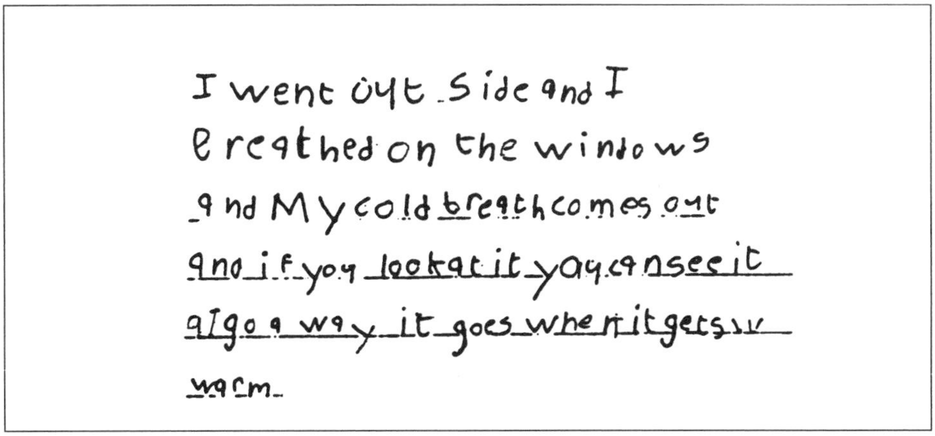

I went oyt Side and I
e reathed on the windows
and My cold breath comes out
and if you look at it you can see it
a go a way it goes when it gets so
warm.

Figure 14.4 A six-year-old's writing about condensation

In Figure 14.5, a ten-year-old's answer to how to slow down evaporation of water from a tank indicates the value of not just asking for writing about what has been observed but posing problems where ideas have to be used:

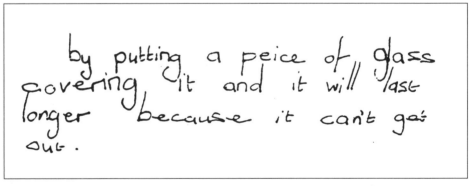

Figure 14.5 A ten-year-old using ideas about evaporation to suggest how to prevent it

Concept maps

Concept maps are another kind of drawing that is useful for finding children's ideas. Concept maps are diagrammatic ways of representing conceptual links between words. There are certain rules to apply that are very simple and readily grasped by children of five or six. If we take the words 'ice' and 'water' we can relate them to each other by connecting them with an arrow to signify a relationship between them. If we write 'melts to give' on the arrow, we have a way of representing the proposition that ice melts to give water, but not vice versa:

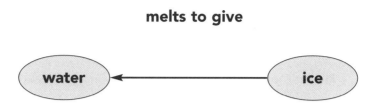

We can add to this by linking other words, so forming a map.

Asking children to draw their ideas about how things are linked up provides insights into the way they envisage how one thing causes another. The starting point is to list words about the topic the children are working on and then ask them to draw arrows and to write 'joining' words on them. Figure 14.6 shows the list and the map that a six-year-old, Lennie, drew after some activities about heat and its effect on various things. It is possible to spot from this that Lennie has not yet distinguished heat from temperature but that he has some useful ideas about what heat can do. As with all diagrams, it is advisable to discuss them with the child to be sure of the meaning intended.

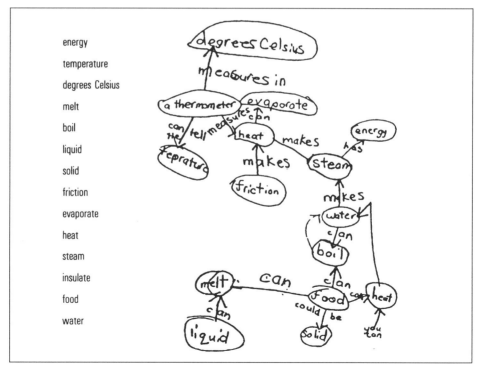

Figure 14.6 A six-year-old's concept map (from Harlen *et al.* 2003: 128)

Concept cartoons

Concept cartoons were devised by Naylor and Keogh (2000). One example is given in Figure 14.7, but a wide range of cartoons have been published and used with both trainee teachers and primary children. Their key features include:

■ representing scientific ideas in everyday situations wherever possible, so that connections are made between scientific ideas and everyday life;

■ using a minimal amount of text, in order to make the ideas accessible to learners with limited literacy skills;

■ using a simple cartoon-style presentation that is visually appealing and empowers teachers and learners to create their own concept cartoons;

■ using published research to identify common areas of misunderstanding, which then provide a focus for the concept cartoon (Keogh and Naylor 1998: 14).

They have various uses, including finding out children's ideas. For this purpose, children can discuss the ideas suggested by the cartoon characters either in small groups or as a whole class and talk about why they may agree or disagree with the suggestions, or give their own ideas. In many cases the situations have no 'right' answer and in all cases the discussion of pros and cons of the suggestions made requires some explanation of why one or another view could be supported.

Children-only discussions

Concept cartoons provide a very useful way of setting up small group discussions that allow the teacher to listen in to the conversation without taking part. Setting groups to work on a combined concept map serves a similar purpose. Another approach was described in the vignette in Box 12.1. Children-only discussions are valuable in freeing children to express their ideas. To quote Douglas Barnes:

The teacher's absence removes from their work the usual source of authority; they cannot turn to him [sic] to solve dilemmas. Thus . . . the children not only formulate hypotheses, but are compelled to evaluate them for themselves. This they can do in only two ways: by testing them against their existing views of 'how things go in the world', and by going back to 'the evidence'.

(Barnes 1976: 29)

When the children are talking directly to each other they use words that they and their peers understand. These, as well as the explanations and reasons that they give to each other, can give clues to their ideas. In the example in Box 12.1 the teacher noted that the children appeared to confuse melting and dissolving, which alerted him to take some action to clarify the difference between these concepts.

Figure 14.7 Concept cartoon: ideas about germinating seeds (from Keogh and Naylor 2000: 30)

Discussing words

Sometimes children use words loosely – as we do ourselves at times. (Who does not talk about 'letting the cold air in' when a door has been left open on a cold day?) In the context of learning science, however, we have to be clear about what a particular word is labelling in the child's mind. In the case of melting and dissolving, have the children not distinguished the processes of melting and dissolving or just not realised which is called melting and which is dissolving? In such cases it is important to explore the children's meaning for the words in order to know what their ideas are. It is useful to ask them to give an example of melting or to say how they would try, for instance, to make sugar melt. This would indicate whether melting is different in their mind from dissolving. Other points about using scientific words are discussed in Chapter 4.

Discussing with children digital photographs of themselves engaged in activities

The ready availability of digital cameras has opened up a new set of opportunities for exploring children's thinking. The speed with which the photographs can be displayed on a computer screen or an interactive whiteboard means that teachers can study images of children within a short time of the event, discuss with the children their thinking at the time or preserve the images for perusal later. An example was described by Lias and Thomas, working with eight-year-olds:

> During the activity (making a 'circuits game' for practising multiplication tables) we took several digital photographs of the children making and testing their circuits to display later. Because there was a PC, an LCD projector and an interactive whiteboard in the room, we decided to show the photographs to the children at the end of the activity... The captured images of particular events helped children to recall what they were doing at a particular time and prevented confusion over which event was being discussed. They also helped to keep the children's minds focused and provided a visual scaffold to support their descriptions and explanations. Compared with previous occasions, the children answered questions far more confidently and fluently, needed far less prompting and support, and their responses were far more detailed and complete.
>
> (Lias and Thomas 2003: 18)

Summary

This chapter has been about methods that teachers can use to gather information about their pupils' ideas in order to make decisions about how to help the children's learning. The main points are:

■ It is important to be clear about the ideas that the children are intended to develop through undertaking an activity.

■ There are many strategies from which to choose to elicit children's ideas. These are listed in Box 14.2.

■ When the teacher is questioning orally or setting a written or drawing task to find out children's ideas, the questions should be expressed as open and person-centred.

■ Setting up situations in which children have to use words in discussion with each other or the teacher enables the teachers to find out how certain concepts are understood.

15 Finding out children's process skills and attitudes

Introduction

In this chapter we continue the description of ways of gathering evidence within classroom activities, turning attention to process skills and attitudes. We first discuss the different considerations that apply because process skills and attitudes can be used and developed in all enquiries and investigations. We then look at the main methods of gathering evidence during activities: using observation, questioning and the possibilities offered by children's writing. In the final section we consider what is involved in planning the collection of evidence as part of lesson preparation.

A structure for assessing process skills and attitudes

The National Curriculum for England describes the skills involved in science enquiry under three headings: planning; obtaining and presenting evidence; and considering evidence and evaluating. In the context of gathering information about these skills for formative assessment we find it useful to consider 'obtaining evidence' and 'communicating' separately. We also include the development of the scientific attitudes of 'respect for evidence and the willingness to change ideas', and 'sensitivity to living things and the environment', which are central to learning through scientific activity – and which apply as much to the work of scientists as to children's learning. Figure 15.1 shows the process skills and attitudes with which we are dealing here and how they relate to the National Curriculum investigative skills.

Gathering evidence about process skills and attitudes

Unlike concepts and ideas, which are determined by the content of activities, the use and development of skills and attitudes are determined by the way in which children interact with the content. But the content does matter because it affects

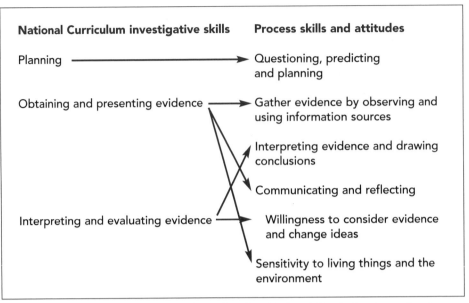

Figure 15.1 Process skills and attitudes related to National Curriculum investigative skills

the extent to which children can use the skills they may have. We don't expect young children to be able to 'process' (that is, use process skills to make sense of) complex phenomena and events, particularly those that can only be understood using mental models. A six-year-old may well be able to draw conclusions about observations in a familiar situation such as rolling toy cars down inclined planes as the angle is changed, but not in relation to patterns of air flow around an aerofoil. *So the children must be engaged in the exploration, investigation or discussion of subject matter within their understanding when their process skills are being assessed.*

The main methods that teachers can use to find out about children's process skills and attitudes are:

■ observation;

■ questioning, using questions that require use of process skills;

■ writing on tasks that require use of process skills.

Gathering information by observing children investigating

First we must acknowledge that the task of making useful observations of each and every child in relation to a range of skills and attitudes, and at the same time fostering their learning, is not just a formidable one, but is impossible. Neither is it expected. The collection of evidence about process skills is made into a manageable task by planning and focusing. At the same time, it is made worthwhile by the benefits to teaching and learning. Knowing where the children are in their development is essential to deciding how to help them, and the evidence gathered indicates the next steps to take (as we shall see in Chapter 16). We deal with planning to gather evidence later in this chapter. At this point we take up the matter of focusing observation.

Identifying significant behaviour

Almost everything that a child does can give some evidence of his or her thinking. But some things are more useful than others and it is necessary to be able to pick out the behaviour of most significance. This can be done with the help of 'indicators', which describe aspects of behaviour that can be taken as evidence of certain skills being used. Such indicators can be even more useful if they are chosen to describe different levels of development of the skills. The kind of thinking and information that this requires can be illustrated in relation to children's skills in gathering information by observing.

Ask yourself: *what would I look for as indications that a child is observing?* The first thought might be that the child seems to be paying attention to details, possibly noticing similarities and differences between things, perhaps using senses other than sight.

Then ask yourself: *how would observation be different for a younger child than for an older one?* For the younger child the similarities and differences might be just the obvious ones, while for the older child we would expect more detail, more accuracy in observation, through the use of measurement and checking results.

Given more time and access to information about the development of skill in observation these statements could be refined into a list of indicators arranged as far as possible in the sequence of development. 'As far as possible' is a necessary qualification because there is not likely to be an exact and invariable sequence that is the same for all children, but it is helpful to have a rough idea. As a result of this kind of thinking, and using shared experience of how children's skills develop, the set of statements of 'indicators of gathering evidence by observing and using information sources' given in Box 15.1 was created. Boxes 15.2 to 15.6 give the results of similar exercises for the other process skills and attitudes identified in Figure 15.1 (note that the statements in Boxes 15.1 to 15.4 are based on ones produced by the authors for the ASE Science Year Primary CD-ROM).

Box 15.1	Indicators of development of skill in gathering evidence by observing and using information sources

Things children do that are indicators of gathering evidence by observing and using information sources:

1 Identify obvious differences and similarities between objects and materials.

2 Make use of several senses in exploring objects or materials.

3 Identify relevant differences of detail between objects or materials and identify points of similarity between objects where differences are more obvious than similarities.

4 Use their senses appropriately and extend the range of sight using a hand lens or microscope as necessary.

5 Make an adequate series of observations to answer the question or test the prediction being investigated.

6 Take steps to ensure that the results obtained are as accurate as they can reasonably be and repeat observations.

7 Regularly and spontaneously use printed and electronic information sources to check or supplement their investigations.

Box 15.2	Indicators of development of skill in questioning, predicting and planning

Things children do when questioning, predicting and planning:

1 Readily ask a variety of questions and participate effectively in discussing how their questions can be answered.

2 Attempt to make a prediction relating to a problem or question even if it is based on preconceived ideas.

3 Suggest a useful approach to answering a question or testing a prediction by investigation, even if details are lacking or need further thought.

4 Identify the variable that has to be changed and the things that should be kept the same for a fair test.

5 Succeed in planning a fair test using the support of a framework of questions.

6 Identify what to look for or measure to obtain a result in an investigation.

7 Distinguish from many observations those that are relevant to the problem in hand and explain the reason.

Box 15.3   **Indicators of development of skill in interpreting evidence and drawing conclusions**

Things children do that are indicators of interpreting evidence and drawing conclusions:

1   Discuss what they find in relation to their initial questions or compare their findings with their earlier predictions/expectations.

2   Notice associations between changes in one variable and another.

3   Identify patterns or trends in their observations or measurements.

4   Try to explain simple patterns in their observations or measurements.

5   Use patterns to draw conclusions and attempt to explain them.

6   Use scientific concepts in drawing or evaluating conclusions.

7   Recognise that there may be more than one explanation that fits the evidence and that any conclusions are tentative and may have to be changed in the light of new evidence.

Box 15.4   **Indicators of development of skills in communicating and reflecting**

Things children do when communicating and reflecting:

1   Talk freely about their activities and the ideas they have, with or without making a written record.

2   Listen to others' ideas and look at their results.

3   Use drawings, writing, models, paintings to present their ideas and findings.

4   Use tables, graphs and charts when these are suggested to record and organise results.

5   Use appropriate scientific language in reporting and show understanding of the terms used.

6   Choose a form for recording or presenting results that is both considered and justified in relation to the type of information and the audience.

7   Compare their actual procedures after the event with what was planned and make suggestions for improving their ways of investigating.

Box 15.5	Indicators of development in willingness to consider evidence in relation to ideas

Things children do when showing the scientific attitude of willingness to consider evidence in relation to ideas:

1 Recognise when the evidence does not fit a conclusion based on expectations.

2 Modify ideas enough to incorporate new evidence or arguments but resist relinquishing them.

3 Check parts of the evidence that do not fit an overall pattern or conclusion.

4 Show willingness to consider alternative ideas that may fit the evidence.

5 Relinquish or change ideas after considering the evidence.

6 Spontaneously seek other ideas that may fit the evidence rather than accepting the first that seems to fit.

7 Recognise that ideas can be changed by thinking and reflecting about different ways of making sense of the same evidence.

Box 15.6	Indicators of development in sensitivity to living things and the environment

Things children do when showing the scientific attitude of sensitivity to living things and the environment:

1 Take part in caring for living things in the classroom or around the school, with supervision.

2 Provide care for living things in the classroom or around the school with minimum supervision.

3 Show care for the local environment by behaviour that protects it from litter, damage and disturbance.

4 Adhere to a code of behaviour that avoids damage to the environment on visits outside the school; replacing disturbed stones, not collecting plants and returning animals caught for study to where they were found where possible.

5 Take responsibility, and initiative where necessary, for ensuring that living things in and around the classroom are cared for.

6 Take part in developing a code of care for the environment, with reasons for the actions identified.

7 Help in ensuring that others know about and observe such a code of care.

Using developmental indicators

In all these lists the earlier statements indicate skills or attitudes that are likely to be developed before the ones later in the list. However, as just mentioned, this will not necessarily be the case for every child. It should also be noted that there are no 'levels', grades or stages suggested: just a sequence expected for children in the primary, and perhaps early secondary, years. For formative assessment it is not necessary to tie indicators to grade level expectation – all that is required is to see where children are and what further progress they can make. Even though the same idea of development runs through the attainment targets of the National Curriculum, the numbers against the statements here do not signify levels in the same way, but they provide more detail of what to look for than the level descriptions. We must remember that their function is different from the level descriptions of attainment targets. See Box 15.7 for some important points about their use.

Box 15.7	Using developmental indicators

- Developmental indicators are not intended to be used as checklists, carried around on clipboards.

- They can serve their purpose best when carried around in teachers' heads, guiding observation during normal activities.

- It is advisable to start by using only one list – say that relating to children's skill in observing and using information sources – and to become familiar with this before using lists relating to other skills.

- Not all investigations give opportunities for all the skills to be used, so observations will need to be spread over several activities.

- As children's engagement with different subject matter will vary, it is important to gather evidence for each skill from several events.

- Indicators can also be used in interpreting evidence from children's oral and written answers, as well as from their actions.

The indicators have two important functions. First, they focus attention on particular aspects of behaviour that signify a skill or attitude in action. Being prepared regarding what to look for makes observing much easier. Second, because they are arranged in a rough sequence of progressive development, they give an indication of where a child has reached. If a child shows evidence of the first few behaviours, but not of later ones, then the change from one set to the other shows where help is needed to make further progress. We look more at this use of the indicators in Chapter 16.

Questioning

In Chapter 14 we identified the most useful questions for probing children's thinking as being ones that are open and person-centred (see page 143). We also noted that some open and person-centred questions were more appropriate for revealing children's process skills than for giving access to their ideas. Questions that help in finding out about skills will be expressed so that, in answering, the children describe or show these skills.

For example, questions relating to gathering evidence by observing will be in the form:

> What differences do you see ...?
> What else have you noticed ...?
> What is the evidence that you used ...?

Questions relating to questioning and planning:

> What questions would you like to answer ...?
> What do you think you need to do to find out ...?
> How will you make sure that the test is a fair one?

Questions relating to interpreting evidence and drawing conclusions:

> What did you find about how ... changed when you changed ...?
> What made a difference to ...?
> What do you think explains what you found about ...?

Using written work

Not all the evidence of process skills needs to be collected through on-the-spot observation. Children's written work often gives useful information, particularly in the case of older children, when the tasks are set to require them to describe their observations, predictions, plans and how they carried them out. The examples in Figures 15.2 to 15.4 illustrate the value of the products. They all come from Paterson (1989).

In Figure 15.2 two predictions are made, both of which can be tested by investigation. The first prediction is based on the everyday experience that it is easier to see things that are closer than those that are far away. However, the basis of the second prediction, about people wearing glasses, is less easy to follow and deserves discussion.

Figure 15.3 shows a child's reflection on an investigation of how far away the sound can be heard of a penny being dropped. Not only does she identify the deficiencies of the investigation carried out, she shows some aspects of planning, including the ingenious use of an instrument to measure the sound level.

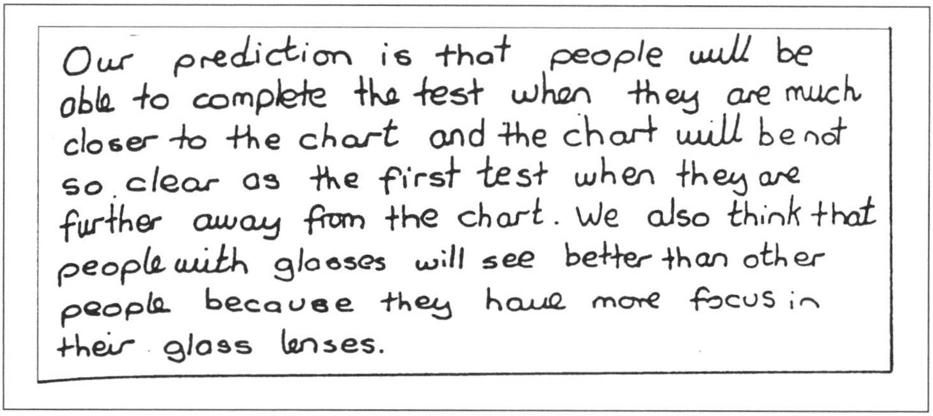

Our prediction is that people will be able to complete the test when they are much closer to the chart and the chart will be not so clear as the first test when they are further away from the chart. We also think that people with glasses will see better than other people because they have more focus in their glass lenses.

Figure 15.2 An 11-year-old's prediction as part of planning an investigation

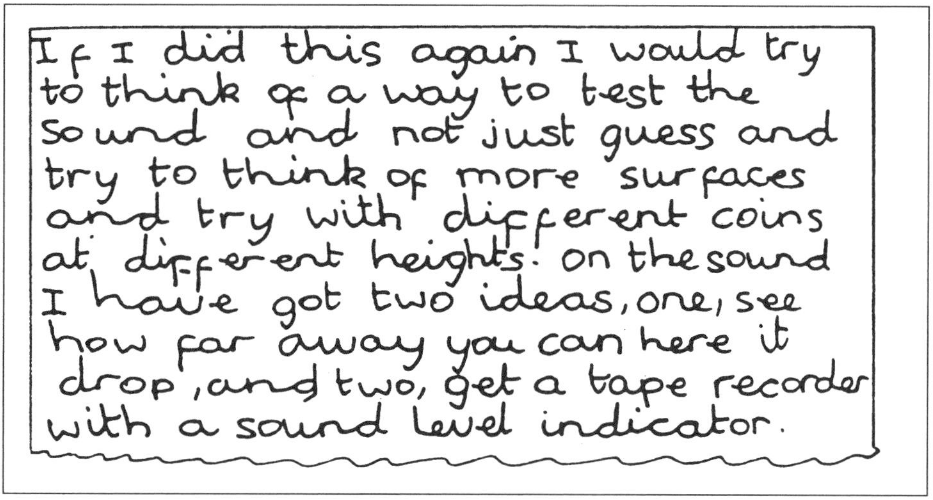

If I did this again I would try to think of a way to test the sound and not just guess and try to think of more surfaces and try with different coins at different heights: on the sound I have got two ideas, one, see how far away you can here it drop, and two, get a tape recorder with a sound level indicator.

Figure 15.3 A nine-year-old's reflection after reporting her investigation

Figure 15.4 shows very detailed observation, using four senses, carefully and vibrantly described so that the reader can almost share the experience.

Planning to gather evidence during activities

Collecting evidence to build up a picture of all children in a class over all skills, concepts and attitudes is a task that requires a thought-out strategy. It will not happen automatically but needs to be planned as part of lesson planning if the result is not to be patchy and only about the readily assessed parts of children's achievement. Three points have to be considered in planning for assessment:

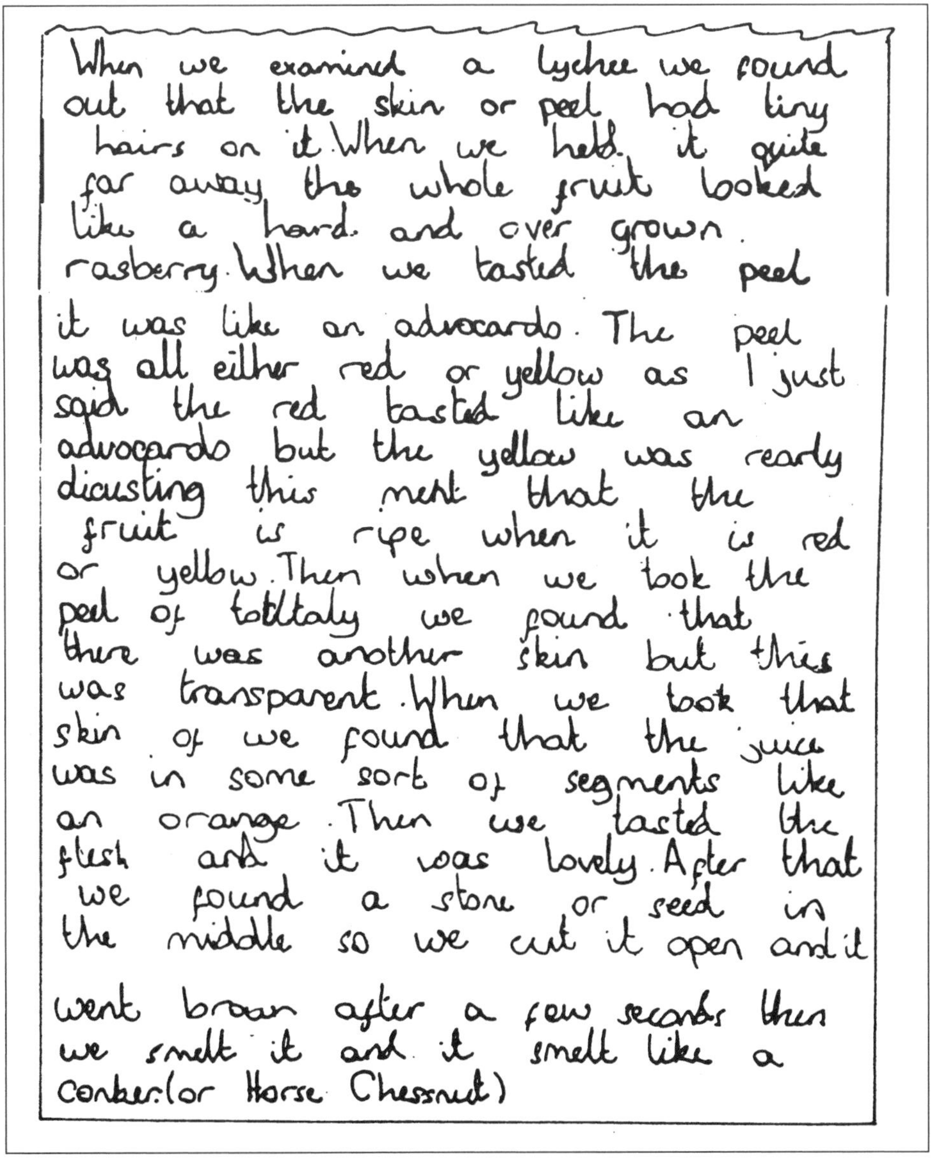

When we examined a lychee we found out that the skin or peel had tiny hairs on it. When we held it quite far away the whole fruit looked like a hard and over grown rasberry. When we tasted the peel it was like an advocardo. The peel was all either red or yellow as I just said the red tasted like an advocardo but the yellow was nearly diausting this ment that the fruit is ripe when it is red or yellow. Then when we took the peel of totltaly we found that there was another skin but this was transparent. When we took that skin of we found that the juice was in some sort of segments like an orange. Then we tasted the flesh and it was lovely. After that we found a stone or seed in the middle so we cut it open and it went brown after a few seconds then we smelt it and it smelt like a Conker (or Horse Chessnut)

Figure 15.4 Observations recorded by two ten-year-olds

- which skills, ideas and attitudes will be assessed out of those that could be assessed;
- which children will be assessed;
- what part children will play, through self-assessment.

The third of these is the subject of Chapter 17. We consider the first two here.

When to assess what

Different aspects of achievement offer different assessment opportunities. It is useful to consider the frequency of opportunities.

■ 'Frequently occurring' events. Since the skills and attitudes relating to investigation can be assessed in many different situations, the opportunity for their assessment will occur as frequently as children undertake investigations. They do not need to be assessed for all children every time they occur, which is fortunate because this would be impossible. Because of their nature, assessing these skills involves, particularly for young children, careful observation on the spot of how they carry out the activities.

■ 'Infrequently occurring' events. Ideas relating to specific subject matter, such as magnetism or seed germination, can only be assessed when activities relate to these things. Information needs to be gathered about all the children working on a particular content while the opportunity exists. Fortunately, these are the aspects of achievement that can be assessed through questioning groups or through children's drawing and writing, things that can be studied after the event rather than assessed on the spot, so that it is possible to collect information about several groups of children or even a whole class during the time the relevant activities are in progress.

In planning what to assess, therefore, it is best to consider, first, the *infrequently occurring* aspects and make sure that information will be obtained about these for all the children concerned, selecting the methods from those discussed in Chapter 14. Then plan for the *frequently occurring* aspects, which will be assessed for some of the children, using methods suggested in this chapter.

Selecting the children

The greatest benefit of planning assessment is perhaps that it ensures that information is gathered equitably about all the children, not just the ones who need most help or claim most attention. It depends upon keeping records and carrying out the assessment systematically.

■ For infrequently occurring aspects, the teacher needs to plan how to collect information about the ideas of all the children at the appropriate points – perhaps at the start of activities. But it may be that he or she already has, from previous activities, evidence of the children's initial ideas and the interest will be in how ideas are developing during the activities. In either case, the planning will involve thinking out the questions to ask and the situations to provide to enable children to express their ideas.

■ For frequently occurring aspects, the teacher might plan to observe and make notes about one group (the target groups) in particular during an investigation, which could spread over several sessions. The children in the target group should not be aware of special attention being paid to them; there is no suggestion of a teacher hovering with a clipboard and refusing to interact with the children in a normal way.

The aim is gradually to collect evidence that can be used to help all the children to develop their skills and attitudes. In one lesson information may be collected about one group; later, other children may be observed, and missing information filled in, according to the opportunities provided by the activities planned. It may take a few months to cover all the skills for all the children. However, as the process becomes an established part of planning and interaction with children it becomes progressively more easy. The need to make notes about individual children, which may be felt at first, gives way later as the information fits into the mental framework that a teacher develops for assessing the children. The process is not, in practice, as demanding as it may seem in abstract, as the example in Box 15.8 shows.

| Box 15.8 | An example of planned collection of evidence for formative assessment |

This example of work with infants (five- to 7-year-olds) is based on work quoted in Harlen *et al.* (1990). The teacher began the lesson by reading to the whole class a story about feet, in which a boy puts his Wellington boots on the wrong feet. After the story, still as a whole class, they talked about the events in the story, about their own feet, about shoes. This was followed by the organisation of group work, with six groups of four children, and the tasks of each group were described before they split up and went to the tables where necessary equipment had already been put out. So as soon as they reached their tables they could start on something, while the teacher began to pass round each group, helping, monitoring and observing.

The teacher had decided that her assessment focus would be group one, which had been given a collection of old plimsolls, Wellington boots, other shoes and slippers to investigate. (Other groups were taking up the subject of feet through different activities, including making shadows of their feet using a torch, measuring them, drawing round them and cutting out the shapes, making a graph.) Group one had the task of discussing which shoes or boots they thought would be most waterproof and this involved feeling and manipulating the materials. When they had made their choice and given their reasons, they were asked to find a way of showing that their idea was correct. So they planned a simple investigation and proceeded to carry it out.

There was plenty of opportunity for the teacher, on her visits to this group, to collect information about the detail of the children's observations, their identification of simple differences, their interpretation of the results (water drops stayed on the surface of smooth and fluffy materials) and the record they made of what they did. At the same time she made notes about individual children; for example, 'Lee – said water soaked though the plimsoll tongue because it's thinner that the other part. Tried out drips on sole and rubber edging – predicted that the water wouldn't go through.' Figure 15.5 shows Lee's record.

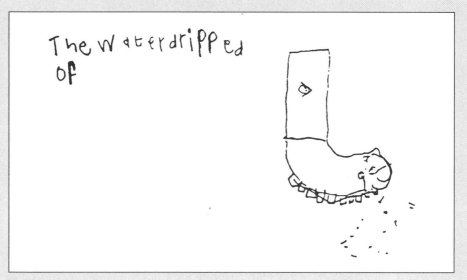

The water dripped
of

Figure 15.5 Five-year-old Lee's drawing

As well as the information about how group one went about observing and investigating, the teacher discussed the children's ideas about materials, particularly in relation to properties which varied among the ones they had been given. In this work on feet the other groups were not working with materials at this time, but the teacher ensured that such opportunities were given through other activities and so enabled her to complete her assessment of all the children's ideas on materials.

An aspect of this approach that may at first seem surprising is that accumulating information over time in this way means that children will be assessed in relation to the same skills and so on while engaged on different activities. Does it matter that group one were investigating materials while group two might be investigating toy cars when their skills are assessed? Or that ideas about materials were assessed for group one using materials different from those other children were handling when their ideas were assessed? The answers to these questions depend on the purpose and use of the information, matters that we take up in the next chapter.

Summary

This chapter has described ways in which evidence about the development of children's process skills and scientific attitudes can be gathered by teachers. The main points have been:

■ The methods for collecting evidence are chiefly by observing how children go about their enquiries, by asking process-based questions and by studying their writing in tasks set to reveal their skills.

■ Observation has to be focused, so it is necessary to be aware of significant behaviours that indicate the skills in action.

■ Indicators of relevant behaviours arranged in a sequence of development can act both to focus observation and to identify points reached by children in their development of skills and attitudes.

■ Evidence relating to skills and attitudes can be obtained from the writing of older children providing the tasks are presented so as to elicit their predictions, interpretations, reflections on methods used etc.

■ The collection of evidence has to be planned as part of the lesson, to ensure that opportunities for accessing ideas about the subject matter are taken when they occur for all the children and evidence is gathered systematically about process skills over time.

16 Using information for formative assessment: deciding and communicating next steps

Introduction

How is the evidence gathered as part of teaching to be interpreted and used formatively to help learning? How are decisions made about the next steps? How are these decisions fed back to the children? These are the questions we tackle in this chapter. In practice interpretation will happen at the same time as the evidence is gathered, but it is important to recognise the difference between evidence and interpretation in order to ensure that decisions have a sound evidence base.

In terms of the formative assessment cycle in Figure 12.3 we are dealing here with the parts labelled 'Judgement of achievement' and 'Next steps in learning'. With the help of examples, we look at interpreting evidence of process skills first, then the development of children's ideas. This enables next steps to be identified. Taking these steps involves feedback into teaching and the kinds of actions to develop process skills and concepts discussed in Chapters 9 and 10. But an important part of taking action is feeding back the judgements and next steps to children. This is considered in this chapter, linking to the involvement of children in the formative assessment of their own work, discussed in Chapter 17.

Deciding next steps in process skills

The indicators of development in process skills, introduced in Chapter 15, provide the opportunity to decide where children have reached in the sequence of development of each of the skills. A useful way of using these indicators in deciding next steps is to regard them as questions to be put to the evidence gathered by observation or from written work. So we could ask in relation to 'observing and using information sources', for instance, what evidence is there that the children: identify obvious differences and similarities between objects and materials; make use of several senses in exploring objects or materials; etc.?

To identify next steps, the evidence gathered about the observations the children are making in their work is scanned in relation to each question in the list. Probably the answer to the first few questions will be 'yes' and there will be a point where the answers turn into 'no'. It is this point that suggests where development has reached and so where the next steps are required. Where answers are a qualified 'yes' (sometimes, but not always) it is useful to consider where the skill is and is not shown, leading to identification of the kind of help needed. These are indeed the most useful answers, since they identify the points where development is fluid. An answer 'no' signals where future help is needed, focusing first on using the skills in more familiar situations.

Although it is not advisable to judge from one event, for the purpose of illustrating the approach we can use the example shown in Figure 16.1. The account gives a good idea of what the children did and we can assume that the teacher was able to observe the investigation as well as reading the account. How might this evidence be interpreted in relation to the child's process skills? We refer here to the developmental indicators in Boxes 15.1 to 15.4.

Figure 16.1 A nine-year-old's account of her group's investigation

Gathering evidence by observing and using information sources (Box 15.1)	Some evidence in relation to statement 3: identifying differences. Apparently only one measurement (statement 5). No evidence from this investigation in relation to statement 4. *Next steps*: Not enough information here to inform a decision.
Questioning, predicting and planning (Box 15.2)	Evidence that a useful approach was taken (3) and the variable to be changed was appropriately selected (4) (although it is not clear how much of the planning was the children's own); some variables controlled. *Next steps*: Give further opportunities for the child to plan a fair test independently.
Interpreting evidence and drawing conclusions (Box 15.3)	Results not interpreted in terms of initial question (1) and no explicit connection between the colour of the paper and the temperature (2). *Next steps*: Question the child about the relation between findings and the question being investigated. Ensure children understand the reason for their investigations.
Communicating and reflecting (Box 15.4)	(Assume evidence for statements 1 and 2.) Evidence of use of drawing to show what was done, but not findings (3). *Next steps*: Discuss with the child how to make drawings more informative and how to structure reports of investigations.

A similar approach can be used for attitudes, but this requires evidence to be brought together from a very wide range of activities and it is not helpful to discuss just one event.

Interpreting information about children's ideas

A good deal of information about children's ideas will come from their explanations of events, whether written, drawn or spoken. In interpreting this information it is first essential to be clear about what the evidence is. We have to be careful to distinguish evidence from interpretations and to be as objective as possible about what the child actually says, writes, draws or does. This means taking a scientific approach to interpretation: clarifying the questions we are trying to answer ('What are the children's ideas about...?') and the evidence that we can use to answer it. Looking at the process in this way reinforces the point that any conclusions that are drawn (about next steps) are tentative and subject to change in the light of further evidence.

For example, if as part of exploring light sources children are asked to draw things that they think give out light, and they include a mirror and the moon in their drawings, the *evidence* is the drawings. The *interpretation* might be that the children do not distinguish between things that give out light and those that reflect it. Before deciding what action to take it would be wise to test out this interpretation. Is this really the problem, or did the children mistake 'things that are bright' for 'things that give out light?' Is there supporting evidence from other things the children have done or from what they say about the things they have drawn? Is it reasonable for children to be expected to know that the light from the moon is reflected light? If the interpretation is confirmed, the next step becomes clear: to provide an opportunity for children to test their ideas by exploring what happens to a mirror in the dark, compared with a torch or other source of light, for example.

Similarly, if a child produces the drawing in Figure 16.2 of an electric circuit with two bulbs, it is necessary to make sure that the connection to the left-hand bulb is not just a mistake in drawing. If the child does not see anything wrong, then the next step might be to test the circuit in practice, following the child's diagram carefully.

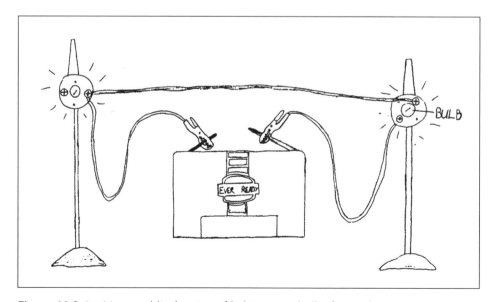

Figure 16.2 An 11-year-old's drawing of lighting two bulbs from a battery

In principle it would be possible to use what is known from research about the development of children's scientific ideas to describe development in terms of indicators, as we have done for process skills. This would require a very large number of lists, of course, and would be unmanageable. A more efficient way is to consider the overall development of ideas as they grow from 'small' ones (which explain particular events or phenomena) to 'bigger' ones (relevant to a range of linked phenomena). In helping this development the aim is to help the children to construct more widely applicable ideas that are shared by others in making sense of the world around.

For each idea, we can think of a sequence in the different ways it is used in giving explanations, reflecting the 'growth' of the idea, such as the following:

1 Little attempt to explain: description only.

2 Attempt to explain but using a preconceived non-scientific idea (about . . .).

3 Reference to the idea (about . . .) but without showing how it explains the event.

4 Uses the idea (about . . .) to explain a familiar event but not related ones newly encountered.

5 Uses the idea (about . . .) to explain situations different from those encountered before.

6 Refers to a larger idea (about . . .) and how it explains a number of linked events.

7 Uses the larger idea (about . . .) to predict events not encountered before.

Here the 'about . . . ' stands for any idea that is the goal of the activity. For an example of using this approach, we refer back to the children's work in Figures 2.6 and 2.7. There the children were giving their explanations of how the drum makes a sound and how we hear it. The two ideas that the teacher was probing were that 'sound is caused by vibration' and that 'we hear sound when the vibrations reach our ears'. We consider the evidence in relation to the first of these.

In Figure 2.6 the child claims to give an explanation but it is really just a description (the sound is very loud). So the next step is perhaps to give some experience of the difference between a drum that is making a sound and one that is not. In Figure 2.7 the word 'vibration' is used directly in relation to the production of a sound. The child has used the idea about sound being caused by vibration in the situation given (statement 4). We have no evidence that this can be applied in other situations (statement 5). So the next step might be to give experience that enables the child to see if the idea explains other events where sound is produced. Identifying useful next steps is the purpose of formative assessment; there is no need to pin down the children as working at a particular level.

Feedback

The essential feature that makes assessment formative is that information from the evidence gathered is used to help children take the next steps in learning. This requires information to be fed back into the teaching–learning process. There are, however, at least three different ways of doing this, all of which need to be considered.

Teacher → (feedback about next steps) → teaching → → learning

Here the teacher uses the feedback as an input into teaching, to adjust the content and interaction with children with the intention of helping further learning.

Teacher → (feedback about next steps) → children → → learning

Here the teacher feeds back the information to the children in a way that enables them to recognise the next steps they need to take and how to take them.

Child and teacher → (decisions about next steps) → → learning

Here the children are involved in gathering information about their own progress and using this to recognise the next steps they need to take and how to take them.

Feedback into teaching

So far in this chapter we have dealt only with part of the first of these types of feedback, the part concerned with identifying next steps. (The second part of this, how the teacher can adjust teaching in order to help children to take these next steps, is the concern of Chapters 9 to 11.) However, an important opportunity for helping learning is missed if this is the only route for feedback into learning. At the very least teachers should share with children their views on their work in such a way that the children understand the feedback and what it means in terms of what they need to do. In the next section we begin to consider this form of feedback. The discussion continues in the next chapter, where we are concerned with the involvement of children in assessing their own work.

Feedback to children

There has been a good deal of research into feeding back information to children through marking their work that indicates that the form of the feedback has an impact on children's motivation as well as on their achievements. The importance of this is underlined by recalling that children have to do the learning and thus their motivation and enjoyment is as relevant to future learning as is information about how to correct errors. Thus the *way* in which feedback is given to children is as important as the focus of the feedback. Indeed, some research shows that feedback can have a negative impact on performance as well as a positive one (Kluger and DeNisi 1996). A study that has influenced thinking about feedback, and which was highlighted in the review of Black and Wiliam (1998a), is summarised in Box 16.1. What the Butler study reveals is that children seize upon marks and ignore any comments that accompany them. They look to the marks for a judgement rather than help in further learning. When marks are absent they engage with what the teacher wants to bring to their attention. The comments then have a chance of improving learning as intended by the teacher. In order to do this, of course, the comments should be positive and non-judgemental, and where possible should identify next steps.

Box 16.1	Research into different kinds of feedback

In a study by Ruth Butler (1987) the effects of different types of feedback by marking were compared. In a controlled experimental study she set up groups, who were given feedback in different ways. One group of pupils was given marks or grades only, another group was given only comments on their work and the third group received both marks and comments on the work. These conditions were studied in relation to tasks that required divergent and convergent thinking. The result was that, for divergent thinking tasks, the pupils who received comments only made the greatest gain in their learning, significantly more than for the other two groups. The results were the same for high and low achieving pupils. For convergent tasks, the lower achieving pupils scored most highly after comments only, with the marks only group next above the marks plus comments group. For all tasks and pupils, comments only led to higher achievement.

Feedback that is formative

The main point to emerge both from research studies and from experience of effective practice is a distinction between feedback that gives information and feedback that is judgemental. Feedback that gives information:

- focuses on the task, not the person;

- encourages children to think about the work, not about how 'good' they are;

- proposes what to do next and gives ideas about how to do it.

Feedback that is judgemental:

- is expressed in terms of how well the child has done rather than how well the work has been done;

- gives a judgement that encourages children to label themselves;

- provides a grade or mark that children use to compare themselves with each other or with what they want to achieve.

Interestingly, praise comes into the judgemental category; it makes children feel they are doing well but does not necessarily help them to do better. It is fine to acknowledge what is good about a piece of work, if this reinforces the goals, but praise in itself will not improve learning. A remark or mark that indicates a judgement on the work will divert children's attention from any comment that is made about improvement. Children are more motivated by comments that help them to think about their work and realise what they can do to improve it, and that give them help in doing this. This means oral or written questions and comments such as

How did you decide which was the best...?

Is there another way of explaining this by thinking of what happened when...

Next time, imagine that someone else is going to use your drawing to set up the circuit and make sure that you show them clearly what to do.

Dos and don'ts of feedback through marking

Some very practical guidelines for marking, particularly applied to science, were proposed by Evans (2001). The 'dos and don'ts' in Box 16.2 are derived from his list.

Box 16.2   Dos and don'ts of marking

Do

1 Plan the task with specific learning goals in mind.

2 Identify one or two aspects for comment and review which are related to the planned learning goals.

3 Comment first (and perhaps only) on aspects specific to *science*, since the task was set to help learning in science.

4 Think carefully about whether or not any other comment is needed at all, such as about neatness or effort, deserving though these may be. By all means acknowledge and encourage effort and progress, but not in a way that diverts attention from how to improve and move ahead.

5 Pinpoint weak aspects, e.g. misuse of a technical term (but don't be pedantic about the use of words) or assertions the children may have made that are not supported by their own evidence.

6 Indicate next steps.

7 Give children time to read, reflect on and, where appropriate, respond to comments.

Don't

1 Give judgemental comments and above all scores or symbols (such as B+ or 7/10), since these divert children's attention from learning from what they have done.

2 Don't pose rhetorical questions ('Do you think so?' 'I wonder why').

3 By all means pose questions, as long as the child understands that a response will be expected and will be read.

4 Don't waste precious time on evaluating tasks that are mainly about reinforcement. Concentrate on work that is really worth evaluating *for its science*. Any other work should be acknowledged by signature, not by the ubiquitous and ambiguous tick, which is often interpreted by children (not to mention parents and others) as commendation.

Feedback to children is more effective in improving learning when children realise the goals of their work and then begin to take part in the decisions about next steps. This leads to the third kind of feedback, which is discussed in the next chapter.

Summary

This chapter has discussed ways in which evidence of process skills and ideas can be interpreted so that next steps in learning can be identified and fed back into teaching and learning. The main points have been:

■ Deciding next steps requires a clear view of the nature of progression.

■ Next steps in process skills can be identified with the help of developmental indicators.

■ Next steps in ideas can be suggested by where children are in the progress from 'small' to 'big' ideas.

■ Learning is helped by providing feedback about next steps to children as well as using it in adapting teaching.

■ Feedback to children on their progress should be non-judgemental and give information about next steps and how to take them.

17 Involving children in assessing their work

The previous few chapters have explored various segments of the formative assessment cycle, and we now come to the centre, where, in Figure 12.3, we placed 'children'. In this chapter we look at the reasons for involving children in assessing their work – both their own and each other's – and at what it involves in practice. We discuss the importance of children knowing the goals of their work, being aware of the standards or quality expected and taking part in deciding their next steps in learning. We give examples of how teachers have approached these aspects of involving children in in self- and peer assessment.

Why involve children in assessing their work?

When asked this question a group of teachers came up with the list in Box 17.1.

Box 17.1	Some reasons for involving children in using assessment to help learning

- The children are the ones who ultimately have to take the actions that lead to learning.

- Knowing their goals puts any learners in a better position to achieve them.

- Research shows that it raises levels of achievement.

- There is less need for feedback from the teacher if the children are involved in assessing their work and deciding next steps.

- Involvement in self-assessment facilitates ownership of their learning and enables children to be responsible for and accountable for their learning.

- It provides for independence and can lead to self-regulated learning.

■ It raises children's self-esteem.

■ It promotes higher order thinking since it requires children to think about how they learn (metacognitive thinking).

The practical reasons were identified in the research studies reviewed by Black and Wiliam (1998a), which highlighted the central role of children in their own learning. The involvement of children in self- and peer assessment was among the successful approaches in raising achievement. In the studies reviewed, there were examples of successful strategies for self-assessment with students from age five upwards.

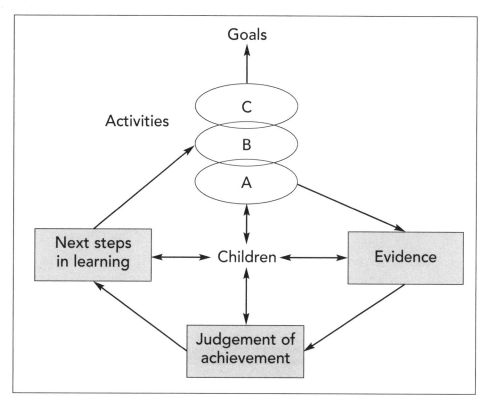

Figure 17.1 Giving children a role in formative assessment

The theoretical reasons for involving children in decisions about their learning derive from general ideas about how people learn. The kind of learning we need to aim for, as discussed in Chapter 7, is not a matter of absorbing information and ready-made understandings. Instead, it involves the active participation of learners in using existing ideas to try to make sense of new experiences. Perhaps the strongest, but almost too obvious, reason is that learning goes on inside children's heads and so they must be willing to undertake it and to make the necessary effort. Children can, of course, be bribed or cajoled into learning by rewards and punishment, but the fact remains that no one can do the learning for them.

These reasons explain the two-headed arrows that we should add to Figure 12.3, as in Figure 17.1. The inward pointing arrows indicate that the children are the subject of the teacher's decisions about goals, evidence etc. The outward pointing ones indicate the children's role in all these decisions.

In self-assessment the focus should be on the work rather than the 'self'. This being so, the way to help learning is to give learners as much opportunity as possible (appropriate to their age and stage) to know what they are intended to learn and how to go about it. Again, this seems an obvious point but it is in fact quite uncommon for children to be able to articulate what the teacher intends them to learn from a particular activity, as opposed to what they are supposed to do (see Box 17.2).

Box 17.2	Distinguishing what to learn from what to do

We have always been very good at telling children what we want them to do and how we want them to do it, thus establishing control and discipline, an essential element when teaching a number of children at once. Without the 'secret' knowledge of the learning intention, however, children have [not only] been deprived of information which will...enable them to carry out the task more effectively, they have also been denied the opportunity to self-evaluate, communicate this to the teacher, set targets for themselves and get to understand their own learning needs: in other words, to think intelligently about their own learning, rather than 'finding out what the teacher wants, and doing it'.

(Clarke 1998: 47)

Sharing goals with children

When any of us try to learn something or improve performance, whether it is a physical activity such as playing a sport or a mental one such as learning another language, we like to be able to tell how we are doing. We can only assess our progress, though, if we have a clear notion of what we are aiming for. It is the same with children: they need to be aware of the goals of their learning. However, as Shirley Clarke indicates in Box 17.2, often children do not have a clear notion of the purpose of their activities. Consequently, classroom activities appear to children as collections of disconnected and often meaningless exercises. To improve understanding of the purposes of activities, teachers need to find ways of conveying goals and standards of quality. What this means in practice is giving children a reason for what they are doing. In Box 17.3 we recall how Graham, the teacher in the case study in Chapter 1, did this.

Box 17.3	An example of communicating goals

Graham set children the task of investigating soils with three instructions about what to do and a fourth that gave a reason for doing it – so that they could think about what makes a difference to how well plants will grow in the soils. Without this fourth part, the children would probably have investigated the soils, but if asked what they were learning would have answered 'about soils'. The reason for the investigations given by the teacher focused their observations on relevant differences and thus not only made them aware of why they were investigating the soils but made the intended learning more likely.

How to communicate content-related goals to children

Communicating goals of learning to students is not an easy matter, however, particularly in the case of young children. It is certainly not possible to do this using the language of official documents. In science it is difficult to share goals without telling children what they have to find. For example, suppose the teacher's goal is: 'For children to learn that the pitch of a sound depends on how rapidly the source vibrates.' What the teacher might say to the children is: 'When you make different sounds with these things, I want you to see if you can find out what makes the sound higher and what makes it lower.' This gives the children a reason for the activity in terms of what they will learn but does not tell them 'the answer'.

Contrast this with: 'Try to make high sounds and low sounds with these things by changing the length of the string or putting different amounts of water in the bottle.' This tells the children what to do but not why. Or: 'When you make different sounds notice that the high sound comes when the string vibrates more quickly and when there is less air in the bottle.' This tells them what they are intended to find and takes away the opportunity to think about the evidence for themselves.

How to communicate process-related goals to children

In the case of activities where the goals include the development of process skills, this should be made clear; otherwise the children will assume that the answers they get are the main aim rather than the way in which they go about finding the answers.

For instance, suppose the teacher's goal is: 'For the children to plan an investigation that will be a fair test of which material will keep an ice block from melting for the longest time.' This might be best shared with the children in this way: 'When you test these materials I want to see if you can do it in a way that the test is fair and you are quite sure that it is the material that is making the difference.'

Reinforcing the goals

It it not enough to talk about goals only at the beginning of an activity. The purpose of what they are doing needs to be reinforced during the activity and at the end. Ensuring that discussion afterwards picks up on these intentions will help to set the pattern of taking the purpose seriously and working towards the intended learning.

One teacher regularly asks the children to explain to others what they have learned, making explicit reference to what they hoped to do or find out. If, as often happens, there was some unplanned feature of the enquiry, she asks them: 'What did you learn from that?' Sometimes she asks the children to think of questions to ask each other about what they have learned; she finds that these are often more probing and difficult than her own questions. All these things combine to reinforce the learning atmosphere and support learning as a shared endeavour.

Involving children in judging the quality of their own work

In order to judge the quality of the work, children need not only to know the purpose of what they are doing but also to have some notion of the standard they should be aiming for. This is less easy in science than in an area such as language development, where children might be told that in a piece of writing they are to use whole sentences or make sure that the events in a story are in the correct sequence. The children then know what to look for in judging their work. In science it is more difficult to make general statements that convey meaning to the children. Thus the required features are better conveyed through examples; over time the children come to share the teacher's criteria. Box 17.4 outlines an approach that can be used with young children.

Box 17.4	Communicating standards of quality with young children

The process can begin usefully if children from about the age of eight are encouraged to select their 'best' work and to put this in a folder or bag. Part of the time for 'bagging' should be set aside for the teacher to talk to each child about why certain pieces of work were selected. The criteria that the children are using will become clear. These should be accepted and they may have messages for the teacher. For example, if work seems to be selected only on the basis of being 'tidy' and not in terms of content, then perhaps this aspect is being overemphasised by the teacher. At first the discussion should only be to clarify the criteria the children use. 'Tell me what you particularly liked about this piece of work.' Gradually it will be possible to suggest criteria without dictating what the children should be selecting. This can be done through comments on the work. 'That was a very good way of showing your results, I could see at a glance which was best.' 'I'm glad you think that was your best investigation because although you didn't get the result you expected, you did it very carefully and made sure that the result was fair.'

Through such an approach children may begin to share the understanding of the goals of their work and become able to comment usefully on what they have achieved. It then becomes easier to be explicit about further targets and for the children to recognise when they have achieved them.

Teachers of older children can more explicitly share with them the criteria they use both in assessing practical skills and in marking written work. One science teacher, for example, did this by writing his own account of a class investigation and distributing copies for the children to mark, looking for particular features. It led to lively discussion and a keener understanding of what was expected in their own accounts (Fairbrother 1995).

Another approach is to use examples of other children's work, which could be collected for the purpose and made anonymous. Alternatively, the examples from the collections published to help teachers to assess work could be shared with the children. These include publications such as *Exemplification of Standards, Science at Key Stages 1 and 2, levels 1 to 5* (SCAA 1995) and *Performance Standards: Volume 1 Elementary School* (New Standards 1997). The discussion of these examples should lead to the children identifying the criteria for 'good work'. If they have done this for themselves, the teacher does not have to convince them of 'what is good'. One teacher printed the list of 'what makes a good report of an investigation' that the children had brainstormed and displayed it on the wall so that when the children were writing their reports they were reminded of how to write them well.

Involving children in deciding next steps

When children have a view of what they should be doing and how well they should be doing it, they are in a position to share in deciding the next steps to be taken. 'Sharing' is meant to convey the point that the responsibility for helping children's learning is ultimately the teacher's, for we are in no way suggesting that children decide what they do and don't do. However, sharing means that the children understand why they are being asked to do certain things and have a firm grasp of what they should do. Moreover, their involvement is likely to lead to greater motivation for the work.

Ways of involving children

In Box 17.5 a teacher of nine- and ten-year-olds describes how she helps the children to decide what they need to do.

Box 17.5	An example of involving children in deciding next steps

I make time to sit down with each group after an activity and talk about what they found difficult, what they thought they did well and what they could have done better. I ask them if they thought about particular aspects relating to the processes and then about how they explain their results. This is important for me because I won't have followed every step of their investigation and it helps me decide how much they have progressed from earlier work and whether they have taken the steps we agreed previously. I then ask questions that indicate my view of what they need to do, but by expressing this as questions, they actually identify what they are going to do. The questions are like: 'What can you do in your next investigation to be more sure of your results?' 'What sorts of notes could you make as you go along to give you all the information for preparing a report at the end?' 'Where could you find out more information to explain what you found?'

Note that the teacher 'makes time' for this, which, she reports, is time well spent. It saves time for teaching and learning in the end by obviating the need to repeat explanations of what children are to do, and the children learn more quickly by thinking rather than from making mistakes. This teacher treats the group as a learning unit and encourages them to help each other. Since the purpose of the assessment is formative, and since they learn as a group, the decisions made together are important for their learning. However, she also looks at the work of each child individually and makes sure that they recognise their own next steps in learning.

Other approaches in which children assess their work to identify next steps are self-marking using 'traffic lights' and peer marking.

Self-marking using traffic lights

This has been developed by teachers for use with lower secondary pupils (e.g. Black *et al*. 2003: 11), but has potential at the upper primary level. It requires some gradual introduction and possible modelling. The teacher might demonstrate what to do: 'Suppose I've finished writing and I read through what I've written and reflect on what I did. If there is something I'm not quite sure about then I put a yellow spot on the top corner. If I really don't understand, then it is a red one. But if I feel it all makes sense, then it is a green spot.' The teacher can explain that the spot is not a mark but a way of helping the teacher to know when to go on or to go over things.

This approach is particularly applicable to the conceptual understanding in an activity and clearly requires a classroom climate where it is acceptable for pupils to discuss what they don't understand (as we noted in Chapter 14).

Peer marking

Peer assessment in the context of formative assessment means something quite different from children marking each other's books. In essence it means children helping each other with their learning, by deciding the next steps to take.

One of the advantages of peer assessment is that it requires less one-to-one attention from the teacher than some other approaches to self-assessment. Children can more frequently discuss their work with each other and help each other to improve. But there are other more important reasons, summarised in Box 17.6.

Box 17.6	Advantages of peer assessment

Saving on teacher time is not the only reason for encouraging peer assessment. Having children talk to each other in pairs about their work requires them to think through the work again and find words to describe it without the pressure that comes from the unequal relationship between the child (novice) and the teacher (expert). It is also consistent with the understanding of learning as being the development of ideas through social interaction as well as through interaction with materials. It can help children to respect each other's strengths, especially if pairs are changed on different occasions.

The paired discussion needs to be structured, at least when it is new to the children. For example, the children can be asked to exchange work and then think about two or three questions on it, reflecting the criteria of quality. For instance, if the work describes a conclusion from something that has been observed or found from an investigation the questions might be 'Can you tell what was found?' 'Does the conclusion help to answer the question that was being investigated?' 'What would help to make it clearer (a diagram, or series of drawings)?' After such a discussion one child commented on having her work assessed by another: 'She said it was hard to understand my investigation so I asked her what sort of thing I should have put to make her understand. Next time I will make sure that I describe things more clearly.'

This approach to peer assessment clearly requires a class atmosphere where cooperation and collaboration, rather than competition, are encouraged. When they have confidence in gaining help from a structured exchange with a peer, children begin spontaneously to ask each other for their opinion. The recognition of being able to help themselves and each other enables learning to continue when the teacher is occupied with those who need extra help.

(Based on Harlen *et al.* 2003: 132–3)

Summary

This chapter has discussed the value of helping children to take part in the formative assessment of their work. The main points have been:

■ There are important theoretical and practical reasons for involving children in assessing their own work.

■ Acting on this means sharing learning goals with the children, conveying an operational meaning of quality and helping them to identify their next steps.

■ Sharing goals means communicating to children a reason for their activities in terms of learning, and referring back to this in discussion at the end of the activity.

■ Helping children to judge the quality of the work requires the subtle communication of criteria of quality through discussion of examples.

■ Involving children in deciding next steps follows from a review of what they have done and how they have done it, and agreeing ways of improving it or moving on from it.

■ Children can take part in deciding their next steps through self- and peer marking.

18 Summing up achievement

Introduction

Assessment for a summative purpose has an important role in children's education, although it is not as 'close to the learning' as formative assessment. In this chapter we consider the purposes of summative assessment and the kind of information that is required to meet these purposes effectively and efficiently. Then we consider ways of obtaining this information: through summarising evidence collected over a period of time, or through giving special tasks or tests, or a combination of these. We acknowledge some of the dangers that accompany the use of children's test scores for evaluating schools, suggest how these can be minimised and note some of the ways in which summative assessment information can be used formatively.

Assessment for summative purposes

Information about what children have achieved at certain times is important for teachers, parents and the children themselves. It might be collected at the end of a unit of work or the end of term or of the school year. It is essentially a summary, and so is much less detailed than the information for formative assessment, but, at the same time, it should refer to the full range of learning goals. As for formative assessment, it is important to keep the purpose in mind. This assessment is intended not to guide learning but to describe it in a way that is useful to those who need this information. It is assessment *of* learning, rather than assessment *for* learning.

Those who use this information generally wish to know what has been achieved and how this relates to expectations, levels or standards that apply to all children. Thus, whatever evidence is used to arrive at the summary must be judged against the same criteria for all the children. In other words, the assessment should be criterion-referenced and not child-referenced, or ipsative (page 125). Comments can be added about the effort put into what has been achieved, but the judgement of the achievement has to relate to the standard of the work and not whether this is 'good work for this child'.

Further, the results may be used to compare children with each other, or to combine results for different children to summarise the performance of a class. This means that the procedure for making the judgements has to be as reliable as possible. Reliability (see Box 12.4, page 127) in this context means that the same result would be obtained by different teachers assessing the work and that the work of all the children is judged in the same way by any one teacher. These points are summarised in Box 18.1.

Box 18.1	Information for summative assessment

The information for summative assessment needs to be:

■ a summary of what has been achieved at a particular time;

■ succinct, giving an overview of progress in relation to the main goals of learning;

■ criterion-referenced to standards or levels that have the same meaning for all children;

■ reliable, ideally involving some procedures for quality assurance.

There are three main ways of obtaining this information:

■ by summarising information already gathered and used for formative assessment;

■ by giving special tasks or tests to check on what has been learned at a particular time;

■ by a combination of summarising over time and checking up.

Summarising learning over time

Pieces of work or observations gathered over time and used as evidence to help learning can also be used as evidence for summative assessment providing that it is reviewed in relation to the criteria for the standards or levels. It is not appropriate to rely on judgements made for formative purposes since these will have an ipsative element; that is, will take into account the individual child's progress and effort. While this does not matter for formative assessment, where identifying the levels at which children are working is not necessary (see page 157), things are different for summative assessment. In summative assessment levels are used as ways of communicating to others what children have achieved, so their work has to be judged against the same criteria for all children. While the *evidence* used for the two purposes might be the same, the judgements in summative assessment are made differently.

In England and Wales teachers are required to summarise their 'teacher assessment' judgements at the end of each Key Stage in the form of a level for each attainment target in the curriculum in science (and in mathematics and English). The ways in which they should do this are indicated in the Assessment Arrangements, quoted in Box 18.2.

Box 18.2 | **Summarising teachers' assessments in the National Curriculum**

The level descriptions in the National Curriculum are the basis for judging children's levels of attainment at the end of the Key Stage. Teachers use their knowledge of a child's work to judge which level description best fits that child's performance across a range of contexts. In reaching a judgement, teachers should use their knowledge of a child's work over time, including written, practical and oral work in the class, homework and results of other school examinations or tests.

The aim is for a rounded judgement which:

■ is based on knowledge of how the child performs over time across a range of contexts

■ takes into account strengths and weaknesses of a child's performance

■ is checked against adjacent level descriptions to ensure that the level awarded is the closest match to the child's performance in each attainment target.

(Key Stage 2, Assessment and Reporting Arrangements, QCA 2004)

Recognising what is significant in children's work

There are various sources of help that teachers can find to assist them in picking out what is significant in the evidence. For example, the *Nuffield Primary Science Teachers' Guides* (1995) all contain a chapter on assessment, which gives examples of children's actions, words, talk, writing or drawings relating to the topic of the guide and discusses aspects that are significant in coming to a decision about whether certain level descriptions in the National Curriculum are being met. The ASE has also produced examples of children's work analysed against National Curriculum level descriptions (ASE 1996). In the USA the *Performance Standards of the New Standards* (1997) serve a similar purpose.

A range of work

In reviewing the evidence accumulated about each child, it is important to look across all the pieces of work relevant to a particular objective and not to judge from just one. So it is more useful to have exemplar material in the form of a portfolio of work from one child (as in parts of Exemplification of Standards, SCAA 1995) than single pieces of work to help teachers to apply the criteria in a holistic manner. Not every piece of work will fit the descriptions and neither will every part of the criteria for a level be represented in the portfolio. This may seem rather a loose procedure, but assessment is not an exact matter and it is better to be aware of the uncertainty than to assume that we can pigeon-hole children when this is not the case.

Summarising in terms of levels

Of course, information is inevitably lost in summarising. But the alternative is too much detail that fails to communicate an overview of achievement. In the case of process skill, reporting on each skill is probably less useful than summarising across them and reporting on 'enquiry skills'. Examples of level descriptions for investigative skills are given in Box 18.3.

| Box 18.3 | Examples of level descriptions for investigative skills in the National Curriculum |

Level 2

Pupils respond to suggestions about how to find things out and, with help, make their own suggestions about how to collect data to answer questions. They use simple texts, with help, to find information. They use simple equipment provided and make observations related to their task. They observe and compare objects, living things and events. They describe their observations using scientific vocabulary and record them using simple tables when appropriate. They say whether what happened was what they expected.

Level 3

Pupils respond to suggestions and put forward their own ideas about how to find the answer to a question. They recognise why it is important to collect data to answer questions. They use simple tests to find information. They make relevant observations and measure quantities, such as length or mass, using a range of simple equipment. Where appropriate, they carry out a fair test with some help, recognising and explaining why it is fair. They record their observations in a variety of ways. They provide explanations for observations and for simple patterns in recorded measurements. They communicate in a scientific way what they have found out and suggest improvements in their work.

(DfEE 1999)

Checking up by testing

A summary assessment can also be arrived at by checking up; that is, giving some special tasks that are devised specifically to assess the point reached in the development of ideas or skills. Even when evidence from regular activities is used, there may be times when teachers feel the need to introduce special tasks when it does not seem to have been possible to collect information in any other way. Commercial sets of test items are available for teachers to use, but usually take the form of short, 'stand alone' items with well-defined 'right answers'. Such question formats are not well suited to assessing science, especially enquiry skills. An alternative is to embed questions in a theme that is more interesting for the children and also cuts down on the amount of reading the children have to do to establish a fresh context for each item.

Minibeasts

Dan and Tammy kept a note of all the 'minibeasts' they found in the Walled Garden. They drew the minibeasts as well as they could.

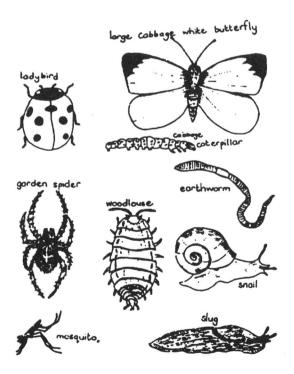

Read about the 'minibeasts' in the project folder before you try to answer the questions.

Later, back at school, they used some books to get information about the minibeasts. They made a special chart, called a table, which showed the information, and put it in the Walled Garden project folder. Here is a copy of it.

Minibeast	legs	where eggs laid	eggs hatch into	sheds skin	adult feeds on
woodlouse	yes	under stones, logs	young woodlice	yes	dead animals and plants
snail	no	soil	young snails	no	dead and living plants
ladybird	yes	plants		yes	live greenfly
slug	no	soil	young slugs	no	dead and living plants
earthworm	no	soil	young worms	no	dead things in the soil
cabbage butterfly	yes	leaves	larva caterpillar	yes	plants
spider	yes	in cocoon on leaves	young spiders	yes	flies
mosquito	yes	on water		yes	

1. Use the information in the table to answer these questions:

   a)   What do ladybirds feed on?...
   b)   In the table all the minibeasts with legs have something else that is the same about them. Can you see what it is?
        ....
        ....

2. When they made the table they could not find all the information about the ladybird and the mosquito.
   Please fill in this information for them on their table:

   a)   A ladybird's egg hatches into a <u>LARVA</u>.
   b)   Adult mosquitos feed on <u>ANIMALS and PLANTS</u>.

3. Dan and Tammy's table shows that snails eat dead and living plants, but it doesn't say whether they like to eat some plants more than others.

   Suppose you have these foods that snails will eat:
   and as many snails as you want. Think about what you would do to find out which of these foods the snails liked best.

a)   Say what you would do to start with? (Draw a picture if it will help.)

strawberries   porridge   lettuce   carrot
                   oats

b)   Say how you will make sure that each food has a fair chance of being chosen:

....
....
....

c)   What will you look for to decide which food was liked best?

....
....
....

4   What other things could you find out about snails by doing investigations with them? Write down as many things as you can think of to investigate.

....
....
....
....

5   Dan and Tammy went to visit their Aunt and looked for minibeasts in her garden. They found them all except for snails although they looked carefully for a long time.

a)   Write down any reasons you can think of to explain why their were no snails in their Aunt's garden:

....
....
....

b)   Their Aunt thought it could be because of the kind of soil
        where she lived; there was no chalk or limestone in it.

What is the main difference between snails and other minibeasts
which Dan and Tammy found?

....

....

....

c)   Why do you think snails only live where there is chalk or limestone in
        the soil?

....

....

....

Figure 18.1 Examples of test items embedded in a theme (Schilling *et al.* 1990: 115–18)

Using tasks embedded in regular work

An example of this approach is given in Schilling *et al.* (1990). Written questions assessing process skills were devised on the theme of the 'Walled Garden', which teachers could introduce as a topic or as a story. Questions were grouped into seven sections about different things found in the garden: water, walls, 'minibeasts', leaves, sundial, bark and wood. For each section there was a large poster giving additional information and activities and a booklet for children to write their answers. Children worked on the tasks over an extended period, with no time limit; they enjoyed the work, which they saw as novel and interesting, in no way feeling that they were being tested. The examples in Figure 18.1 are of the questions on 'minibeasts'. They can be used as guides to setting process-based tasks in other contexts to suit the class activities.

Special tasks for checking up on process skills can be written or practical. Practical tasks designed to require all the process skills to be used, to the extent that children are able, were employed in the APU surveys (DES/WO 1983) and for research purposes (e.g. Russell and Harlen 1990). As they require the full attention of an administrator/observer they are not practicable in the classroom as regular tests. Their value to teachers is in the ideas and hints they give about the kinds of tasks, and the ways of presenting them and of questioning children, that can be adapted and applied in planning children's practical work.

National tests

National tests are used to check up at the end of each Key Stage in England and Wales. They are intended to provide 'a snapshot of a child's attainment at the end of the Key Stage' (QCA 2004). In Scotland, where the school programme is not divided into key stages, children are tested when the teachers' ongoing assessment shows that they are ready to succeed in the tests at a certain level. In both cases, standardised written tests are given (in mathematics and English only in Scotland, to date) and administration is controlled so that results are 'fair' for all children.

The effects of 'high stakes' testing

When information about children's achievement is made public and used to draw up league tables of schools or in other ways to imply quality of teaching or teachers (i.e. it has 'high stakes'), there is a well known tendency for the children's activities to be focused on what is tested, for time to be spent on practice tests and for 'teaching to the test'. What is less well known is the impact on children's motivation for learning. A review of research focused on this issue, by Harlen and Deakin Crick (2003), shows 'strong evidence of a negative impact on pupils' motivation' (ARG 2002: 2). The main findings of the review are summarised in Box 18.4.

Box 18.4   The impact of high stakes testing on motivation for learning

Findings from a review of research (Harlen and Deakin Crick 2003).

- The introduction of Key Stage 1 tests was associated with a reduction in self-esteem of those pupils who did not achieve well.

- When tests pervade the ethos of the classroom, test performance is more highly valued than what is being learned.

- When tests become the main criteria by which pupils are judged and by which they judge themselves, those whose strengths lie outside the subjects tested have a low opinion of their capabilities.

- The results of tests that are 'high stakes' *for individual pupils*, such as the 11+ in Northern Ireland, have been found to have a particularly strong impact on those who receive low grades.

- Pupils are aware of repeated practice tests and the narrowing of the curriculum.

- Low achievers become overwhelmed by assessments and demotivated by constant evidence of their low achievement. The effect is to increase the gap between low and high achieving pupils.

■ The use of repeated practice tests impresses on pupils the importance of the tests. It encourages them to adopt test-taking strategies designed to avoid effort and responsibility. Repeated practice tests are, therefore, detrimental to higher order thinking.

Box 18.5	Suggestions for actions to avoid the negative effects of testing

Teachers should:

do more of this	and do less of this
Provide choice and help pupils to take responsibility for their learning. Discuss with pupils the purpose of their learning and provide feedback that will help the learning process. Encourage pupils to judge their work by how much they have learned and by the progress they have made. Help pupils to understand the criteria by which their learning is assessed and to assess their own work. Develop pupils' understanding of the goals of their work in terms of what they are learning; providing feedback to pupils in relation to these goals. Help pupils to understand where they are in relation to learning goals and how to make further progress. Give feedback that enables pupils to know the next steps and how to succeed in taking them. Encourage pupils to value effort and a wide range of attainments. Encourage collaboration among pupils and a positive view of each other's attainments.	Define the curriculum in terms of what is in the tests to the detriment of what is not tested. Give frequent drill and practice for test taking. Teach how to answer specific test questions. Pupils judging their work in terms of scores or grades. Allow test anxiety to impair some pupils' performance (particularly girls and lower performing pupils). Use tests and assessment to tell pupils where they are in relation to others. Give feedback relating to pupils' capabilities, implying a fixed view of each pupil's potential. Compare pupils' grades and allow pupils to compare grades, giving status on the basis of test achievement only. Emphasise competition among pupils.

Assessment Reform Group (2002: 8)

Reducing the negative effects of testing

These effects have to be avoided as far as possible, since they clearly impair enjoyment of and willingness to continue learning, as required for lifelong learning. Some general advice for avoiding the negative impact is given by the Assessment Reform Group (2002), and this is reproduced in Box 18.5.

Using summative assessment for formative purposes

The requirements for summative assessment by testing can be turned into positive value for learning if the process is used formatively. For instance, the preparation for tests, revising earlier work, can be an opportunity for children to assess their own understanding, using the 'traffic lights' approach mentioned in Chapter 17 (page 180). The children's self-assessment means that they can seek help where it is most needed. Some of this help can come from other children, if they work in groups to explain to each other what is happening in certain activities or situations. Selected concept cartoons (Naylor and Keogh 2003) can be used for this. Teachers can use test results formatively if afterwards they analyse returned scripts to pinpoint errors in children's thinking that will inform aspects of their future thinking. Other ideas for the formative use of summative assessment can be found in Black *et al.* (2003).

Summary

This chapter has discussed some practices and issues in using assessment for summative purposes. The main points have been:

- Summative assessment is essentially a summary for giving information about a child's attainment at a certain time. Compared with formative assessment it has to be more succinct, strictly criterion-referenced and as reliable as possible.

- Summative assessment can be obtained by summing up evidence gathered over time and across a number of contexts, or by giving special tasks or tests that give a snapshot of what has been attained at a particular time.

- In either case, criteria have to be applied uniformly so that comparable information is provided about each child.

- The overuse of tests, particularly when they have 'high stakes' attached, has adverse effects on children's motivation for learning.

- Teachers can take steps to minimise the negative impact of testing on children's learning and use some summative assessment information formatively.

Part 4　Practical work and using ICT

19 The role and organisation of practical activities

Introduction

Practical activities are at the heart of primary science because they provide first-hand experience, the channel through which a great deal of learning takes place in children. Interaction with materials is important to learning, but it has far greater value if it is accompanied by social interaction that helps in making sense of it and making links between ideas from one situation and another. This chapter begins by elaborating this point, placing practical activities in the context of learning activities in general. As classrooms now include more and more adult support it is essential that a teacher fully understands this so that he or she can communicate clearly to other educators in the class. We move on to mention briefly recent insights from research in primary and secondary sciences, including some warnings that primary science educators need to heed. We then look at different kinds of practical work, beyond 'fair testing', and finally consider the issues arising in the organisation of practical activities relating to group size and composition.

The role of first-hand experience in children's learning

Seeing for oneself is the most direct way of knowing that something exists or happens. This still applies to adults even though our experience makes it more likely that we can learn about new things in other ways, such as by reading or hearing others tell about them. We can use our experience of similar things or events, and our imagination, to envisage something we have not seen. For children, who have much less experience, things are different. Words can conjure up false images and misunderstandings are common unless children see for themselves. We only have to recall the children who link milk with cartons and supermarkets rather than cows, and those who have no idea of the size of objects that they have only seen in photographs.

Seeing or, more widely, observing is only one kind of direct experience. More significant for learning science is physical 'interaction', when you see the results of carrying out some action on an object. Interaction opens up the possibility of explaining things in terms of cause and effect; and science is about explaining, not just describing, things. But physical interaction alone is not enough to develop ideas that help children to understand the things around them. Social interaction has an important part to play. The give and take in sharing ideas has a double benefit. It is a very common experience for adults as well as children to clarify their own understanding by explaining to others what they think. In addition, listening to others, particularly peers, brings the further benefits of access to alternative views and of using these to create a shared understanding. Murphy *et al.* (2000) looked at effective classroom practitioners and concluded that the most effective in developing children's understanding were those who promoted interaction, where classroom talk was a central feature of classroom enquiry.

Box 19.1   **Ideas about sound and the string telephone**

Sue was working with a class of six-, and seven-year-olds looking at string telephones. The children had been given a variety of 'phones', some with long and some short strings, some made from tin cans, some with paper cups and some with plastic cups. The class enjoyed discovering that they could speak to one another through the phones. After a while Sue asked them to start thinking about what was happening. They then gathered together, with the telephones, to discuss their ideas. An enthusiastic discussion ensued.

Robert: It was pressing through the string gaps.
Teacher: Little gaps in the string?
Hayley: When we said something the sound bounces along the string (indicates with hand).
Louis: I thought I saw a bit of electric going along the string.
Teacher: Louis thought he saw the string moving.
Robert: I thought it was following along the string.

. . .

John: There is a crack in the bottom of the cup and the voice gets out.
Teacher: How could you test it?
John: Try a thin gap and a bigger gap and see if it gets through.
Alex: It went along the string and bounced.
Claire: It goes along the gap.
John: We could try a metal cup. If you speak into a metal cup it will be better because if you tap it it (shows vibration with hand).

Sue recognised that John was beginning to consider the idea of vibration and that the children were ready to begin to test out their ideas. The discussion moved on as the children were asked about ways to test out their ideas. Different tests were considered and pairs of children decided what they would like to try.

(Qualter 1996: 73)

In the lesson described in Box 19.1, as in all classrooms, the value for learning of direct experience and physical interaction with materials is vastly increased by discussion among children as well as between teacher and children (see also Chapter 4). This has important consequences for the organisation of practical work. It is not enough for children to use and investigate materials; time must be spent on discussing what sense they are making of what they have found. This may mean less time for doing, but increased learning from what is done. It becomes even more important to select and plan activities carefully, with a clear idea of the learning intentions. In recent years the role and value of practical activities have come under scrutiny, so we can learn a good deal from research in both secondary and primary science.

Recent insights from research

There is a tendency to assume that practical work is valuable in itself. Yet research into the impact of conventional laboratory work in secondary science does not support some of the ambitious claims made for its value in learning. Osborne (2004) argues that whole investigations are only used in secondary schools for the purposes of assessment and that their value for learning is seriously undermined. He states that using 'such a limited set of practicals [to] develop or exemplify the wide range of skills and scientific practices that constitute science is a bit like reducing the teaching of performance in music to three standard scales on a recorder'. The response from a number of secondary school teachers in a discussion forum indicates that many see practical work not as exploratory but as illustrative, and that it is therefore appropriate for students to undertake the 'recipe-like' practical work Osborne so criticised.

Among the claims for practical work are the development of students' skills and conceptual understanding and increased motivation for learning science. Most secondary students report that they like practical work; it is often because they like the freedom to work in groups at their own pace rather than appreciating that it helps their understanding. This is because their focus is often on the detail of completing the investigation and getting it written up in the required format.

There is little time given to talking about the work and often, and possibly as a consequence of this, students don't understand the purpose of the practical work. What they understand the exercise to be about is getting the results expected by the teacher; otherwise the experiment would be a failure and they would feel they had learned nothing.

Is practical work worth doing?

It seems almost heretical to question the value of practical work in primary science. Yet the pressures on teachers to cover large swathes of content and some of the arguments in relation to secondary science about how much learning actually takes place mean that the question must be answered. Martin Wenham argues the case for practical enquiry:

First-hand investigations as part of the educative process give pupils the opportunity to use both creativity and critical thought, often together with practical and observational skills to solve a problem or find an answer to a question.

(Wenham 1993: 231)

The arguments put forward for practical work can be summed up as:

1 It allows learning by seeing and doing.

2 It encourages discussion and debate.

3 It is motivational.

One of the barriers to learning identified in secondary science is the use of complex equipment, which can lead pupils to focus on technical difficulties and not on what they are learning from the activity. Although in primary science we tend not to use overly complex equipment, with the exception perhaps of some ICT equipment, it is inappropriate to assume that pupils will learn what the teacher intends simply by undertaking the activity. Miller and Luben (1996) found that pupils between the ages of seven and 13 did not tend to change their conceptions as a result of practical investigations. This may well be because teachers were not engaging in the kind of exploration of ideas characterised in Sue's lesson (Box 19.1). Miller and Luben argued that practical work should only be used to develop procedural understanding. Even here, though, it is crucial that pupils understand the teacher's intention that they develop their process skills. Goldsworthy *et al.* (2000), as part of the AKSIS project, found that often children's understanding of the purpose of an investigation was not that intended by the teacher. They give the example in Box 19.2, where the teacher's focus was on the pupils developing particular process skills.

Box 19.2	What is the investigation about?

Interviewer:	Whilst Daryl is running around, tell me, what do you think you are learning in this investigation?
Robert:	How fast you can run.
Jody:	The length of your legs.
Interviewer:	What about the length of legs?

444444

444444444

444

Jody:	Well, if there are bigger legs you can run faster and with shorter legs you can run a bit faster.
Interviewer:	And anything else you think you are learning?
Jody:	How much muscle it needs to go, how fast it can take.
Robert:	About forces.
Interviewer:	What about anything about doing investigations? (Interrupted by Daryl returning from running) Do you think you are learning anything about how to do an investigation?
Jody:	Yes.
Interviewer:	What sort of things are you learning?
Jody:	Hot and cold and stuff.
Robert:	Body.

(Goldsworthy *et al.* 2000: 1)

It is clear that learning by seeing and doing is much more successful if the pupil knows the purpose of the activity and can therefore focus on what is important (see Chapter 14). Again, the AKSIS project (Goldsworthy 1998) found that teachers tended not to teach the skills of investigating explicitly, yet this is the key to pupils knowing what to attend to. It seems that teachers having a clear view of what it is they want pupils to learn from practical work and communicating this clearly is the way to ensure that children really do learn by seeing and doing.

Learning by doing, when properly supported, is powerful; such learning can be taken further by discussion and debate. This is not simply a matter of putting children in groups, but also one of finding ways to encourage them to exchange ideas. Elizabeth Jurd (2004) promotes an open-ended problem-solving approach to practical work in her class, and explicitly encourages children to organise their own thought process consciously by:

- relating thinking to previous experiences;
- making predictions based on existing knowledge;
- making observations and giving reasons for what is observed;
- asking questions, especially in a form that can lead to further investigation.

When Elizabeth probed the children's thinking during investigations she found that many were not thinking in this way or using language to make sense of their experiences. The majority of children need intervention by an adult to model the kinds of questions they need to ask themselves and each other. Here the use of prompt cards can remind children of the kinds of questions they should be asking. The increasing numbers of other adults in the classroom can be made use of here, but only if the teacher is able to explain the value of this kind of discussion. Siraj-Blatchford *et al.* (2002), for example, found that the most effective settings in early years encouraged sustained shared interaction between children and adults, but that the adults need to understand how to initiate such interactions or to take up ideas initiated by the children.

Feasey (1998) argues that it is crucial that science investigations are set in a social context, thus providing a purpose and a specific audience, where children have responsibility to that audience and so must communicate appropriately. This contextualisation provides a platform for authentic discussion and debate. It is perhaps the lack of real contexts that results in less time being given to the consideration of evidence than to planning and doing. Consider the example of Daryl and his friends given above (Box 19.2): perhaps a much more lively discussion with more focus on how to investigate it would have been achieved if the children were responding to a suggestion by the head teacher that on school sports day pupils should be in teams of similar heights rather than as usual in year or class groups. In this way pupils get to exchange and challenge each other's ideas, to construct appropriate ways to investigate their ideas and to develop theories based on that evidence. This learning about how science works should be implicit in the way science is taught, but made explicit through reflecting on how experiments help to build theory, and how theories then lead to other experiments (Hodson 1993).

In recent years a worrying trend has been observed in terms of attitudes towards science. It seems that children are being 'turned off' science as young as eight or nine (Galton 2002; Jarvis and Pell 2002). One explanation for this is that there has been an emphasis on subject knowledge coverage in order to pass tests. Murphy and Beggs (2001) found that Northern Irish primary school pupils' attitudes to science were more positive than their English counterparts'. They suggest that this may be due to the heavier emphasis on science assessment in England. It would seem that this emphasis is leading teachers to more direct teaching and less practical work. This is confirmed in a study by Braund and Driver (2002), who found, in telephone interviews, that some teachers did no practical work in the final year of primary school because they were preparing for tests: 'At primary school we didn't do experiments just sheets and we had no equipment' (Secondary school pupil, Braund and Driver 2002). That undertaking practical work is motivational is clear, but it is not simply recipe following practical work that is important. Braund and Driver also found that pupils want to be challenged by new ideas and finding things out for themselves. This is particularly the case for more able pupils, who thrive on being encouraged in the higher order thinking skills that come with discussion and debate (Coates and Eyre 1999).

The messages from recent research point to the need for careful consideration of what learning is intended and a decision as to whether practical experiences are the best way to achieve them, and then consideration of how to ensure that the activities are motivating and how learning can be maximised through the encouragement of interaction. So what lessons for primary science can we learn from this recent research? Some obvious ones are:

■ Decide whether first-hand experience is the best way of achieving the learning intended. There are many other kinds of activity that can help children's understanding besides direct interaction with materials; for example, games, simulations, drama and acting out, visits and demonstrations.

■ If first-hand experience is appropriate, decide what kind. While all practical work should involve investigation, not all investigations are of the same type.

■ Share with the children the purpose of the work and ensure that it is answering a real question for the children.

■ Involve the children in decisions about what to do and planning how to do it. There is then no risk that they don't know why they are doing things, since they decided this for themselves.

■ Use simple and familiar equipment. In Chapter 21 some of the issues relating to the use of ICT are used to underline this point.

■ Encourage discussion and debate among the groups, exchanging and sharing their ideas from initial ideas to those developed as the investigation progresses (ensure that all adults in the class know how to model and promote such discussions).

■ Organise small group and whole-class discussion of what has been learned both from the findings and from the procedures used.

Types of investigation

To investigate is to observe, study closely or examine. All the practical work involving first-hand study of materials would therefore be called investigation (or enquiry, since this is defined in terms of investigation). There are different kinds of investigation, however, which emphasise different process skills and are appropriate for investigating different kinds of questions. Although different people have suggested slightly different classifications the main types are broadly: information-seeking; comparing or fair testing; pattern-finding; hypothesis-generating; how-to-do-it investigations.

Information-seeking investigations

These are investigations carried out to see what happens, either as a natural process unfolds or when some action is taken. Examples are seeing eggs hatch, raising butterflies or silk worms, observing the expansion of water on freezing, seeing what things dissolve in water. Usually these concern the behaviour of particular living things or substances and there is no comparison between things.

Box 19.3	A bird box in the classroom

Despite their rural location, the five- to seven-year-old children in Sally Buckle's class were unfamiliar with the diversity of life around them. Raising their awareness, sensitivity and care for living things was a key aim. With the help of a grant a solution was found by setting up a bird box in the school grounds with a micro camera placed in it linked to a monitor in the classroom showing the blue tits who set up home in the box in real time. The monitor was constantly switched on and became like another window in the classroom. Children were able to record the nest building, egg laying and hatching, and feeding of the fledglings. Although the death of the adult male meant that most of the fledglings did not survive, the whole community were by that time enthralled by the experience.

(Based on Barker and Buckle 2002: 8–10)

The fact that the whole school and wider community were fascinated by the nesting birds demonstrates clearly that information-seeking is relevant at all ages, building up a stock of personal experiences that are needed to make sense of later experiences. In this case information-seeking was an end in itself, but in other situations it might be a forerunner for hypothesis-generating investigations; for example, about what it is that makes things float.

Comparing or fair-testing investigations

Finding out which is the best floor covering for the kitchen or which wind-up car goes furthest is probably the type of investigation most familiar to many primary teachers. Such investigations involve the manipulation of variables (the amount of sugar, the number of stirs, the amount of water), yet care must be taken not to present these questions in isolation. The first step is for children to engage with the question; for example, we need a new carpet for the class to sit on, which of the ones available is best? Once the question is a real one the next step is to consider what we mean by 'best'. In this situation there could be more than one 'best'; children might suggest the least irritating on their legs, the most easily cleaned of the mud brought in on shoes and many more. By starting with a real and important question pupils gain ownership of the problem and a formulaic approach, perhaps with a workcard offering a 'recipe' for finding the answer, will be avoided.

Pattern-finding investigations

These apply where there is a relationship to be found between variables associated with the behaviour of a thing or substance. Examples are: the note produced by blowing across the top of a bottle and the amount of water in it; the direction of a shadow cast by the sun and the time of day; the number of turns given to a wind-up toy and how far it will go. These investigations involve the same skills as 'comparing' investigations, since the effect of changes in one variable have to be tested fairly, with other variables or conditions kept the same. However, there is additional emphasis in these investigations on the interpretation of findings, and they provide valuable opportunities for developing the skills of presenting data in the form of graphs, tables or charts, and for considering the extent to which conclusions about cause and effect can be drawn. Generally there is not a direct relationship, and there is another step in the chain of events. So while the clockwork toy car may go further, the more turns of the key, the effect of turning the key is to give the car different amounts of energy, which enable the car to move different distances. Similarly, the fact that trees of the same kind with more growth rings tend to be taller does not mean that one causes the other; there is another factor that links the two. So these investigations provide experiences that help children to distinguish between an association between things and a cause and effect relationship.

Hypothesis-generating investigations

These investigations can often begin with 'I wonder why?' questions, where the first step is to consider possible reasons why and then to test them out. 'I wonder why footsteps echo on the path in some conditions' or 'I wonder why the mirror in the bathroom steams up when I have a shower' can lead to some open-ended exploration. What surfaces get wet: towels, bathroom tiles, the wooden laundry basket? Further discussion can lead to suggestions, such as 'The mirror and the bathroom tiles are cold so the "steam" turns back to water.' This hypothesis can then be tested out. For example, if the hypothesis is that the echo is caused by the kind of surface of the path, do you find an echo in all places where there is this kind of surface? The hypotheses surviving this first testing are then the subject of further investigation, which might well involve some fair testing. Sometimes the end product is making something happen, such as a making an object that sinks in water float, or vice versa. This involves trying different things based on possible explanations of why things sink or float.

How-to-do-it investigations

These are investigations where the end product may be an artefact or a construction that meets particular requirements: a model bridge that will support a certain load, for example. These are problems of a technological nature, though they involve many scientific process skills and ideas. It is not necessary to make a clean distinction in children's activities between science and technology, but it is important for the teacher to be aware of the difference and of the particular learning that can be developed through these activities.

Organising practical work

When you are making decisions about organising practical work it is important to keep in mind the features that enhance the value of first-hand experience: the physical interaction with materials, discussion and social interaction.

Group size and composition

Group size has to be a compromise between what is desirable and what is possible in terms of the size of the whole class. Groups of four are ideal for the youngest children but 8- to 12-year-olds can be in groups as large as six if this is necessary, although a smaller number is desirable. Where work with equipment such as the computer is involved, smaller group sizes may be necessary. The potential for genuine collaborative work, where the work is a combined effort and not a collection of individual efforts carried out by children working in proximity, diminishes the more the group size increases above the optimum, but it can also be influenced by the way a task is set up and the encouragement of the teacher, who can support ways in which pupils can most effectively challenge one another's ideas.

In relation to the composition of groups, there are quite different approaches practised and advocated both by teachers themselves and by others. Some are in favour of groups of mixed ability and others in favour of groups based on similar attainment. In an important study of group composition and learning, researchers compared the change in ideas of groups of children, some of whom were in groups of similar initial ideas and some in groups composed of children with different ideas about the topic of the task to be undertaken (Howe *et al.* 1990, 1992). The research provided strong and consistent evidence that children in groups whose ideas were initially different progressed markedly more than those in the groups with initially similar ideas to each other. The findings enabled the researchers to conclude with confidence that there was more advance in the ideas of children who worked with others holding different ideas from their own than in those of children in the groups where the ideas were the same.

What is particularly noteworthy in the Howe research is that the differential progress was more apparent at a later date than during the group work. When children were assessed immediately after group work as well as six weeks later, there was no evidence of immediate change in ideas, but this did appear, to a significantly greater extent in the groups with differing ideas, later. 'Thus, there is a strong suggestion that progress took place after the group tasks, indicating that interaction when concepts differ is a catalyst for development and not the locus of it' (Howe 1990: 27). The researchers followed up the obvious alternative explanations for the differences (for example, that further work at school, or experience at home, was responsible) but found nothing that could account for them.

If we judge only from the way the group work goes then there is very little to choose between one basis for grouping and the other. However, the exposure to different ideas from their own appears to lay a foundation for greater learning in all children over a longer period of time.

Allocating group activities

The questions here are:

■ Should all groups be working on science at the same time?

■ Should groups be working on the same activities as each other?

The questions are interconnected and so best considered together. Again practicalities will modify any theoretical ideal. Where specialised equipment is needed and available only in limited quantities, or requires close teacher supervision, then there is no alternative to having one group at a time using it. What other children will be doing and whether groups will take turns at the same activities remain more open to teachers' decisions.

When these restrictions do not apply, which is most of the time, opinions vary about these questions. One school of thought advocates that the amount of science going on at one time is best limited to one or two groups, with others engaged in non-science activities. However, some arguments against this arise from experience: the science work can be a distraction to others; the teacher's attention is too widely divided; and there is no opportunity for whole-class discussion of experiences shared by everyone.

A more effective alternative is to have groups working on science all at the same time, with the activities of each being different but all linked to a single theme (as in the case of Graham's class, Box 1.1, and Sue's class, Box 19.1). The reasons for this being preferred are easy to see, since it solves the problem of distraction and enables class discussions to take place on a shared theme, with enough differences between groups to create interest in each other's findings.

Written instructions

A key message running through this book is that pupils' ideas are crucial and that teachers and children exploring ideas within interesting, relevant contexts is likely to be the most fruitful approach to engendering motivation, creativity, conceptual change and learning. This can present a teacher with a problem. How can we encourage and enable freethinking while at the same time providing support through instructions, workcards, worksheets and other means of giving help? The role of these aids is best decided in relation to the purpose of the activity. If, for example, a teacher simply wants the children to learn a technique, instructions from published schemes can be projected on to a screen, but if the exploration of materials is desired then the 'instructions' should contain 'action questions' and 'problem-posing questions', but should not give instructions as to what to do. When you are producing or adapting worksheets etc., the questions should be a written form of the teachers' questions suggested in Chapter 3 for finding out children's ideas and for promoting thinking and action.

In the case of Sue's lesson on string telephones (Box 19.1) she did not know what ideas the children would come up with and so could not prepare worksheets in advance. What she did was to use a basic 'experiment sheet' with the headings 'I want to find out', 'To make it fair I will', 'What I did' and 'I found out'. Then in discussion with the groups she helped them to add extra instructions; for example, John's group needed tin cans, paper cups and strings of the same length. Using a computer and a digital projector would enable the whole class to give advice here. What this approach does is to provide attention focusing and an indication of the materials they need to collect, while at the same time ensuring that they retain ownership of the problem they are addressing. It must be disheartening to spend ten minutes discussing exciting possibilities and then to find that the investigation to be carried out is the one that was in the teacher's head all the time.

Instructions on cards can also give children ideas about how to organise themselves to share ideas. Varying devices can be suggested, such as: 'Get one person to write down all the ideas in the group and then decide which you all agree with and which you don't', or 'Each write down your ideas on a slip of paper and stick them on one piece. Make sure you understand all the ideas even if you don't agree with them.'

However, when the purpose of the practical work is to give children an experience of carrying through a complete investigation of their own, a workcard is unlikely to be appropriate. Such investigations have to be drawn from the children's own questions and ideas, and guidance is best given in discussion with the teacher, when new ideas for procedures or explanations can be 'scaffolded' by the teacher as necessary. The action to be taken coming from the discussion could then be written down as an *aide-mémoire* or as a checklist to remind children of what was agreed. This is a useful device to ensure that matters relating to safety and care of equipment will not be forgotten. Such 'tailor-made' workcards are specific to particular groups of children and should be prepared by the teacher and children together, not written by the teacher beforehand.

Summary

- Children of primary school age learn best from first-hand experience and so practical work has a central role in their science education. The value of the practical experience is, however, increased by discussing and sharing ideas about how to make sense of what is seen or done.

■ Recent research provides a warning that practical work may not improve learning unless its purpose is clear to children, and teacher and children are involved in the planning, so that they know why certain steps have to be taken and what to look for in finding results.

■ The key to developing understanding of processes and concepts is to ensure that pupils are challenged by questioning and testing their own ideas and those of others. In this way children are also more likely to enjoy their science as well as to learn from it.

■ Although fair tests are the most popular types of investigation they are not always appropriate for answering a question. Other types are inform-ation-seeking, pattern-finding, hypothesis-generating and how-to-do-it investigations.

■ Practical work is best organised, if possible, with children working in mixed ability groups of four or five, engaged on aspects of a common problem. They achieve more than any one group alone by sharing their findings and adding to a wider understanding of the problem.

■ Written instructions, where used, should pose questions that provoke enquiry and should avoid giving a set of instructions to follow. They are best seen as *aides-mémoires* of planning in which children have been involved.

20 Equipment, safety and visits

Introduction

Objects and materials from the environment and equipment and resources for investigating them are the basic essentials for scientific activity in the primary school. The importance of first-hand experience of these things is a theme running throughout this book. How we decide on the materials and resources and how we choose to employ them depends largely on the view we have of learners and learning and the role this implies for teachers. In this chapter we are concerned with three aspects of resourcing primary science: the selection and storage of materials in the school; access to things outside that cannot be brought in and need to be studied *in situ*; and matters relating to safety both within and outside school.

Equipment and materials

The Ofsted handbook for schools inspection (1993) indicates that resources in school can be evaluated in terms of their availability, accessibility, quality and efficiency of use. These factors are in some sense interdependent, but first we consider what sorts of things have to be provided and stored.

Selecting resources

Clearly the resources used in primary science are dictated by the planned activities, which are in turn guided by the intended learning outcomes. Hence planning and resourcing are closely linked. Good published schemes tend to provide lists of resources needed (e.g. DfEE 1998). These can provide a helpful starting point even if teachers do not stick rigidly to the scheme. If we have in mind the kinds of practical activities discussed elsewhere in this book, such as floating and sinking, growing plants, dissolving materials or using string telephones, it is clear that the resources we need are everyday. Some of these resources can be used over and over again: others, such as flour or pieces of wire, will be used up. A shortage of these things causes the greatest frustration because this is what many of the children's activities are all about, so some money needs to be set aside for their purchase throughout the year.

In addition to the 'everyday' items there are some more specialist items that can enhance learning without being so difficult to use that they act as a barrier to learning. Work on electricity is an obvious example, and measuring instruments such as stop clocks or lightmeters can provide clear and accurate recordings that would not otherwise be possible. In addition there is now a dazzling array of software, posters, models and of course books available to support learning. Box 20.1 provides brief lists of the resources you might need.

Box 20.1	Resources for science		
Everyday objects and materials	*Consumables*	*Specialist equipment*	*Support resources*
Boxes, plastic bottles, other containers, string, scissors, rulers, paper clips, sticky tape, drawing pins, elastic bands, glues, card, Plasticine, plant pots, spoons, straws, marbles, toy cars, rocks, pieces of fabric etc.	Flour, bicarbonate of soda, soap powder, plaster of Paris, mirror card, wood for hammering, batteries, wire for shaping, aluminium foil, fruits or flowers for cutting, seeds for planting etc.	Pooters for collecting insects, torches, mirrors, glass blocks, triangular prisms, hand lenses, measuring cylinders, spirit thermometers, tuning forks, stop clocks and watches, springs, bathroom scales, pulleys, filter paper, gardening and other tools, magnets, bulbs, wire etc.	Software to show events (e.g. volcano or plant growth), software that models phenomena (e.g. the solar system, or trajectories), models (such as aprons of the digestive system, or a 3D eye), hardware such as data loggers, posters, books and other paper resources

The lists in Box 20.1 are not extensive; the first column in particular could be much longer, including items brought in from the seashore or from visits to grandparents, or objects brought in by the teacher. The list could be endless, but the storage space is not. Hence the imperative is to consider what needs to be in the collection of resources. In addition to lists in schemes of work other help is available from organisations such as CLEAPSS (Consortium of Local Authority Provision of Science Services: www.cleapss.org.uk). The Association for Science Education (www.ase.org.uk) provides a good deal of support; ASE conferences are the ideal venue for finding and trying out resources and finding out how others have used them.

In all this the key is to link resource needs to planning and so to intended learning outcomes. Here the science coordinator or subject leader has a key role. It may, for example, not be value for money to buy something like a model of a human eye if it is only to be used by the oldest pupils once in a year. It may be better to arrange to borrow one from the local secondary school. The issue of ICT resources is discussed in more detail in the next chapter.

One area of concern that has emerged in recent years is the issue of science books for children. Newton *et al.* (2002) showed that many science textbooks do not show a concern for explanatory understanding. That some present a rag-bag of unconnected facts, and, according to Peacock and Weedon (2002) many require children to be able to interpret the whole page, including making links between the visual elements and the text. This skill needs to be taught, yet in the National Literacy Stategy, for example, very little time is given to visual literacy. These issues need to be considered carefully when you are selecting books that are intended to help children to learn science and to be used in teaching literacy; meeting the requirements of both is a challenge. Many teachers find the book reviews in *Primary Science Review* helpful, as well as some of the articles (e.g. Wardle 2000).

Storing equipment and materials

Access is the key word in deciding a system of storage for equipment and materials. There are various possibilities and the advantages and disadvantages of each in a particular case will depend on the size, physical layout and curriculum planning of the school. We can do no more here than point out options.

A central store?

A decision has to be made about central storage versus distribution of the equipment among classes. Apart from the physical availability of a central store a major consideration is having someone to look after it. There are obvious advantages in sharing expensive items that are only infrequently used but some of these advantages are lost if the equipment is not kept in good order. Clearly the science subject leader, or coordinator, has to be willing and able, in the sense of having the time, to organise a central store and to check that items are not 'lost' by being put back in the wrong place or in an unsatisfactory condition.

Giving children access

Another decision is whether children should have access to the equipment. The problems of maintaining an orderly central store can be exacerbated by too many having access, yet the teacher will want children to help in the collection and return of equipment. Appointing a few children to be 'monitors' or 'storekeepers' may be a solution. If the store is within each class the same considerations apply.

If children are to have access then the labels used to classify the equipment should be ones that they will relate to and understand. There are considerable dividends for the initial investment of time when children are, perhaps, involved in drawing up lists of what equipment there is and creating rules for using the store.

Whether or not there is a central store, within a class the equipment for a certain session needs to be accessible to the children. The demands of providing group activities for all the children at once are of course considerable and require planning and preparation. The materials and equipment needed for a set of activities can be anticipated and a suitable selection made available without limiting what the children will be able to do using their own ideas. It is handy to have these materials on a trolley if possible so that they can easily be put safely out of the way when not being studied. When the equipment is being used the teacher should be able to depend on the help of the children to take responsibility for choosing, collecting and later returning it to its proper place. Building up a system for this is important in developing children's ability to take a part in facilitating their own learning, as well as for the teacher's sanity. It involves making sure that children know what is available, where, and how to look after it and keep it tidy.

Topic boxes

A third major decision point, which applies where a school or class organises science within topics, is whether equipment should be boxed by topic or stored as separate kinds of items. The topic box is a great convenience, but can tie up equipment that could be used for work outside the topic. This can lead to 'plundering' from the box, with the chance of the item not being there when that topic is being used. The effort put into developing topic boxes is also a disincentive to changing topics, when perhaps they have outlived their freshness. The device of temporary topic boxes is a useful compromise. The box exists for as long as the topic is being used and is dismantled when moving on to another topic.

Visits and field trips

Most teachers will attest to the value of taking children out of school and into interesting places providing links between classroom activities and everyday life, to learn new things that cannot be covered in class and to see science in action. It is now proving to be very expensive to take children out on school trips, because hiring transport is so costly. This does not mean that school trips should be abandoned; it means that any such trip must be made the most of. A visit should, of course, be great fun, and it must also make the most of the learning opportunities available. This means careful preparation, a clear purpose for the visit that the children understand and, most importantly, appropriate follow-up work. Many museums, galleries, city farms and hands-on centres provide materials to support follow-up work (see Chapter 21). However, many of those running these places report on a too low uptake of such opportunities. Places to visit can be divided into:

- natural locations (parks, seashores, woods etc.), where there may not be a formal structure for visitors;

- places of work (factories, farms, supermarkets, airports etc.), where there will be someone on the premises to accompany the children;

- science museums or centres, zoos or wildlife centres, where groups can be supervised by teachers with or without help from museum staff, but where there is usually material available to support the visit;

- other locations (castles, historic buildings etc.), which do not at first appear to link to science but where there is a science potential.

Preparing for a visit

When you are selecting a possible location it is important to check that your children can be catered for. Early years groups may find that a visit to a building site is not possible because the hard hats are too large. It is always worth talking to colleagues about visits they have undertaken, but most importantly teachers should make a visit well in advance of taking the children. Some places, such as museums, science centres, zoos and some conservation areas, offer courses for teachers who are thinking of taking their classes. These can be extremely useful, as they provide expert knowledge of the site and often have prepared materials, which can be used or modified to suit particular groups.

The key to a fruitful visit is preparation, whether you are visiting a wood, a section of the coastline, a science museum or the local cake shop. There will be a wealth of possible things to notice, to do and to follow up. The teacher needs to consider:

- What do I want the children to notice?

- What do I want them to investigate (on the spot or back in the classroom)?

- What ideas do I want them to develop?

Based on the answers to these questions, more detailed planning needs to include:

- Questions to ask the children to stimulate their observation, their investigation, their questioning.

- Preparation in terms of skills they will need (such as the use of a hand lens or pegging out a minifield).

- Equipment they need to take with them.

- Materials, such as worksheets, that the children might use. A digital camera used on a preparatory visit helps to produce useful, tailor-made resources.

Such worksheets, if used, should not be so time consuming that the children are not invited to raise their own questions and make their own observations.

■ Strategies for informing classroom assistants and parent helpers about what to look for and what questions to ask.

The school will have procedures and regulations relating to out-of-school visits. In addition to following these rules, there must be time before the visit for the teacher to work with the children to:

■ set the scene;

■ collect all the necessary equipment and ensure the children know how to use it;

■ explain, and insist upon compliance with, safety measures, parts of the Countryside Code and considerate behaviour;

■ introduce sources of information for use in the follow-up work after the visit;

■ undertake some classroom activities before the visit to raise questions and whet appetites.

Box 20.2	A visit to a brickworks

A mixed class of five- to seven-year-olds were studying a topic on homes. They focused on the building materials. Their teacher organised a trip to a local, traditional, brickworks. She visited the site and undertook a risk analysis. She identified a place outside the plant where the children could observe stones being delivered (the start of the process), she saw clay being prepared and how it was extruded in a long square sausage ready for cutting into bricks, she looked at the kilns, taking great care to ask lots of questions about the process and about safety precautions.

In school she gathered together drawing materials for the children to use to capture the stages in the process, she collected a few containers for the children to bring samples back, she wrote letters home and she arranged for some parent helpers to come along (with a five-minute briefing before the visit).

In discussion with the children she explored their ideas about the properties of bricks, how they might be made, what the raw materials were and where they came from. Most children were unclear about this and so were keen to find out during the visit. They discussed how the clay might be shaped and, at their suggestion, explored extruding square shapes of play dough through unifix cubes. The class was well prepared for and very enthusiastic about the visit and so able to gain a great deal from it.

Natural locations

When the teacher is wholly responsible for the kinds of activities the children will undertake during a visit to a natural location, it is useful to plan experiences rather like a 'nature trail' so that attention is drawn to particular objects or features. The activities and questions at these places have to be thought out beforehand. In some circumstances this is usefully carried out with the children so that questions are raised before the visit. This has the effect of making the visit more purposeful for the children and hence more interesting. Rangers in many areas have prepared 'trails' that can be used. Such trails might invite children to observe or investigate, for example, different kinds of vegetation, folds or cracks in rocks, evidence of erosion, fossils, animal tracks or holes and living things in a pond. The teacher needs to decide how children will record their observations, and answer their questions. This could be by using cameras (digital or disposable if preferred). They could use worksheets, although these should not detract from observations, and clipboards might be needed, as well as some protection from the weather. Follow-up work in the classroom is an essential part of the visit, so having some record to refer to can be valuable.

Places of work

Visits to factories, small industries, supermarkets or farms involve liaison with those at the site. During the pre-visit it is as important for the teacher to tell those involved at the place of work about the children and the aims for the visit as it is for the teacher to find out what the children can do and experience (as seen in Box 20.1). This avoids unrealistic expectations on either side and will enable the teacher to set the scene for the children and prepare focusing questions. Safety is always important on visits, but never more so than in workplaces. Farms present both physical hazards (from machinery and slipping on mud) and health hazards (infections can be picked up by stroking animals or touching surfaces that might be contaminated with dung). These risks may be small but should be taken seriously and can be largely avoided by ensuring that children follow safety codes, such as those set out in the ASE's publications on safety, *Be Safe* (2001, Scottish Edition 1995) and *Safety in School Science for Primary Schools* (1994).

Safety in and out of school

Despite the fact that science is now taught by most primary teachers and in all primary schools, it remains very safe. Teachers and others take sensible precautions and hence very few accidents are related to science activities. However, this situation should not lead to complacency. Part of the reason why science is so safe is that there is a good deal of high quality advice available to support science coordinators and teachers. The ASE produces and updates the essential guide called *Be Safe* (ASE 2001), and there is also an INSET pack (ASE 2002a). A school may have a health and safety policy or statement. Teachers and other educators in the school must be aware of the issues, and Peter Burrows (2003) argues that every school should have at least one copy of *Be Safe* which is a short booklet setting out the main points (see Box 20.3). More detailed information can be obtained from regular publications distributed to member schools by CLEAPPS, of which all local authorities in England and Wales are members, or SSERC, which has a similar role in Scotland.

Box 20.3	Topics covered in *Be Safe* (ASE 2001)

Be Safe contains essential safety codes for using tools, glues, sources of heat, chemicals and electricity. It also covers the preparation of food in the classroom and related matters of hygiene. Precautions to take in studying 'ourselves' are set out. There is an important section on the selection and care of animals kept in the classroom and a list of those that should not be kept. Advice is also given about growing micro-organisms. Finally, there is information about poisonous plants and safety codes for working out of class and for visits and field trips.

Safety in science is not achieved simply by reading booklets, no matter how good. It requires the application of common sense. Peter Burrows (2003) comments that an activity that is safe for a group of children with high levels of literacy may be less so where many of the children are early bilinguals or refugees with limited experience of formal schooling. Notes to this effect can be added to the school scheme of work for science (see Chapter 22), but staff training is essential to ensure that all know about and can apply safety procedures. This applies as much to support staff and parent helpers as it does to teachers.

Safety is not only a matter for the staff to consider: these considerations need to be shared with the pupils. Health and safety rules should not simply be presented to the children. Most curriculum guidelines require the explicit development by children of ideas relating (for example) to road use, mains electricity and the health hazards of smoking or drug abuse. All these ideas need to be discussed with children in such a way as to encourage understanding and therefore self-discipline in terms of obedience to the rules. Rules and obedience to them are necessary where safety matters are concerned, but the sooner compliance becomes voluntary the sooner the temptation to break them is eliminated. The construction industry, for example, has recently recognised that inviting school groups to visit local projects not only encourages much needed interest in the trade, but also reduces children's temptation to trespass by satisfying their curiosity and explaining some of the dangers. The prime importance of safety should be not to curtail children's investigations but to ensure that the necessary precautions are taken and that children gradually come to understand the reasons for them.

Summary

■ When you are selecting materials for use in primary science it is important to keep in mind the centrality of first-hand experience. Children learn best when they explore things around them, so simple, familiar utensils are to be preferred over more complex laboratory apparatus.

■ When you are building up a stock of resources it is essential to consider the curriculum and the activities planned and to ensure that consumables are available as appropriate.

■ Care must be taken to maintain and store equipment and materials in good condition. A clear responsibility for maintaining resources must be allocated. This is particularly so if a central store is to be used. Children should be involved in keeping all the things in good order.

■ Funds need to be set aside for teachers to purchase consumables when needed.

■ There is great value in making use of a variety of out-of-school visits. These need a thorough pre-visit by the teacher, careful planning of questions that will help pupils to engage with these new experiences, attention to safety and follow-up work afterwards.

■ A wide view of safety has been taken, so that risks involved in certain activities can be minimised without inhibiting children's experience. Helping children to understand reasons for safety codes has to be seen as an important part of learning in science.

21 The role of ICT

In this chapter we look at the role of information and communications technology (ICT) in the teaching and learning of science. What we have to say about using ICT is firmly linked to the discussions in Chapter 7, where we considered the importance of learning with understanding constructed through children's thinking and in particular with the link to the development of the skills and attitudes of science as discussed in Chapters 8 to 11. Thus we argue for a pedagogical model for science teaching that requires that ICT be used to support and enhance science learning rather than as a teacher of science knowledge.

This chapter is divided into three broad sections. The first discusses the different ways in which ICT can be used within science and the different types of ICT this might involve. In the second part the focus is on particular applications, reflecting current experience, in learning science in the primary school. Here we look at using ICT to support classroom-based enquiry, to enable access to the wider world and to bring experience from outside into the classroom. In the third part we look at the role of ICT in supporting the professional development in science of primary teachers.

Current practice: how well are we doing?

ICT is now a well-established feature of the primary school curriculum; that is, if policy documents, reports by inspectors, the huge push around the world to increase the availability of new technologies in schools and the amount of research being undertaken on the topic can be believed. But worryingly, the place of ICT in science teaching does not seem to be as well established in primary schools as it might be. The IMPACT2 project (Harrison *et al.* 2002) found that the level of ICT use in science for seven- to eleven-year-olds in England was lower than in maths and English both within lessons and more widely in school and homework. In addition, the type of use made of ICT in science tended to be highly focused on developing subject knowledge related to testing. High use of ICT was correlated with higher test performance in English and maths but no such relationship was found for science. Perhaps the issue is not simply the use or otherwise of ICT, but the ways in which it is used in science education. One of the difficulties faced by educators is the rapid pace of change. Research shows, for example, that primary school pupils tend to be more familiar than their teachers with the Internet (Murphy and Beggs 2003). Murphy (2003) argues that most of what we know works in classrooms comes from practitioners, with very little research evidence to extend and support our understanding.

The functions of ICT

Useful accounts of the various applications that are available appear in journals and magazines (e.g. Hemsley 1994; Hart 2003) and on a number of websites for teachers (see page 228). It is difficult to keep up with the pace of change, for example the widespread introduction of digital microscopes and interactive whiteboards since the previous edition of this book presents many opportunities but also makes it important to have some way of thinking about how ICT can be used to support science learning. Ball (2003) categorises the role of ICT as a *tool*, including spreadsheets, databases and data-logging; as a *reference source*, using CD-ROMs and the Internet; and as a means of *communication*, with digital cameras, e-mail, word processing, desktop publishing and interactive white-boards. Newton and Rogers (2001), in a book that focuses on secondary school science and ICT, provide a useful link between the various functions of ICT and the role of the learner, from which Box 21.1 is adapted.

Box 21.1　The functions of ICT and the role of the learner

Teaching use of ICT	Learner's role
Obtaining knowledge Visual aids, such as data projectors Information CD-ROM, through a Database Browser (using Internet websites)	*Receiver:* this need not be a passive role as software can present information in interesting ways and can demand interaction from the learner.
Practice and revision CD-ROMs, web	*Receiver:* again the learner can be active in trying out puzzles and quizzes to test their knowledge.
Exploring ideas Simulation and modelling software,	*Explorer:* the learner is testing out ideas; this can be done in groups, who can

and spreadsheets and databases, that let pupils test out ideas, e.g. the trajectory of a cannon fired at different angles, or testing the effects on fox numbers of reducing the number of rabbits

then discuss these ideas and build on them.

Collating and recording
Spreadsheets and databases (using data-logging equipment) to collect, record and present information

Receiver: this can really only be made active if the pupils fully understand what is happening in the experiment and how graphs and charts are produced.

Presenting and reporting
Desktop publishing, word processing

Creator: here pupils are synthesising information and finding innovative ways to present it to themselves (for discussion and modification) and to others.

This approach helps us to see that different forms of ICT can serve different purposes in learning and teaching in science. However, it is not always easy to see how best to plan science teaching in such a way as to make the best use of ICT. In the following section the focus is on thinking about ICT when planning science activities.

Integrating ICT in planning

When planning ICT use in science it is important that the view of science learning that the curriculum is intended to promote is kept firmly in mind (MacFarlane and Sakellariou 2003). A curriculum that values hands-on experiences and emphasises the importance of children's own ideas should guide the approach taken to the integration of ICT. A number of useful maps have been drawn up to aid planning this integration, for example Grace Woodford developed two grids (for Key Stages 1 and 2) for integrating ICT in a topic on 'Food and Farming'. Many case studies now appear on websites such as those provided by the Quality and Curriculum Authority (QCA) and the Department for Education and Skills (DfES), as well as groups such as the British Educational Communications and Technology Agency (BECTA).

One way of sorting out the various roles that ICT can play is to make explicit links between the process skills of inquiry as discussed in Chapter 7 and where and when ICT can usefully contribute to science learning.

Box 21.2	Linking process skills and ICT uses	
Process skills	*Activities*	*Possible ICT use*
Questioning and planning	Exploring a new topic, collecting information, raising questions	Using CD-ROMs or web
	Drafting plans, making changes on reflection after discussion etc.	Word processing Interactive whiteboard
Gathering evidence	Making observations of the unknown, new or even familiar	Using a digital microscope, time lapse photography etc. to enable close observation Using sensors and probes to measure light, sound, movement etc. (see Box 21.4). Data-logging to capture information. Digital cameras (see Box 21.3), video or audio recorders
	Surveying, measuring, recording	Collecting data from simulations (such as food chains) Gathering evidence from websites (e.g. weather data)
Interpreting evidence and drawing conclusions	Organising, presenting and recording results Using models and simulations to try out ideas	Spreadsheets linked to software to present graphs, charts etc. (see Box 21.5). Spreadsheets to collect and manipulate data (e.g. finding mean, median and mode), e.g., using CD-ROM simulation of electric circuits to test out ideas further
Communicating and reflecting	Making posters, sending letters, writing reports, presenting graphs etc. to share in discussion with others or to inform others	Desktop publishing. Clip art to enliven reports Interactive whiteboard to share findings (see Box 21.1). Multimedia presentations of findings taking images from web, video, digital cameras or including sound recordings or interactive presentations. E-mail to send or exchange information. Creating website

No simple mapping system such as the one above is comprehensive, so it is important to focus on what science needs to be learned and how or if teaching and learning can be enhanced by the use of ICT. Feasey and Gallear (2002) give an example of a science activity in which cinder toffee is made using the reaction between vinegar and bicarbonate of soda. The speed of the reaction is such that without a digital video recorder to play back the event children would not be able to study the permanent change that is taking place. This is a rare example of there being no alternative to using ICT. Mostly there are alternatives, and on many occasions these alternatives, such as pencil and paper, or the use of drama, offer better possibilities for learning. Good medium- and long-term plans developed at school level with the ICT coordinator supporting and cross-referencing to the planning for science are important. This will ensure that teachers know what is available, that there is proper progression in ICT use through the school, that children are not hampered in their science learning by ICT demands that they are not prepared for and that software can be purchased that is going to give maximum value.

Box 21.3	ICT use in a reception class

Greg's reception class (four-year-olds) were looking at materials. They had a variety of everyday objects, such as coins, postcards, plastic cups, pencil sharpeners and erasers, and were discussing the materials they were made of. In groups the children observed their objects closely, discussing the properties of the materials and developing appropriate language to describe them. They then used a digital camera to take images of their objects to put on the computer. Greg made some files containing descriptions based on what the children had said. The images were then sent through a data projector on to an interactive whiteboard. The children recognised their objects and together the class discussed their observations and findings. Children were asked to use their 'magic fingers' to move the images of the objects around the board, to group them in different ways and to link their objects to the labels and descriptions that Greg had made using the children's words, which were then projected on to the white board. In this way the sharing of ideas was encouraged and decisions about materials and their descriptions could be discussed. The children loved using their magic fingers, finding it much easier than manipulating a mouse and more visually attractive because of the large screen. They could save their work, and print it off for display.

Greg's approach ensures that his children have hands-on experience of materials and are able to explore them directly. The use of the digital camera helps the children to make the link between the two-dimensional image and the actual object. The children were able to discuss the properties of the materials and how they would group and describe them together by manipulating images on the interactive whiteboard. This enabled language development, discussion and reflection.

Box 21.4	Using ICT to measure sound levels

A class of nine- and ten-year-olds were presented with a problem relating to the local steel factory. It had recently installed a very noisy machine. The safety officer wanted to find the best sound insulator to use to improve the company's ear protectors. The children knew they would need to test out different sound insulators. After discussion with their teacher to review their understanding of how sound travels and to reinforce the need for a fair test, they set about planning in groups. When they presented their ideas to the whole class it was agreed that the best approach was to record themselves shouting into a laptop and take the highest reading each time. The distance between the sensor and the source of the sound had to remain constant, as did the volume of insulation material used. The pupils decided to resolve the problem of keeping different types of material constant in volume by placing the sound sensor in a small box.

Each group had the opportunity to use the computer, sound sensor and software to record results. After they had tested each material, the teacher asked them to discuss and predict the next results. Then they entered the results into a spreadsheet, found the average of each reading and generated a graph. To complete the lesson, the pupils discussed why they thought cotton wool was the best sound insulator.

The pupils produced a word-processed report using imported graphs from the spreadsheet to display their results.

(Based on a study from www.ncaction.org.uk)

One of the advantages of word processing is that, pupils can make notes during planning or practical work, draft their ideas, present and discuss them and then redraft without the tedium of writing the whole thing out again. Keogh and Naylor, writing in 1996, reported that, at that time, primary children engaging in 'hands-on' science investigations rarely had the opportunity to plan their investigations in detail or to evaluate them fully. The introduction of word processing, and more recently PowerPoint, as a common feature of primary work is helping to bring a better balance to practical work in school by enabling drafting and redrafting without the tedium of writing everything out again, and providing opportunities to discuss and share ideas with the class on enquiries completed.

Data-logging is one of the more common uses of computers in science. As the case study in Box 21.4 suggests, it involves sensors or probes linked to a computer with the appropriate software to record the information. It has considerable advantages over data-logging by hand in terms of speed, memory, accuracy and perseverance. Probes that respond to sound, temperature, light, rotation, pressure, humidity and so on, open up to children direct experience of some variables that would not be available to them through conventional measuring instruments. They can, for example, use a light-sensitive probe to investigate the intensity of light before and after it passes through a coloured filter, helping them to test out the idea that children often have that the filter adds something to 'colour' the light. The reduction in intensity after passing through the filter may lead them to consider the alternative idea that some light is absorbed in this process.

Connecting probes to computers, using suitable software, provides a screen display of data that changes in real time. This means that the children's attention can be given to the trends and patterns as they appear, whereas if they are, say, using a thermometer to take temperatures at different times, their attention has to be on the mechanics of using the instrument and reading the scale. However, children still need to make sense of what is happening and to maintain the essential link between what they see on the screen and the real events taking place.

The interpretation of evidence rests on an understanding of the nature of the evidence collected. An emphasis on understanding is also crucial in terms of the use of spreadsheets. Children in primary school are generally required to use spreadsheets but not to create them. Investigations in primary classes do not tend to produce data that can usefully be analysed in this way. Poole (2000) suggests that children need to go through the preliminary stages of selecting the best axis scales and deciding on the most useful type of graph. Without this children are confused and much of the learning opportunity is lost. There is, therefore, a key role for the teacher in ensuring the link between the nature of the evidence and its interpretation and presentation.

Box 21.5	Using temperature probes to enhance investigative skills

Children in four different classes were all comparing the cooling of warm water in identical bottles covered with different materials. In two classes the children were using thermometers and representing the falling temperatures by drawing line graphs. In the other two classes the children were using portable computers, temperature-sensitive probes and software that recorded and plotted graphs of their findings. Before the work started all the children were asked questions to assess their ability to identify events from a temperature–time graph. The researchers found that, at the start, 'most children were completely unable to gain meaning from line graphs, with many unable to identify the data line as the significant part of the graph'.

Those using the temperature probes then explored their surroundings with them and were encouraged to find ways of making the line on the screen go up and down. They quickly discovered how to do this and were able to make predictions as to the effect on the line of placing the probe in certain places. They then devised an investigation to compare the effect of the covers on the bottle. The other children in the other two classes had help from their teachers, who were 'extremely inventive in getting children to present data in an imaginative way'. Both groups, when questioned after their investigations, showed improvement in their ability to interpret line graphs, but those using the computer significantly more so. In addition to this advance, the researchers concluded that:

it was apparent that using IT reaped advantages in terms of the children's observed ability to work in a genuinely investigative way. They became more accepting that it is 'OK' to make predictions that turn out to be incorrect. They were willing to adapt and re-run their investigations, as they could immediately see the outcomes of changes made. Perhaps most crucially, they demonstrated a sound understanding of the relationship between variables, together with the ability to manipulate them for various purposes; this might not, perhaps, have been anticipated in children of this age.

(Warwick and McFarlane 1995: 24)

Using ICT to bring the outside world into the classroom

Museums

CD-ROMs and websites designed for children provide information that children can use in a variety of ways. When they are seeking factual information it is important for the children to have clear questions in mind if they are to locate what is useful to them. The process of clarifying questions by seeking information via a computer is as important as is the identification of investigable questions when seeking answers through enquiry. But these sources do far more than provide readily available factual information. For example, the Natural History Museum's QUEST website creates an environment in which children can explore and investigate objects that actually exist in the museum but are presented on the screen. They can use a selection of 'virtual tools' to investigate them. The website also provides an on-line notebook where 'children can record their ideas, thoughts and questions about an object. They can read those of others and respond to them' (Hawkey 1999: 4). Murphy (2003), in a review of primary science and ICT, points out that simulations and virtual reality are probably the least exploited uses of ICT in primary science classrooms. This may be changing as schools increasingly have access to faster and more reliable connections and intranets that guard against children accessing inappropriate websites when using the Internet.

Real and virtual visits

Museums and science centres, wherever they are, often provide materials to help teachers to prepare for visits, resources to support the visit and ideas for follow-up lessons. The Eden Project provides all these, for example the follow-up lesson suggestions for seven- to eleven-year-olds include a series of three lessons in which pupils analyse the ingredients of a pizza, identifying the origin of the food, the part of the plant that provides the food, the manufacturing process etc. Pupils need to study the foods at first hand, research them using books, CD-ROMs and the Internet and then make up a database that can be interrogated by others. Useful web links are provided and links to other areas of the curriculum, such as geography, where pupils can study the economic impact of trade in, say, coffee on parts of the world. Even if the class cannot visit Eden, a virtual tour and some other work can help to bring this resource to the school. Similarly, museums, galleries, science centres and others provide wonderful facilities to enhance and extend pupils' experiences and so their learning opportunities. The website www.24hourmuseum.org has links to lots of museums, science centres and galleries in the UK.

Talking to others

Children use computers to communicate via e-mail with other children or with scientists or other experts. This can expand their experience in a particularly friendly way. For example, children recording the precise time between sunrise and sunset would probably find it intriguing to exchange this kind of information with children in another part of the world. There are many opportunities for children to learn from each other by using e-mail; for example, about the variety of animals, plants and habitats in different places. This is less formal and more immediate than conventional correspondence and has far more impact than reading about such things in books. Direct links to scientists are sometimes arranged but obviously have to be used with consideration for the adults involved. In some cases, however, schools can help to collect survey data of value to scientists. In the USA the National Geographical Society's Kids' Network programme gives elementary and middle school children opportunities to learn about globally significant science topics. In another US example, middle-school girls use e-mail to connect with women scientists who act as role models and encourage the girls' interests in science and technology.

Teaching resources and ideas

One of the ways in which ICT can enhance primary science learning is as an aid to teaching. For example, teachers can prepare tailor-made resources for groups of pupils, share ideas and materials with other teachers, get ideas for lesson plans and develop straightforward, centralised, recording systems for assessment. Further, ICT can be used directly to enhance teaching. We have already discussed the use of interactive whiteboards and other devices to aid teaching. In another example, Lias and Thomas (2003) showed how taking photographs of pupils carrying out experiments and then talking about them with the children enabled teachers and pupils to describe their understanding and to assess it.

The role of ICT in professional development

Professional development can be seen as having two forms – structured and informal. Structured professional development includes accredited distance learning programmes and materials developed specifically as a course of study but not accredited as such. Informal can range from websites dedicated to providing information for teachers to special interest e-mail groups.

Structured provision

Increasingly, CD-ROMs and on-line programs are being developed to support science teaching, to supplement conventional courses for professional development and to extend the value of certain TV programmes. This trend will increase further in England with the development of National and Regional Science Learning Centres. Initially these will focus on secondary school teachers and primary science coordinators and much of the provision should be on-line. However, other systems have been up and running for some time. In Scotland a CD-ROM with Internet links system was trialled in a number of regions. The Science On-Line Learning Network (SOLN) had many valuable features, such as access to resources, to expert advice and to discussion forums (Plowman *et al.* 2000). A difficulty was the quality of the technology and the level of teacher expertise in using it, which inhibited full use being made of the system. However, systems are now much more capable of coping with this kind of provision and there are similar initiatives around the world. These include the TOPS (Teaching On-line Primary Science) in Victoria, Australia, and in both England and the USA (e.g. Washington state) teachers can use centrally provided professional development credits to purchase on-line training programmes. The ease of access when and where required, rather than at the time and place where a course is being offered, makes CD-ROM and web-based alternatives extremely attractive to busy teachers. The question as to how effective these programmes are is still an important focus for research. Box 21.6 gives an example of such a project.

| Box 21.6 | On-line versus conventional professional development |

Try Science was developed as a substantial (13-week) module within a master's programme for primary teachers. It was carefully designed to be delivered on-line by a module facilitator, with a science specialist offering support. Harlen and Altobello (2003) compared the quality of learning experiences and the learning outcomes of teachers studying Try Science on-line with a group of teachers studying the same course content in a conventional face-to-face course of 13 weekly three-hour sessions. The main findings, reported in Harlen and Doubler (2004), were that:

■ the on-line group were involved more frequently in reflecting on their learning than the face-to-face group;

■ on-line participants experienced, appreciated and commented upon their collaborative learning; and did not feel that they were working alone;

■ there were changes in their understanding of the science content of the course for both groups, but this change was significantly greater for the on-line participants;

■ participants in both courses considered that their understanding of enquiry in science had been increased;

■ the confidence that teachers expressed in their capacity to teach science through enquiry increased during the course, significantly more for the on-line than for the face-to-face participants.

As the study described in Box 21.6 shows, on-line courses should be seen not as a poor substitute for face-to-face learning, but as a valuable alternative, which, if done well, can provide real advantages. Often there is an opportunity for occasional face-to-face encounters with a tutor or with other teachers (as in Try Science), but even without this the popularity of web-based courses is rapidly increasing. Of course, much depends on the construction of the website and the facilities offered. It is certainly not enough to transfer course notes to an electronic form. It is generally advocated (e.g. Bober 1998) that the website should provide at least e-mail links to tutors and fellow participants, activities on-line and off-line, interactive activities, many relevant examples, frequently asked questions, lists of resources, opportunities for participants to contribute ideas and examples and, if the course is for credit, assignments, sample projects and assessment details.

In addition to accredited programmes such as the one described in Box 21.6, a number of organisations have constructed what might be termed 'off the shelf' programmes. Astra Zeneca, for example, has developed CD-ROMs for science coordinators to use with their staff (see www.azteachscience.co.uk/PDU/pdu). ASE produced a CD-ROM for Science Year, which includes sections to guide INSET (ASE

2001; see www.ase.org.uk). In addition, Astra Zeneca has developed short INSET courses for early years teachers on teaching science. BECTA has recently developed an on-line INSET pack in science for Key Stage 1 and 2 teachers (http://forum.ngfl.gov.uk/). Many more will come on stream over the next few years.

Informal provision

Over the past few years the number of websites devoted to giving advice to teachers has burgeoned. Teachers are using these sites more and more to download lesson plans and schemes of work, or to get ideas for teaching and learning. There are also a number of discussion forums dedicated to primary teaching and some dedicated to primary science teaching. These change over time but can generally be found on specialist gateways (sites that suggest links to other sites). All these sites provide opportunities for informal, unstructured professional development. The difficulty with simply surfing the Internet for sites is that it can take an inordinate amount of time, and some sites are significantly better than others. This is why at least initially it is useful to use recommended websites that provide appropriate information and tested links to other related sites, such as those in Box 21.7

Box 21.7	Useful websites that lead to others

Website for teachers: www.teachernet.gov.uk/

Qualifications and Curriculum Authority (QCA): www.qca.org.uk/ages3-14/subjects/science

National Grid for Learning gateway: www.ngfl.gov.uk/

Astra Zeneca science teaching: www.azteachscience.co.uk/

Standards site: www.standards.dfee.gov.uk/

ASE website: www.ase.org.uk/

Many more informal opportunities exist through the Internet and CD-ROMs for learning science and learning about science teaching. However, it is clear that, as with young people, teachers learn by sharing ideas, and discussing them with others and exploring them in practice is important to development. We would hope, therefore, that informal continuing professional development does not entirely replace the more formal structured provision that face-to-face or on-line programmes can provide.

Summary

- It is important to place the role of ICT in the pedagogical model that is adopted. Hence ICT should be used to enhance science learning rather than as a teacher of science knowledge.

- Different forms of ICT can be used to explore ideas through simulations, models, databases and spreadsheets, to collect and collate information, to report information. ICT can also be used to obtain knowledge and to revisit ideas, although this should be done carefully and interactively.

- When they are using ICT, e.g. seeking information from a CD-ROM, it is important that children have a clear question in mind.

- ICT, especially the Internet and CD-ROMs, can be used to widen children's experience by bringing the outside (such as museums or the deep seas) into the classroom.

- ICT, such as e-mail, is a useful way to take the inside out, to communicate with others (scientists, other schools etc.).

- There is an increasing role for ICT in the provision of continuing professional development for teachers. Used well it promises to support learning, planning and the sharing of ideas.

Part 5 Planning and managing primary science

22 Planning a school programme

Introduction

In this chapter we discuss issues relating to planning provision for science. The concern is mainly with long- and medium-term planning and with matters where decisions need to be made at the school or phase level or between schools or phases. Detailed discussion of lesson planning is reserved for the next chapter. We begin by looking at long- and medium-term planning and the role that published schemes can play. We then consider issues relating to curriculum coverage, the extent to which science can be taught within or with other subjects and how topic work, once dismissed as not leading to sound science, is being reconceived. Finally, we consider matters relating to ways of supporting continuity in children's experience at points of transfer from one phase to another.

Overview of planning

One of the noticeable trends over recent years has been the change from curriculum planning being treated as a matter for individual teachers to its being treated as a whole-school responsibility. Indeed, it is considered essential that all staff are involved in discussions about the curriculum and teaching, although generally the responsibility for putting it all together lies with the subject leader or coordinator.

Some decisions are best made at the school level in order to ensure continuity as children move from class to class. These include the broad topics and the concepts to be covered, time and timetabling and the extent of integration with other subjects. Teams of teachers from a year group or groups, or phases, can use the long-term plans to develop medium-term plans. In some cases teachers continue to work together to develop their short-term planning. This, of course, depends on the way the school is organised, its size and the approach taken to curriculum planning generally. A further decision is whether the school develops its own scheme of work or adopts a ready-made one such as that provided by the

QCA scheme of work (DfEE 1998). This sets out a scheme of 33 units and four short (revision) units that cover the National Curriculum at Key Stages 1 and 2. Each unit takes about half a term to complete and the suggested sequence gives a reasonable balance during each year of activities in biological and physical science.

Other decisions are the subject of medium-term planning that is concerned with the activities that will be included in a topic or unit. These decisions are made several weeks in advance so that they can be coordinated across classes. Short-term planning is the province of the individual teacher and concerns the detailed plans of lessons that put the medium-term plan into action. The QCA scheme provides suggestions somewhere between the medium- and short-term levels of planning by identifying, for each unit, a series of possible teaching activities, with learning objectives and learning outcomes for each one. Thus teachers have access, if they wish to use it, to a good deal of help from outside the school for their individual planning.

Long-term planning

Long-term planning concerns the overall framework for the school's programme for science. The decisions about matters of content to be covered are bounded by the national or local curriculum or guidelines or by early learning goals, but the school retains control of decisions about how this is organised and taught. The majority of schools have a well-planned whole-school scheme that maps the relevant externally devised curriculum on to the phases and year groups of the primary stage. In this way planning for progression can be assured, with indications of points at which children will have the opportunity to revisit concepts and where meaningful links across curriculum areas can be identified.

The management of long-term planning is generally the responsibility of the science subject leader or coordinator. The role of the science subject leader is discussed in more detail in the next chapter. However, it is important to note that the long-term planning within the school is the first level of implementation and interpretation of the school's policy for science, it is the articulation of the school's view of what primary science is. How this is developed depends on other influences, such as changes in the school's circumstances (for example, the acquisition of a computer suite) or changes in the externally prescribed curriculum, such as with the introduction of distinctive early years goals, or changes in other subject areas (as was observed with the introduction of the literacy and numeracy strategies a few years ago). All this means that, even if the school has adopted a published scheme, this will be modified and added to over time.

Medium-term planning

Medium-term planning is the first major step in moving from the broad brush strokes of the longer-term plan to the detailed activities of the lesson. It is at this stage, when thinking about a block of time, say half a term, that a clear view is needed of the learning objectives, how progression towards them can be achieved, the particular activities that might be used, the knowledge and understanding required by the teacher and the assessment opportunities that exist. Issues of timetabling and resources need to be addressed at this stage and any visits (with permission slips sent home) or visitors planned for.

The QCA scheme of work for science is, in some senses, between the medium-term and short-term planning levels. Yet no scheme, however detailed, can properly take account of the particular pupils in the school and their previous experiences and learning, or any special circumstances of the school. At Brindishe School (see Box 25.1), for example, working in the environment is highly valued and the school benefits from the close proximity of an environmental centre. The school therefore includes a rolling programme to ensure that each class visits the centre once every two years; this clearly influences medium-term planning.

Hollins and Whitby (2001) provide a detailed discussion of the ways in which the QCA scheme might be used to guide medium- and short-term planning. The key point they make is that 'In all schools, teachers are best placed to judge whether the learning objectives meet the learning needs of the individual children' (p. 163). Many teachers have noted that appropriately differentiated learning opportunities for the more and the less able cannot be planned for in isolation of knowledge of the children concerned.

Box 22.1 gives the background within which one school and teacher developed medium-term plans based on the QCA scheme of work.

Box 22.1   Medium-term planning using a published scheme of work

Alice has a class of 22 ten- and eleven-year-olds in the autumn term of their final year in their newly built primary school. The school uses the QCA scheme of work as a guide to coverage of the curriculum, but teachers are all aware of the fact that each of the classes has a wide range of abilities, from children who are defined as gifted and talented (Alice has two such children) to those with learning difficulties (Alice's class includes about eight such children). A significant number of children come from disadvantaged backgrounds and can be challenging to teach.

Alice's class had the opportunity to explore materials and change in previous years and had just finished a unit of study similar to the QCA 'More about dissolving'. They had used and consolidated their previous experience of dissolving, mixing, evaporation and filtration, and gone on to explore ways in which solids can be recovered from a solution by evaporation. They had explored through investigations the factors that affect the rate at which solids dissolve. They had used a variety of process skills to help them to investigate, including observation, prediction and recording findings, including drawing tables and graphs.

The children had enjoyed their work on dissolving and were beginning to feel very confident in their own skills and knowledge.

In this unit Alice wanted to move on to look at 'reversible and irreversible changes', Unit 6D of the QCA scheme of work. She was keen to ensure from the start that the children should consolidate their understanding of the concepts they had developed in previous work and that they were confident in using the terms involved. She also felt it important that the children had the opportunity to make careful observations. She knew from previous assessments that some would need help to observe closely. She wanted to assess their skills in this area, and also to ensure that they had a real sense of ownership of the science investigations they were undertaking.

Alice's medium-term plans are very similar to those presented in the QCA scheme. However, she put more emphasis on assessment and she identified slightly different learning outcomes for groups of pupils. She also puts more emphasis on children understanding the scientific language and on links with their everyday experiences. The second lesson in the QCA scheme suggests a discussion about retrieving sand and salt from water. Alice changed this, intending to challenge the children to solve this problem practically. In the scheme the activity is simply intended to consolidate their knowledge from the previous unit, but Alice wanted to give the class some valuable experience in undertaking a whole investigation. This is because she was aware that, in the previous year, the disruption to the school of the rebuilding had limited the children's opportunity to undertake whole investigations. In this same vein she also ensured that activities were repeated (i.e. those from session one were demonstrated again in session three, rather than the children being expected to remember them). This is because she knew that some of the children needed the concrete reminders and some were absent on the day of the first lesson. Thus, in a school that adhered to the published scheme of work, delivering science as a separate subject with few links to other subjects, quite significant changes were made to specific aspects in order to meet better the needs of the children.

The amount of detail included in the medium-term plans depends on the needs of the teachers involved. For example, Alice is a science graduate who feels very confident with the topic. However, other teachers might need to research the background knowledge required and to make more detailed notes in their plans. The science subject leader can contribute here by supplementing medium-term plans with detailed notes on background science and alternative resources (useful websites are given in Box 21.7).

Another approach to developing medium-term planning is through a team of science coordinators from a number of schools as part of a joint project. This is likely to become more common as the idea of networked learning communities is developed (www.ncsl.org.uk). Clusters of schools working together to develop medium-term plans that suit the pupils of the area have the distinct advantage of combining the knowledge and expertise of a group of specialists. These plans provide more detailed guidance for teachers, but individual subject leaders or coordinators would still need to consider them in the light of the needs of their own pupils; that is, to modify or develop them to suit the staff and children of their own school.

| Box 22.2 | Medium-term planning across a group of schools |

The RASKALS Project
This project involves a group of science coordinators in Bournemouth who worked together on a project supported by Astra Zeneca. One of the products of this project was a set of medium-term plans for science for primary age children. Linked to the National Curriculum for science, the plans are presented for teaching science as a separate subject.

Headings for boxes on the plans include the link to statements in the National Curriculum, the year group and term, the learning outcomes, the range of levels covered, teacher background knowledge and vocabulary. Possible starter activities are then listed with a heading under which possible reasons for misconceptions are given. This is followed by 'possible activities for diagnostic teaching'. One of the activities, it is suggested, can be used as part of the literacy/guided reading work of the children.

(www.swgfl.org.uk/raskals/default.htm)

Planning and curriculum coverage

One of the major dilemmas facing teachers in recent years has related to the difficulties of ensuring coverage of the whole curriculum. Since the introduction of national curricula, national guidelines, learning goals etc., teachers have struggled to find a balance between meaningful learning opportunities and 'delivering' curriculum entitlement to all children. This problem is seen as particularly acute where the curriculum is defined in terms of discrete subject areas, such as the National Curricula for England and Wales, and perhaps somewhat less so where curriculum guidelines are less subject specific. One of the ways in which such tensions might be overcome is to take advantage of any overlap between subjects and any reinforcement that learning in one area can offer to another by planning through topic rather than separate subjects.

Topic work means that different aspects of work are linked together, or remain undifferentiated, so that they reinforce one another and are studied within a context that has meaning for children in relation to their experience. The different forms of topic work arise from the breadth and variety of what is included. Cross-curricular topics link most subject areas (usually with the exceptions of physical education and music), with equal emphasis on the components. Environmental studies topics leave language and mathematics to be taught separately. There can also be science-based topics in which, while other areas of the curriculum are inevitably involved, their role is incidental rather than planned. The approach of one school is described in Box 22.3.

Box 22.3   **A school view of cross-curricular planning**

Dalton St Mary's primary school includes in its prospectus a clear rationale for teaching through topic work. They indicate that their topics are 'carefully selected and planned in a structured way to provide opportunities for children to study a broad and balanced curriculum in increasing depth as they progress through the school'.

Planning thorough topic work allows the school to make maximum use of its local environment, places with which the children are familiar, with topics linked to the local abbey, to farms and to ponds. The topic often starts with a class visit to one such place. Topics are usually history, science or geography led, with science topics entitled 'Homes', 'My world and me', 'Woodlands and seashore', 'Forces'.

Pupils in the school achieve high standards in terms of external tests, and an inspection report from 2001 indicated that children's development in terms of science process skills was good.

(www.daltonstmarys.cumbria.sch.uk/science.htm)

The school described in Box 22.3 is, according to an inspection report, well organised, with experienced subject coordinators and good management. It is in this context that staff are able to achieve such high standards. It is clear that cross-curricular work requires a good deal of careful planning, and a knowledgeable staff who are committed to working in this way.

At the time of the introduction of the National Curriculum in England and Wales, and equivalents in other parts of the UK, there were mounting criticisms of the previously prevalent approach to planning and teaching in primary schools through integrated topics. Criticism came from researchers and from schools inspectors. Topic work was accused of being overambitious, trying to cover too many elements at once and making rather spurious connections between subjects (DES 1989). However, since 2000, evidence has emerged that schools that adopt a flexible approach to curriculum delivery are more likely to achieve high standards than those that stick to single, separate subject teaching. This shift in emphasis is apparent in a DfES report 'We want schools to feel freer... To take a fresh look at their curriculum, their timetabling and their organisation of the school day and week' (DfES 2003: 12). What is clear is that, in whatever way a school chooses to deliver the curriculum, there needs to be:

■ an agreed system of planning that is consistent and well structured to ensure progression and continuity;

■ discussion and sharing of ideas, expertise and workload between teachers;

■ whole-school agreement about subject coverage and balance;

■ clear links with national or district curriculum requirements;

■ an avoidance of slavish adherence to topic or separate subject work, such that useful links are made but spurious links are avoided;

■ planning referring to learning outcomes and to assessment.

What seems to be happening these days is that schools are looking again at opportunities to maximise learning by linking subjects, either by the expedient of teaching subjects separately but making links between them (such as using the data from a science experiment to support the teaching of graphs), or by teaching through carefully planned topics linking subject areas only where appropriate. For practical as well as pedagogical reasons linking science and literacy or numeracy is commonly suggested.

Science and other subjects

Literacy and numeracy

Concern for the development of numeracy and literacy skills in primary schools over recent years has led to an increase in the proportion of time teachers spend planning for these subjects and has tended to move science to the afternoon, when children are less alert (Sutton 2001). On the other hand, the emphasis on the 'three-part lesson' in literacy and numeracy teaching has meant that teachers are now less likely to overlook the important plenary session in their science lessons. In addition, there is evidence from an ASE survey to suggest that the National Literacy Strategy (NLS) has led to more children seeking out and using science texts to gain information.

Children are taught to use non-fiction texts in literacy lessons. In this way, it is argued, they will increase their knowledge of other subjects. However, care needs to be taken if the intention is to teach science through literacy in this way. The AAAS (1989) found that texts rarely contributed to effective learning. This could be explained in a number of ways. Newton *et al.* (2002) found, for example, that school science texts, like many schemes of work for primary science, do not show a concern for explanatory understanding. That is, they provide information on 'how 'and 'what' but not 'why'. In addition Peacock and Weedon (2002) found that nine- to ten-year-old pupils who had been taught the use of non-fiction texts did not use science texts well to gain information. This, they concluded, was because what is needed is the development of visual literacy, or what Aldrich and Sheppard (2000) call graphicacy. Most science books include more pictures, diagrams and symbols than they do words, yet little emphasis is placed on visual literacy in the NLS. It is therefore important that teachers actively teach children to use science information books, making links between labelled diagrams and text, and seeking to discuss the possible explanations for the phenomena being presented within the pages. These skills are becoming more and more important with the ever-increasing use of the Internet and CD-ROMs, which are even more likely to rely on visual images, and demand the ability to read information in a range of presentational forms.

Increasingly teachers are finding ways to integrate literacy and numeracy teaching with their science teaching. The challenge is to ensure that, by focusing on literacy skills, the science covered will not be trivial. What is important is to look for ways in which science learning can be enhanced or can contribute to literacy and numeracy learning. For example, data from science experiments can be used in numeracy lessons to construct graphs, diagrams and charts. The example given in Box 22.4 shows how science work can inspire literacy work, which can in turn help learning in science. The ASE has two publications that provide useful support to ensure that the science learning remains central, and the goals of developing science skills and ideas are taken seriously, by taking science activities as their starting point (Feasey 1999; Feasey and Gallear 2000).

Box 22.4   Science learning supported in literacy work

Chris Wardle's class of six- to seven-year-olds had been working on the topic of 'light and dark' in the previous term. They had looked at various light sources, explored shiny objects and noted how these cannot be seen in the dark. The class then used their science work to develop some alliterative list poems. In this way the children were able to recap on science work, consider the meanings of science words and use dictionaries, thesaurus and science information books to find more useful words.

> Light is...
> Shining sun
> Twinkling torches
> Laser light
> Magical match
> Golden glows

(Wardle 2000: 27)

Science, mathematics and technology

Science has its own distinctive characteristics but this does not mean that it is independent of other ways of knowing about and reacting to the world. Its closest relationship would seem to be with mathematics and technology. But while there are many occasions when science, mathematics and technology are brought together in one activity, they still remain distinct human enterprises, distinguishable from one another by several characteristics. For example, whereas for science the physical world is the ultimate authority by which its theories and principles are to be judged, for mathematics the ultimate test is the logic of relationships and numbers; there is no need for the descriptions of mathematics to relate to the real world.

Because science and technology have been intimately linked in the activities of primary school children, there often appears to be difficulty in distinguishing between them. There would certainly be difficulty in disentangling them, especially in relation to their role in practical activities in which children are not only devising ways of problem-solving and investigating but also constructing devices to implement their ideas. But there should be no difficulty in distinguishing between science and technology, for they are quite different in aims and the kinds of activity through which their aims are pursued.

Scientific activity, as we have seen, aims at understanding. Technological activity uses 'knowledge and skills effectively, creatively and confidently in the solving of practical problems and the undertaking of tasks' (Layton 1990: 11). This statement sums up with remarkable clarity and economy of words the important aspects of technology. The main points to note are:

- The mention of 'knowledge and skills', not scientific knowledge and skills. Certainly scientific knowledge and skills are used very often in technology but they are not the only kinds; it is this that makes technology an aspect of the whole curriculum, not an adjunct of science. In Layton's words, technology is 'a freshly-conceived, broad, balanced and progressive set of experiences designed to empower students in the field of practical capability and enable them to operate effectively and confidently in the made world'.

- The reference to the effective, creative and confident use of the knowledge and skills. These qualities include not only aesthetic sensitivity but the ability to find solutions to problems where compromises have to be made because of competing requirements, where resources are limited and where there are no existing guidelines to follow.

- The aims are described in terms of solving practical problems and under-taking tasks. This goes beyond the definitions of technology as solving problems relating to human need. Many tasks that are accomplished through technology (e.g. putting the letters in a stick of rock) have little to do with human need but are to serve other purposes, often commercial competition, personal preference or national status.

An important difference between science and technology lies in the way in which a solution to a problem is evaluated. As Layton (1993) points out, the overriding concern in science is that a theory or explanation should 'fit the facts'. But the products of technology must not only function as intended but also meet other criteria, such as 'environmental benignity, cost, aesthetic preferences, ergonomic requirements and market size. "Doing science" is different, therefore, from "doing technology"' (Layton 1993: 48). He goes on to state that scientific expertise 'is no guarantee of technological capability'.

Coming back to the classroom, we see some of these characteristics of technology in progress when children are building models, especially working ones, but in fact at all times when materials are used. There is some application of knowledge of materials, skill in fashioning them, compromise with the necessity of using the materials available and creativity in doing this to achieve the end result intended within the constraints of time and cost.

Distinguishing technological from scientific activities is important in teachers' minds because they are, as the above tries to show, different aspects of children's education. It makes sense, however, to continue to pursue both within the same topics and activities, just as these will also serve certain aims in mathematics, English and other subjects.

Other subjects

Looking at the relationship with other subjects from the point of view of helping scientific activity and understanding science, the matter does not end with mathematics and technology. History provides insights into how the accumulation of knowledge over the years has led to greater understanding of how things around us are explained. There are two aspects of this: how new ideas have emerged and what these ideas are. These two are the reasons given by the American Association for the Advancement of Science (1993) for including historical perspectives in *Benchmarks*.

There is also a strong relationship between science and art in its various forms, in that both help to reveal patterns in things around us that help in making links between one object or event and another. These patterns enable us to make predictions, not as much about what will happen in the future as about what we may find happening now if we try to find it. Science and art are also connected in the use and nature of the human senses and in a particularly enthralling way in such phenomena as optical illusions, colour perception and resonance.

Transition and transfer

As discussed earlier in this chapter, it is essential for continuity and progression that school staff work together to develop a shared vision of primary science. Once this shared vision has been negotiated, teamwork and mutual support continue to be needed to devise long-term plans and to transpose these into effective medium-term plans. Within a school that works together in this way the experience of pupils as they move up the school should be of smooth progression in terms of the concepts, skills and experiences of science. This was indeed one of Peacock's (1999) findings in a study of progression in schools in York. One way in which the transition from one teacher to the next can be achieved is through good quality record-keeping that all teachers use (see Nimmons 2003) and regular reviews of the curriculum.

It is perhaps because teachers in the same school often work together as a team to develop long-term plans that ensure continuity and progression that the problems of transition for pupils as they move from one school year to the next do not seem to be significant. However, difficulties for children have been much more keenly felt at transfer between primary and secondary schools, and more recently reported between early years and Year 1. It has been noted that there is reduction in the rate of improvement in pupils' attainment after transition from primary to secondary school. Galton *et al.* (2003) suggest that the reasons for this could include pupil anxiety, different teaching styles and teachers' ignorance of each other's curriculum content. In response to this a number of 'bridging projects' have been established to link the end of Year 6 with the start of Year 7. Many have used the Science Passport developed by ASE (Heslop 2002) for pupils to record their experiences and achievements inside and outside school to take on to the secondary school.

Box 22.5   A project to support transition from primary school to secondary school

Teresa Phillips and Graham Bray obtained funding for their outreach work with a number of secondary schools and their feeder primary schools. Teachers from the schools worked together to plan a bridging project that involved using the QCA scheme of work unit on reversible and irreversible change and the secondary school QCA scheme unit on energy resources. Pupils used data loggers to study temperature changes as they observed the irreversible change of washing soda added to vinegar, and magnesium ribbon added to vinegar. The data were plotted using appropriate software and analysed by the children.

In Year 7 the pupils considered energy released as a result of the irreversible change caused when burning fuel. They measured the rise in temperature of water heated by the fuels using data loggers.

Questionnaires given before and after the project revealed that the attitudes to science of boys in particular had been significantly improved, as had the attitudes of girls to the use of ICT. Teachers valued the smoothing of the transition for pupils.

(www.standards.dfes.gov.uk/keystage3/strands/?strand=science&year=trans23)

The key feature of all the bridging projects reported by Braund (2004) and others is that:

■ they result in a shared understanding by teachers of each other's curriculum and teaching styles;

■ they result in an increased confidence and understanding of the assessment information passed to secondary school;

■ pupils look forward more to the move to secondary school science.

All those reporting agree with McMahon and Davies (2003: 9) that 'It is unlikely to be enough for other schools to take up this project, or any other bridging project as a package without taking ownership of it through some process to establish a trusting relationship between teachers at each end of the transfer.'

Summary

This chapter has discussed the issue of long- and medium-term planning of science teaching. We have explored in particular the issues of topics and single subject teaching and put forward some arguments for both. The main ideas are:

■ Long-term planning within the school is the first level of implementation and interpretation of the school's policy for science. It is the articulation of the school's view of what primary science is.

■ Long- and medium-term planning must be considered in the light of the school's circumstances and the needs of the children.

■ Teamwork, sharing expertise, experience and ideas, enhances planning and helps to ensure a smooth transition from year to year, stage to stage and school to school.

■ Externally developed schemes of work are useful in supporting planning. But these must be adapted by the school to suit the needs of the learners and teachers.

■ There is value in making links between subjects, such as science with literacy or with numeracy. It is important to ensure that these links maximise learning opportunities in science and avoid the trap of making the science learning trivial.

■ Science has clear links with other subjects (especially with technology, but also with art, history and geography). It is important to ensure that, in planning, the particular characteristics of the individual subjects are not lost or confused. This makes considerable demands on teachers' knowledge and understanding.

23 Planning at the class level

In Chapter 22 we discussed the importance of long-term planning at the school level, and how this is translated into medium-terms plans, beginning the process of turning the school's approach to learning and teaching science into practice. The medium- and long-terms plans build in progression through the school and ensure that there are opportunities to revisit and develop earlier concepts. Lesson planning is done within this overall framework.

In this chapter we are concerned with the detailed planning that a teacher does in thinking through the purpose and aims of a lesson, what it is intended the children will learn, how this is to be achieved and what assessment opportunities will be taken. In Chapter 5 we took a *post hoc* look at the decisions a teacher made when planning a lesson. As we noted there, experienced teachers may not write everything down, but this does not mean that they do not plan in detail. We begin by considering the questions a teacher needs to consider as the planning process proceeds. We then consider, through some examples, how this is translated into planning notes, and how the lesson will be reviewed.

Thinking through planning a lesson

We can think of the planning process as falling into four stages. First, it is important to consider how the lesson arises from and contributes to the overall topic; then the specific learning objectives for the lesson need to be identified, appropriate activities selected and the broad outline of the lesson sketched out. After the lesson, the review and evaluation of what happened is an important input into future lessons and forms a link between the planning of one lesson and another.

Box 23.1	Stages in planning a lesson

Putting the lesson in context

1 What are the main 'big' ideas, skills and attitudes to be developed through this topic?

2 What have the children done before on this topic?

Setting the learning objectives (aims) and starting points

3 What do the children know and understand about the subject?

4 What ideas might they have?

5 What skills have the children developed?

Selecting the activities

6 What activities will engage the children's interest?

7 What questions will stimulate thinking?

8 What resources will be needed?

9 What are the opportunities for assessing children's progress?

Outlining the lesson

10 Thinking through plans.

11 Writing plans.

Putting the lesson in context

What are the main 'big' ideas skills and attitudes to be developed through this topic?

In answering this question the teacher needs to consider the long- and medium-term plans and the broad general topic to be addressed. For example, the class might be looking at transport as a topic, focusing on forces and movement, particularly on pushes and pulls. The areas of skills development might be predicting, gathering evidence by observing and interpreting evidence. The scientific attitudes include a willingness to consider evidence and to change ideas (see Chapter 6, page 67).

What have the children done before on this topic?

This is where the record-keeping of other teachers comes into its own. Clearly, when starting a new topic it is important to have some idea as to what topics have been covered, and in what depth, in order to establish an appropriate starting point. It is also useful to know the sorts of activities the children have done to avoid seeming to repeat work. If, for example, the children feel that they are rolling cars down slopes yet again, they will be less motivated to engage with the activity.

Setting the learning objectives (aims) and starting points

What do the children know and understand about the subject?

Within a topic ongoing assessment records are essential to ensure that children are not being asked to move on to bigger ideas before they have grasped the simpler ideas. This became apparent in Chris's lesson on ice melting (see Chapter 1, Box 1.2) where she noticed that some children needed more opportunities to explore ice, while others were able to consider the factors that affected melting and possibly the insulating properties of materials.

What ideas might the children have?

As we discussed in Chapter 2, children have a range of ideas that result from their attempts to make sense of their experiences. Research tells us, for example, that in many children's experience sound travels only through air. This would suggest that a lesson on sound, where the goal is to develop the idea that sound travels as vibrations through solids, liquids and gases, should include opportunities for children to observe sound travelling through different materials – the string telephone, for instance.

What skills have the children developed?

It is important to recognise that some children will have developed skills of planning, observing and collecting evidence to a higher degree than others. This may, for example, be important in determining how much support individual children will need during a lesson. When planning her topic on dissolving, Alice (see Box 22.1) knew from her assessment that certain children had not developed the skills of observation as far as others. This helped her to decide which children to support during the early part of their investigation.

Selecting the activities

What activities will engage the children's interest?

We took a preliminary look at the features of activities that make them learning experiences in Chapter 5. Activities that engage children need to be interesting, linked to their experience and accessible to all. One way to do this is to make the activities relevant to the broader topic and to what is happening in the children's daily lives. For example, children may be interested in what makes a snowman melt in winter, but on a hot day in summer they may be more engaged, and see the links more easily, if they consider how to avoid their ice-lolly melting. A quiz in the form of 'Who wants to be a millionaire' might engage children's interest more than a worksheet full of questions. This approach can also allow the teacher to target questions for particular children. When you are selecting activities, key scientific words can be identified that might also be introduced during the lesson (see Chapter 4).

What questions will stimulate thinking?

As we discussed in Chapter 3, the form and content of teachers' questions should match the purpose and the kind of response the teacher is seeking. It is therefore important to take the time to consider how key questions might be phrased, ensuring that questions are generally open and person-centred. It is no simple matter to formulate the best questions for finding out children's ideas and for developing them. So some 'starting' questions need to be thought out. These will match the stages of the lesson. For instance:

- Questions to elicit the children's current knowledge and understanding will include questions such as 'Have you noticed?' 'Do you remember when we . . . ?' These are followed by questions that ask for children's ideas about phenomena e.g. 'Tell me what you think happens . . . '

- Questions to encourage exploration of materials will include attention-focusing questions, such as 'What do you notice about your ice cube now?'

- During investigations, questions will encourage the children to think about what they are trying to find out with the observations and measurements they are making, e.g. 'What does this tell you about how the sound gets from here to there?'

- In the reporting and discussing stage, questions will help children to link their findings to what they were initially trying to find out, e.g. 'So what have we learned about the kind of soil that helps seedlings to grow best?'

- For reflecting on how the investigation was done: 'If you were to do this again, what would you change to make the investigation better?'

During the lesson more questions will arise, and it is not possible to anticipate exactly what ideas and questions the children will contribute. Being able to react to and work with children's responses to questions, and to the ideas and questions that they pose, is much more likely when lessons are well planned. One teacher wrote 'Being open and flexible, and willing to allow the children to follow their own thinking was an integral part of my planning' (Boctor and Rowell 2004).

Identifying appropriate resources

This is something that needs thinking about in advance. For example, in the lesson described in Box 19.1 the children were given a variety of cups and cans of different sizes, as well as string of different lengths, when exploring string telephones, and these needed to be carefully selected beforehand.

Identifying assessment opportunities

As we discussed in Chapter 13, when assessment is used to assist learning (formative assessment) decisions about what information to collect must be linked to the learning intentions of a lesson. It is important to decide beforehand what aspects of children's learning can be assessed and how this can be done by:

■ scrutinising children's written work, drawings and concept maps;

■ asking children questions and noting their responses;

■ observing children working;

■ discussing findings with children.

Teachers should also think about how to use any opportunities for helping the children to assess their own work (see Chapter 17).

Of course a teacher cannot gather detailed information by observation, questioning and discussion for all the children, so it is necessary to identify which group or individuals to focus on in a particular lesson. This is where looking back at assessment records can be useful. Thus, for example, when Alice thought through her lesson (see Box 22.1) she identified, from her records, which children might struggle with observation. She knew they would need her support and so decided to take this opportunity to assess their observation skills and use this to see how best to help their progress.

Outlining the lesson

Thinking through plans

As we have mentioned above, experienced teachers may not write down everything they plan to do down in meticulous detail. One teacher, when asked about her plans, said 'Oh, I didn't plan it'. Yet she immediately went on to say:

I mean, once you have the objectives clear in your head then you start to think about just what might grab them, and what activities we can do. I can be walking down the street and suddenly I see something that would be perfect for a particular lesson... I like to be a bit flexible, to have space to move a bit. I like to go by their ideas too.

Clearly, what this teacher meant was that she did not write the lesson down in detail, but she has quickly described the first part of the planning process, determining the aims and selecting the starter activities. Her actual written plans were sketchier, with resources listed and some key questions written out. What the process of writing lesson plans does is to facilitate thinking, to help to order ideas and to ensure, through some sort of planning pro forma, that all aspects have been covered.

DATE: 9/2/04   TIME: 1.30- 3.15   SUBJECT: Science

YR GROUP: Six

Any inclusion issues? 7 of the 24 children in this class have special educational needs.

■ Details given for classroom assistant (CA)
All of the above children respond very well to praise and a positive, secure classroom environment.

Assessment that has informed this lesson/prior learning. Work already undertaken in this unit has informed the planning of this lesson; see medium-term planning for details of previous lessons. Assessments recorded by last year's class teacher, especially of Unit 5D.

Lesson objectives:

■ To understand ways in which solids can be made to dissolve faster.

■ To plan and carry out a fair test.

■ To decide what apparatus to use and to make careful measurements.

Vocabulary: soluble, dissolve, fair test, reliable, average, rate, volume, particle, factors, control, variable	*Deployment LSAs:* CA will monitor ch's listening during whole class activities (particularly those who have IEPs for behaviour). CA to work with Blue group. Assess understanding of the processes (fair test, careful measurements)
Introduction/starting points: As a starter activity/recap, children will respond to statements on interactive whiteboard with either true or false cards. Establish what happens when a solid dissolves in a liquid. Show slide 25/26 PowerPoint. ■ Share the lesson objectives. Ask the children to suggest everyday examples of dissolving solids in water, *sugar in tea, salt in water for cooking.* ■ Ask children to suggest ways in which they could make a solid dissolve faster (establish factors: stirring, temperature, size of particles, volume of water; *PowerPoint slide 36 to reinforce factors*).	*Resources:* vacuum flasks, stop watches, beakers, spoons, measuring jugs, range of sugars, thermometers, planning sheets

Development/main activity (including differentiation):
Children are grouped by ability.

■ Guide children towards specific questions they will investigate, e.g.
  – Does the temperature of water affect how quickly the sugar dissolves?
  – Does the number of times you stir affect how quickly sugar dissolves?
  – Does the size of the sugar particles affect how quickly sugar dissolves?

■ Children will go back to their seats and work in groups to establish the factors they will change and control, and what they will measure. Discuss each group's planning board and reinforce the children's understanding of the importance of controlling factors to ensure a fair test.

■ Children will be given a differentiated planning sheet and will begin to plan their investigations carefully. CA to support SENs in their planning. Higher ability children will have to choose apparatus more carefully as they will be provided with equipment that they may not need. Work with each group to ensure they are planning a fair test.

■ Children begin to carry out their tests. On each table, children will split up into two groups looking at the same factors. Each group will carry out the test. Ask children why they might repeat their tests. Instead of repeating test, the two groups on each table will swap their results and then an average can be found.

■ Children put their results into a table. Blue group will have a pre-prepared results table to complete. Red group will have the framework. Green group will have to construct their own tables to record results.

■ Children will complete their tests and draw conclusions. Blues will have a cloze passage to complete related to their investigation. Reds and Greens will be expected to record their own conclusions.

Plenary: draw together the results. Talk to the children about their findings. Start off with group exploring size of particles, use PowerPoint slides 39/40. Describe the relationships between the various factors and the rate at which sugar dissolves. Complete sentences on interactive board. Look at slide 80 to finish. Link back to learning objectives.

Assessment opportunities: Through open and closed questions, group work, individual work.	**Cross-curricular links:** Maths – interpreting results, data handling.

Figure 23.1 Julie's lesson plan: rate of dissolving

Writing plans

In this section we look at two example lesson plans. The first is written by a teacher who has a Year 6 class for the first time in her four-year career (Figure 23.1). Her planning, using the school's lesson plan structure, helped her to think through the lesson as well as to communicate to others (in particular the classroom assistant) what it is she intended to do in the lesson. We can consider Julie's plan in relation to the headings discussed above.

Putting the lesson in context. Julie's lesson plan is clearly situated in the medium-term plans and is linked to previous work in earlier years. She also wants the children to collect data, which will form the focus of the next lesson on understanding and using line graphs and bar charts.

Learning objectives (aims) and starting points. Julie has used her medium-term plans, along with the previous teacher's assessment, to determine the broad learning objectives of the lesson. Her starter activity involves a quiz on the interactive whiteboard, which allows her to check the children's understanding, and enables them to recall work done on the topic in the previous year. This is to be followed up by a more open discussion making links to children's everyday experiences. In this way she can assess the children's current understanding and quickly move into the investigation.

Selecting activities. Assessment evidence suggested that most of the children's ideas about dissolving were well established. In this lesson her focus was much more on developing and reinforcing their process skills. In order to underline the need for care and accuracy science equipment (beakers and stirring rods) was used.

Julie has made clear reference in her planning to the assessments to be made by the classroom assistant, but is somewhat less detailed about how and what she will assess. However, during the lesson she used the starter activities to assess knowledge about dissolving; this was done through the quiz, where she was able to select specific questions for individuals. She then focused on observation and questioning to assess understanding of fair testing and accuracy of measurement. She asked questions such as 'Do you think you would get exactly the same result if you did the experiment again?' 'Do you think the amount of stirring matters?'

Chris has been teaching for over twenty years. She currently teaches a year 2 class. Her lesson is described in Chapter 1, Box 1.2. Her lesson plan (Figure 23.2) was far less detailed than Julie's, but it reflects the detailed thinking that is the crucial element of planning.

Putting the lesson in context. The lesson fits in with the wider cross-curricular context, although this is not articulated in the plan.

Lesson objectives and starting points. The lesson was a risk, in that Chris had not approached this topic in quite this way before, although she was quite clear about her objectives. She wanted to set the scene on the topic of ice to enable literacy and science to be drawn out of it. Lots of 'icy' words and ideas about ice were central.

Appropriate activities. The outline of the lesson consists of notes that would not communicate much to others. However, it is interesting that she actually writes down some of the questions she will ask. She had printed out cards with 'Questions from the penguins' on them, but she did not use these in the lesson,

Class 2W	Date 8 Feb	Time 30 mins a.m. 1.10–3.15 p.m.	Staff Sally (a.m. only)
Topic Penguins and ice			

Subject focus a.m. Science and literacy (see daily plan for literacy p.m. Science	**Links to scheme** QCA – grouping and changing materials
	Cross-curricular links Literacy

Objectives
- To develop words to describe ice and water (cold, wet, hard, melt, runny)
- To describe how ice feels
- To understand that ice is frozen water
- Make predictions
- Begin to understand 'fair testing'

Activities and Organisation

Iceberg ⟶ cold places ⟶ what do we know about ice?

'Look after this ice cube'

Penguins (big book) ⟶ equal chance, fair test

Insulation
Can we help penguins to keep ice for longer? Do you think ice cubes melt more or less quickly in a hot place or a cold place? How could we find out which is the coolest place to keep the penguins' ice cubes

⟶ Big ice cube (fair test)

Investigation
What do we know about ice now? Can we get it back? How can we get the ice back for the penguins?

Resources Bag of ice Trays of ice cubes, one large ice cube Dishes – jug to collect melted ice in Extra paper towels Question sheet Prediction and results sheet	**Desirable outcomes** Can describe ice (all), know that ice melts in warm (all) Understand idea of making a fair test (most) Can make a prediction and say why (some) Can record prediction on sheet (few)
Assessment opportunities	

Figure 23.2 Chris's lesson plan: penguins and ice

as her open questioning indicated that children would struggle to engage with the questions, and that if they did tackle them it might detract from their hands-on experiences with the ice.

Assessment opportunities are not detailed, although, after the lesson, Chris was able to identify the children who had difficulty with predictions and those who did not comprehend the investigation fully.

Evaluation and review

Inevitably the discussion of this post-lesson reflection comes at the end of the chapter. However, the end of one lesson is, in many cases, the beginning of the next. Throughout a lesson, and afterwards, teachers reflect on how it went. The notion of reflection in and on practice is central to continuous professional learning (Shön 1993). Lesson evaluation is often overlooked in the hurly burly of the day, but it is crucial to ensuring quality in teaching.

When you are evaluating the lesson it is useful to keep in mind the criteria given in Chapter 5, pp. 49, 50. Were the activities interesting? Were they linked to their experience? Were they accessible to all? (Julie felt that the purchased quiz questions used at the start of the lesson were fun, but could have included some more challenging questions for the high achievers.) Could the children interact with materials? (The classroom assistant felt that some blue group pupils needed a little time to explore dissolving all over again before starting to plan their investigation.) Could they develop their scientific ideas? Could they develop their investigative skills? Could they develop scientific attitudes? Could they work cooperatively and share ideas in a supportive atmosphere?

Thinking through assessments made during the lesson and linking observations to the evaluation of the lesson can be a powerful way to begin the process of deciding where to go next. For example, when Chris considered her lesson she realised that some of the children had little experience of ice and needed more time to explore. This meant that they did not have full access to the investigation and so could not develop their scientific ideas as much as they might have done. She decided to set up an 'ice table' (including an ice balloon) for the rest of the week to provide further opportunities for exploration. When judgements have been made based on in-lesson assessments a record needs to be made to inform future planning (this is discussed further in Chapter 24).

Summary

This chapter has been about the process of planning lessons. Written plans are the product of thinking through the details of the children's and the teacher's parts in the lesson. Ready-made plans, such as are available on the Internet, cannot replace a teacher's own thinking and planning. The main points have been:

- Lesson planning should be done within the supporting framework of the long- and medium-term plans.

- The process of lesson planning has stages: setting the lesson in context, identifying the learning objectives and starting points, planning the sequence of the lesson and the activities within it. Planning the questions to ask is an important part of the process, as is planning for assessment to help learning.

- Planning is a process that takes place in the teacher's head. Written plans support that process because writing helps thinking. They also enable plans to be shared with others.

- Evaluation and review of each lesson feeds into the planning of future ones.

24 Recording and reporting

Introduction

Recording systems are crucial to ensuring continuity and progression for individuals and groups within a class and, as with formative assessment, they need to be built into the teaching process. The form and structure of a recording system needs to be tailored to the requirements of the school, to the curriculum organisation that is in place and to the teaching methods that are employed.

Record-keeping needs to be the subject of whole-school discussion. The science subject leader working with other subject leaders will wish to establish an appropriate general approach to recording that works for all subject areas and that teachers understand and feel comfortable with. It is also important that individual teachers feel able to adapt the system to suit their needs in their day-to-day recording. What is essential is a system that staff (including support staff) can use easily and that will be valuable in supporting planning. Most schemes of work provide suggested recording systems, although it is unlikely that any one would fit the requirements of a school without some modification. In this chapter we present a general discussion of the issues, rather than a review of different systems, focusing on the different purposes served by the records kept in school.

We first consider the various purposes or functions of recording. We then move on to discuss records of activities, which are distinct from records of what children have learned from their activities. Records of what children have learned are discussed in the subsequent sections. We then consider ways in which children's involvement in their own learning can be supported by encouraging them to keep records of their own development, and conclude with a brief comment on summative records, particularly reports to parents.

Functions of a record

Any record is a means of communication and can serve a number of purposes. Box 24.1 indicates the different audiences for recorded information. The amount of detail required increases as we move down the table to that required by the class teacher. The needs of children and parents are somewhat different, as we discuss below. We will begin by considering the record a class teacher needs in order to plan appropriately.

Box 24.1	Audience, purpose and form of record required	
Audience	*Purpose*	*Form of record*
The local authority/or government agency	To enable: • comparisons to be made across schools and areas; • targeting of additional support where performance in particular areas is poor	Summary data drawn from test results and teacher assessment at set points submitted in a standard format
The school management (subject leader, school governors)	To inform the school development plan, to identify areas of strength and weakness and so help in long- and medium-term planning	Summary data indicating aspects of the school scheme of work that are particularly effective and those where improvements might be made
Future teachers (including those in other schools)	To ensure smooth transition between year groups and schools, to aid planning at the appropriate level for the child and to avoid repetition	Broad indications of attainment, and activities experienced by each child
Other educators working with the children (e.g. special needs coordinator, or 'gifted and talented' teacher, 'catch-up' lesson teacher)	To pass on concise information about attainment and teacher and pupil insights about attitudes and motivations	Indications of attainment in knowledge and understanding of concepts and processes, as well as attitudes
Class teacher	To recall previous achievement, to ensure appropriate coverage of ideas, and so to aid planning To establish what aspects have been covered in order to avoid repetition, and select appropriate future activities	Sufficient detail to enable planning to take account of different pupils' needs Details of what has been covered in terms of activities

| The children | To ensure that children are actively involved in their own learning (see Chapter 14) | Simple record that children can understand and use, linked to the learning outcomes communicated to the child during lessons |
| Parents and carers | To keep parents/carers informed and involved in their children's education | Detail about progress and next steps in a language that communicates with non-specialists |

Records of activities of individual children

Unless all the children in a class invariably work on the same activities as each other, there is a need for a system that records what individuals have actually been engaged upon. Indeed, even if the activities were the same for all it would be no guarantee that their *experiences* would be identical, since children attend selectively to different parts of the work, extend some and give scant attention to others. They also become diverted into unplanned avenues to follow their own questions. This is a useful reminder that we can never know exactly what each child has experienced, and in order not to give the false impression that we can it is better to record activities encountered than to pretend to be more precise about exactly what each child has experienced through it.

Box 24.2   Keeping track of coverage

An early years class was undertaking a topic on 'our new school', in which they considered a wide variety of aspects of the Foundation Stage Curriculum, including knowledge and understanding of the world. A new school building was being erected in the grounds of their very old school. The children talked to parents who had attended the school as children, discussed old photographs and considered how people felt about their old school being knocked down. Within 'knowledge and understanding of the world' the focus in science was to 'investigate objects and materials by using all of their senses as appropriate' (DfEE/QCA 2000). The children explored building materials and thought about how to build a stable wall. Within the topic there were many opportunities to develop understanding. For example, an activity table of various play bricks was used to encourage building and testing the strength of a wall. The children were also able to test the properties of different materials (squashy, breaks easily, goes runny when wet) to see which might be good to build with. By the end of the week teachers wanted to be sure that all children had experienced each of these activities. They kept a chart for each activity table, so that children could record their visit to the table (using laminated name labels to stick on a wall chart). At the end of the week gaps could be easily spotted and recorded.

It is not always possible, or appropriate, for every child to undertake every activity. For example, in the class exploring string telephones, as described in Box 19.1, the children put forward ideas they wanted to test and each pair conducted a different investigation. Children then presented their findings to the rest of the class. In this case the different activities were intended to address the same concepts. In other cases activities undertaken in different contexts can be seen as equivalent, in the sense that they are intended to meet the same objectives. For example, the class described in Box 24.2 were to address the same objectives in another topic in the next week on 'The gingerbread man'. They would have the opportunity to investigate ways to keep a gingerbread man dry and, in baking, would examine a variety of materials using their senses. What is to be avoided is the same children missing out on all experiences relating to materials for any reason, such as absence or lack of engagement with an activity.

In the early years when most work is cross-curricular there is an obvious need to keep a record of activities; however, the same is true for older children. In many cases groups of children will have undertaken the same activities but the individual record means that absences and changes of group composition are taken into account. Certain activities will probably be regarded as equivalent to each other (as in Figure 24.1), while in other cases it may be that the context is so different that repetition is desirable. Taking these things into account, the teacher will use the record to keep an eye on the gaps in the activities of individual children and act on this, either in planning the next term's work or by having one or two sessions in which children are directed to activities they have missed.

It is helpful to distinguish between topics (such as 'feet' or 'movement') and the particular activities within them. By listing topics and activities, a record such as Figure 24.1 indicates the context in which the activities were carried out. Such a record could include all the activities within a topic, but it is less cumbersome if different records are kept for the science, language, mathematics and other activities within the topics.

Ongoing records of children's achievement

The records kept concerning the ongoing achievements of individuals in a class are necessarily detailed. Ongoing assessment used as formative assessment involves making judgements about achievement, which in turn inform the next steps in learning. During a single lesson the teacher may use on-the-spot assessments to move children on immediately. However, lessons are time-limited, while learning should continue from one lesson to another, term to term and year-to-year. It is for this reason that recording systems are so important. It must therefore be kept in mind that:

■ the overriding purpose is to help the teacher to remember where each child has reached in his or her development so that suitable activities and encouragement can be given;

Class ....   Term ....

Topic	Our New School (Week 4)		The Gingerbread Man (Week 6)		
Activity	Build a wall	Explore building materials	Baking	Rain cape for Gingerbread	Judge the best Gingerbread man
Goals	Prediction Describes what they did	Investigates using senses Appropriate language	Uses senses to explore Appropriate language	Investigates materials Prediction Describes what they did	Describes simple features Compares features
Ali					
Sam					
Charlene					
etc					

Figure 24.1 Record of science activities undertaken within topics

- these records are for the teacher's own use and so the level of detail can be adjusted to suit the individual's ways of working;

- they will be summarised for other purposes, for school records passed from class to class and for reporting to parents.

Teachers vary as to how much information they can carry in their head and how much they like to write down, and this may be one of the factors which leads to a preference for a checklist, or for a more detailed pro forma that gives space for comments, caveats and explanations. However, systems for recording achievement need to be simple and, in most cases, understandable by others. This is particularly important in cases where a classroom assistant or other adult is to undertake the assessment. For example in Julie's lesson (see Figure 23.1) she indicates that the classroom assistant would undertake an assessment of the less able group he was working with. The class teacher and her assistants in the nursery class described in Figure 24.2 use a simple record for each topic, as shown in Fig 24.2. These records form the basis of discussions between the class teacher and her assistant and in turn contribute to the individual records for each child (looking down the columns) and help to identify aspects to focus on in forthcoming topics (looking across the rows).

Nursery – Mrs Cole and Mrs Kahn - Week 4

Building a new school –

Knowledge and Understanding of the world

Objective	Ali	Sam	Charlene	Kylie 1	David	Liam	Leanne	Kylie 2	India
Tests Strength of materials	✓	✓	✓	✓	✓	✓	✓	O	✓
Able to make prediction	✓	✗	✓	✓	✓	✗	✗	O	✓
Describes what he/she did	✗	✓	✓	✓	✓	✓	✓	O	✓
Investigates objects/materials using all senses	✓	✓	✓	✓	✓	✗	✓	✓	✓
Uses appropriate language to describe objects/materials *(Smelly Squashy hard, Cold etc.)*	✗	✓	✓	✓	✓	✓	✓	✓	✓
Comment	Facial expression etc. but not speaking					Needs to slow down too rushed		Did not do wall.	

Figure 24.2 Simple topic record sheet

As we saw in Chapters 22 and 23, teachers may focus attention on one group at a time and will rarely have the opportunity to observe and assess all the children in a class in this way during a single activity. Records need to be kept in order to identify and fill the gaps. Keeping track of assessments made, particularly in respect of process skills and attitudes, which develop throughout the year, is important to building up a full picture of the child's progress.

Individual records of the sort in Figure 24.3 can serve these purposes. They are designed to be used to record assessment against the indicators of development discussed in Chapter 16. In observing children in her Year 2 class (see Box 1.2) Chris noted that some children were holding their hands out to try to test the temperature in different parts of the room. She noted these children earlier exploring their ice cubes by looking at them, feeling them and tasting them. She could feel sure that these children had demonstrated their ability to use a range of senses in exploring objects. Further observation in lessons where children were being asked to compare materials might demonstrate better-developed skills among some of the children. As many teachers today keep their records on computer it is a simple matter to update records at regular intervals. In this example the record would be in terms of development in gathering evidence from observations and information sources. The areas of knowledge covered will not be the same from half term to half term, but the 'ideas' can be written in as appropriate. However, the skills and attitudes are likely to be widely relevant and so should be covered whatever the subject matter of the activities.

Science profile. Child's name: Date:

	Indication of Development Write in indicators applying
Ideas about	
Living things and life processes	
Interaction of living things	
Materials	
etc.	
Process skills and attitudes	
Gathering evidence by observing etc.	
Questioning, predicting and planning	
Interpreting evidence and drawing conclusions	
Communicating and reflecting	
Willingness to consider evidence and change ideas	
Sensitivity to living things and the environment	

Figure 24.3 Individual science profile: cumulative record

Many teachers will feel that the problem of records of this kind is not that they contain too much information but that they contain too little. The richness and complexity of children's performance can rarely be captured in a brief note (and even less by a tick). In many systems, therefore, these records are only a part of the material that is available to a teacher about individual children. Samples of work, chosen by the child and/or the teacher, and more extensive notes may be kept in a file for each child.

Involving children in keeping records

In Chapter 17 we discussed the importance of involving children in assessing their work. It is now common practice for teachers to share the learning goals with their children at the start of the lesson. As we saw in Chapter 23, Julie's lesson plan (Figure 23.1) includes an explicit mention of sharing goals with the children. In Chris's plan (Figure 23.2) she began by asking the children what they know about ice and ended the session asking 'What do we know about ice now?' In Chapter 17 we discussed the various strategies teachers can use to teach children how to make judgements about the quality of their work, how they might consider how to use criteria to make these judgements and how, for older children, this can involve interrogation of the criteria set down in local or National Curriculum guidelines.

We made mention earlier in this chapter of nursery class children recording the completion of particular activities by posting their name on a chart. The next logical step is for children to keep their own records of their achievements, although perhaps when the children are a little older. A number of approaches have been adopted to facilitate this. In some schools the learning objectives are always written on the bottom of worksheets, or put on the board. These objectives are often presented in child-friendly language. Children are asked to indicate with smiley (or otherwise) faces, ticks, comments or traffic lights (see Chapter 17 page 180) how far they feel they have achieved the goals. Teachers can then moderate this judgement as they make their own records. Children may then mark off the objectives met on an appropriate recording device. In one school even the general class records are couched in terms that the children might use (Nimmons 2003). This is not strictly necessary as these are the teacher's records, not those of the children. It simply reflects the fact that teachers have 'translated' the learning outcomes into a language that the children can understand and use. Because the teachers regularly discuss these outcomes with their children, this teacher, out of habit, has used them in her records.

The record in Figure 24.4 is a group record. Individual children can keep records that are more appropriate to their own needs. One approach to this was published by the ASE (Willis 1999). This takes the form of the statements relating to the programmes of study of the National Curriculum. Each statement is written on a 'brick in the wall', with statements moving from the bottom of the wall (Key Stage 1) to the top. Children can shade in the 'bricks' when they believe they have achieved them. This is probably best done in discussion with the teacher. Willis's wall was devised before the current version of the National Curriculum was published, but the principle remains a useful one.

Year 5 – Changing state Unit 5D

	Marilyn	Kirsty	Jerode	Shanize	Chas	Tracy	Emilie	Suzanne	Fedel	Shinade	Monique	Adeel	Nathan	Jamie	Santino	Soubhagya	Soraia	Namrata	Khalid	Jerome	Felix	Survir	Valdrini	Rielle	Asher	No. not achieved
I have experimented to find out about some of the differences between ice, water and steam	✓	✓	✓	✓	✓	✓	✓	✓	✓	✓	✓	✓	✓	✓	✓	✓	✓	✓	✓	✓	✓	✓	✓	✓	✓	0
I know what happens when water 'disappears'	✓	✓	✓	✗	✗	✓	✓	✓	✗	✓	✓	✓	✓	✓	✓	✓	✗	✓	✓	✗	✓	✓	✗	✗	✓	6
I have found out how other liquids evaporate	✗	✗	✗	✗	✗	✗	✗	✗	✗	✗	✗	✗	✗	✗	✗	✗	✗	✗	✗	✗	✗	✗	✗	✗	✗	25
I have investigated different conditions that can affect the rate of evaporation	✓	✓	✓	✓	✓	✓	✓	✓	✓	✓	✓	✓	✓	✓	✓	✓	✓	✓	✓	✓	✓	✓	✓	✓	✓	0
I have found out how to boil and also evaporate water and then change it back to water again	✓	✓	✓	✓	✓	✓	✓	✓	✓	✓	✓	✓	✓	✓	✓	✓	✓	✓	✓	✓	✓	✓	✓	✓	✓	0
I have found out about the water cycle. I know what 'evaporation' and 'condensation' mean in it	✓	✓	✓	✗	✗	✓	✓	✓	✗	✓	✓	✓	✓	✗	✓	✓	✓	✓	✓	✗	✓	✓	✗	✗	✓	6
I know the 'boiling temperature' and 'freezing temperature' of water	✓	✓	✓	✗	✗	✓	✓	✓	✓	✓	✓	✓	✓	✗	✓	✓	✓	✓	✗	✓	✗	✗	✗	✓	✓	7
I know how to change water into ice and make it into water again	✓	✓	✓	✗	✗	✓	✓	✓	✓	✓	✓	✓	✓	✗	✓	✓	✓	✓	✗	✓	✗	✗	✗	✓	✓	7
I know how to make chocolate liquid and make it solid again	✓	✓	✓	✗	✗	✓	✓	✓	✓	✓	✓	✓	✓	✗	✓	✓	✓	✓	✗	✗	✗	✗	✗	✓	✓	7
I can use a temperature sensor, and create a graph on the computer	✗	✗	✗	✗	✗	✗	✗	✗	✗	✗	✗	✗	✗	✗	✗	✗	✗	✗	✗	✗	✗	✗	✗	✗	✗	25
I can suggest what might happen and explain why	✓	✓	✓	✗	✗	✓	✓	✓	✓	✓	✓	✓	✓	✓	✓	✓	✗	✓	✗	✓	✓	✓	✗	✗	✓	6
I can write clear accounts and explain my results using my scientific knowledge	✓	✓	✗	✗	✗	✓	✓	✓	✓	✓	✓	✓	✓	✗	✓	✓	✓	✓	✗	✓	✗	✓	✗	✓	✓	8

Resource implications: no temperature sensor in school.

Targets: suggest what might happen and explain why.
begin to use science knowledge to explain results.

Figure 24.4 A completed end-of-unit record sheet with coordinator's action points (adapted from Nimmons 2003)

The most important factor in pupil records of attainment is that they are able to see how they have developed and are aware of how they may develop in the near future. This will no doubt contribute when teachers are preparing summative reports for parents and other teachers, but the main purpose, as specified in Box 24.1, is to promote the active involvement of children in their own learning.

Summative records

In this section we focus on reviewing and summing up of records of ongoing assessments made by teachers. This may, from time to time, include information from tests, either devised by the teacher or externally published tests. This information can contribute to an overall view of a child's performance, and is often used to moderate teachers' judgements. But the value of regular ongoing assessment and recording should not be underestimated. Teachers' records will cover a wider, more comprehensive range of opportunities for children to demonstrate their learning. This evidence should then have primacy in the construction of summative records to be passed on to other teachers and schools. As can be deduced from Box 24.1, there are two purposes for summative records:

- those for use within the school for keeping track of the progress of individual children as they move through the school and to other schools;

- those which are intended for reporting at a particular time to a specific audience, such as local education authorities or national agencies.

There has been a significant increase in recent years in the sophistication and detail with which data are gathered and manipulated for the purposes of comparing the performance of schools or specific areas. These data are now used extensively by head teachers, often in negotiation with local authority officers to set targets for the attainment of year groups of children within the school. These charts and tables can enable teachers to compare their school's performance with other similar schools, but it must be borne in mind that more and more sophisticated analysis of assessment data will not in itself improve performance, and remains only as good as the assessment information put into the system.

For cumulative records that are designed to keep track of progress, the same structure can be used as in the ongoing record from which it is derived; that is, in terms of the aspects of learning which have been achieved, adding information at different dates to a record such as Figure 24.3. A slightly different and simple approach is to list all the target or goal statements at each level on a form for each child and to highlight those achieved, using a different colour at the end of each year (a very similar approach to the wall described above for children to use).

One of the observations often made by secondary school teachers is that the records that come to them from primary schools are too detailed and so are not useful. Part of the reason for this is a lack of shared understanding of the meaning of the records received. This is discussed briefly in Chapter 22 (page 245) in the section on transition. Where documents are being transferred within school this problem should be less acute, but receiving teachers may find it difficult to use detailed information because they have the records for a whole class to take on board. A summary of levels of achievement may be most useful, providing that all teachers involved have a consistent interpretation of the meaning of the levels. Additional information is important, pointing out the particular help that a child may need or the kinds of encouragement to which he or she responds. More detailed information, for reference if required, could be provided by supplying, in addition, a copy of the cumulative record.

Science

Throughout the year David has participated in a range of scientific activities. He understands that scientific ideas are based on evidence. He is willing to change his ideas when the evidence suggests it. He is usually able to carry out a fair test. When writing up his investigations he can suggest a number of ways of presenting information and usually chooses a good method of recording information.

He has gained a good knowledge of life processes and living things. He can name the major organs in the human and can show where they are in the body. He can describe feeding relationships using food chains and knows what words such as 'predator and prey' mean. He made an excellent poster about food chains with his group that is still up in the corridor.

He describes differences between properties of materials with confidence and can explain how we use these differences to classify materials. He can describe a number of methods to separate mixtures. He has a good level of knowledge and understanding of the physical processes.

Next steps

In the next term we will be carrying out more investigations. David should concentrate on fair testing and thinking about the best way to record information. He might like to take home the activity box 'Inventors and inventions' as I am sure he would enjoy it.

Next term our topics will be Sound and Music and the Earth, Sun and Moon.

Figure 24.5 End-of-year report to parents or carers

Reporting to parents or carers

In recent years schools have placed increased emphasis on working closely with parents, and helping them to understand the school's approach to teaching and learning and how important parents are as the principal educators of their children. Many schools invite parents to join in activities such as science weeks, or trips to places of interest. Schools provide a good deal of information to parents in newsletters, on websites and at open evenings, and many now send activity boxes home for parents and children to use. School reports continue to provide a valuable opportunity to give a snapshot of a child's progress in school. These reports need to be straightforward, informative and focused on the child.

Parents may find the detail of different aspects of achievement too great to answer their main need to know how their child is doing in science. Remembering that parents will have to be taking in information about all areas of the curriculum, there is clearly a limit to how useful it is to subdivide each one to any extent. Open comment is important to help to summarise and interpret the meaning of the 'levels' achieved and to add other information about attitudes, effort and extracurricular activities. Figure 24.5 shows the report for a nine-year-old boy. The teacher has used quite a lot of the language of the National Curriculum, but has added personal notes – for example, about the poster – that indicate David's skills in communicating evidence. She has also given information about the topics to be covered next and the next steps in David's learning, in particular in terms of process skills. She has used this opportunity to suggest some work at home that might help to move David on within Attainment Target 1 of the National Curriculum statements of attainment. A reply slip and individual parent–teacher interviews a week or so after the reports are sent home encourage dialogue between parents and teacher.

Summary

- It is important to separate records of activities undertaken from records of learning achieved.

- Teachers' own records of assessments made as part of teaching need to be recorded in sufficient detail for them to be useful in aiding planning.

- Summative records serve different purposes and the level of detail is less than for formative purposes, depending on the use to be made of the information.

- Cumulative records of learning can be made on a single record pro forma by adding information at different times.

- As part of their involvement with their own learning, children should be aware of and play a part in the assessment process. They can usefully keep ongoing information that enables them to record their activities and monitor their achievements.

- Summative records for other teachers and for parents indicate what has been achieved at a particular time and useful next steps.

25 The science subject leader

In this chapter we discuss issues in relation to planning provision for science from the point of view of the subject coordinator or subject leader. The concern here is with both the developing philosophy of the school in terms of the direction in which primary science is moving (this is perhaps the leadership element of the role) and the more technical management issues that need to be addressed for science to be properly planned and implemented in school. The science coordinator has the role of leading and supporting science in school.

The roles of the subject leader

Since 1998 there has been in England and Wales a national framework for the role of the teacher who takes on a subject leadership, which is relevant to all subjects. This sets out the role in an extensive, and somewhat daunting, list of tasks under four headings. Some examples of the tasks are:

Strategic direction and development of the subject

- Develop policy and practices.
- Create climate of positive attitudes to the subject and confidence in teaching it.

Teaching and learning

- Ensure curriculum coverage and progression for all pupils.
- Ensure teachers are clear about objectives and sequences and communicate these to pupils.

Leading and managing staff

- Help staff achieve constructive working relationships with pupils.

■ Establish clear expectations and constructive working relationships among staff.

Effective and efficient deployment of staff and resources

■ Establish staff and resource needs for the subject and advise the head teacher.

■ Advise the head teacher on the best use of colleagues.

(TTA 1998)

These are decidedly demanding tasks but indicate the intention that individual teachers should have support in the school and that the overall programme should be planned and coordinated. The sheer range of tasks to be performed means that it is easier to consider the subject leader as fulfilling several roles.

The coordinator as a leader

A key message from schools inspectors and others who visit schools is that the quality of science teaching depends not simply on individuals but on the teachers and other staff in a school having a shared understanding of what the subject is and what they are trying to achieve. This vision comes from a knowledge of the subject area and what it contributes to the whole child, and what the options are for implementing the vision. In the view of Nimmons (2003), one element of this is keeping up to date with new ideas, resources, research findings and learning from best practice, and sharing these insights. The subject leader, whatever the subject, should be in a position to lead, help and advise on issues related to their subject.

There is no point in having a clear view of the strategic direction for the school if this is not communicated or shared with colleagues, yet according to a study by Ritchie (1998) most coordinators saw their role mainly as writing or reviewing the science policy, producing or modifying schemes of work, ordering and looking after equipment and advising staff, with most of their time taken up with equipment issues. Fletcher (2000) argues that most primary teachers do not see their role as leader in the sense that others should follow; teachers feel happier with a collegial approach in which, perhaps, one member of staff oversees development but all are working together to a common aim. This is not in conflict with the role of leadership as long as the school structures promote this collegiality. One example of a structure that promotes collegiality is reported by Barr (2003) in Box 25.1.

Box 25.1   The role of one subject leader as part of a team

At Brindishe School a system of teams with team leaders is used to manage all subject work throughout the school. The science and technology team consists of three teachers, a classroom assistant, the school's 'housekeeper' and the subject leader.

The planning cycle in the school begins in June with a whole-school INSET/ development day. During that meeting the development plan is reviewed, enabling all team leaders to reflect on their own area of responsibility and on achievements throughout the year. The staff (including classroom assistants as well as senior teachers) then start to put forward ideas for the following year. These are collated and drawn together by the head teacher when revising the school plan for the year. The team leaders then arrange meetings with their team to develop the plans for the coming year. Because everyone is part of more than one team, plans within any subject area are not independent of what is being developed by other teams.

Although the subject leader has a number of responsibilities in this school (analysis of assessment data, liasing with senior managers, staff development , lesson audits etc.), the team approach ensures a shared understanding and a shared sense of achievement.

The science subject leader as an advisor

A major element of the subject leader's role is to advise other colleagues. This requires sensitivity, as some teachers may feel less than confident, for example, about their subject knowledge of science concepts and about process skills. Some may feel a lack of confidence in teaching aspects of the science curriculum, in terms of teaching the concepts of science, but many teachers also lack confidence in teaching enquiry skills. On the other hand, newly qualified teachers may, because of an increased emphasis on subject knowledge in the initial training curriculum, arrive with a sound knowledge of the subject but be in need of mentoring and guidance to understand how children learn and how to approach teaching them science. How the subject leader addresses this issue partly depends on the view of what is needed to be an effective primary science teacher.

The question of the extent to which a primary teacher who is a generalist has the knowledge to provide learning activities containing the necessary challenge for children throughout the primary school is a contentious issue. The arguments are clouded when the concept of 'teacher's knowledge' is reduced to knowledge of the subject matter, with little regard for other kinds of knowledge that are involved in teaching.

It is through the work and writing of Lee Shulman and some other science educators in the USA that the kinds of knowledge needed in teaching have been set out. Writing in relation to science teaching, Shulman (1987) lists the following kinds of knowledge as being required by the teacher:

■ content knowledge, about science and of science;

■ general pedagogical knowledge, about classroom management and organisation, non-subject specific;

■ curriculum knowledge, guidelines, national requirements, materials available;

■ pedagogical content knowledge, about how to teach the subject matter, including useful illustrations, powerful analogies and examples;

■ knowledge of learners and their characteristics;

■ knowledge of educational contexts;

■ knowledge of educational goals, values and purposes, including the history and philosophy of education.

It is significant that Shulman puts content knowledge first in this list, since several of the subsequent items depend on it. But what he emphasises is not as much the mastery of each and every aspect of a subject as an understanding of what it is that identifies science; how the discipline of science differs from other disciplines; its boundaries, its limitations and the different ways in which it can be conceived (that is, scientific literacy, which should be part of the education of everyone; see page 61). With this grasp teachers can develop pedagogical content knowledge, which Shulman characterises as building 'bridges between their own understanding of the subject matter and the understanding that grows and is constructed in the minds of students' (Shulman 1991).

Teachers' subject knowledge

In the 1990s disquiet about the effects of poor teacher subject knowledge was causing some concern among policy-makers and educators. This tended to increase the pressure on schools to use specialist subject teachers in the upper years in particular. The disadvantages of separate subject teaching are that science can come to be seen as something different and separate from other subjects and possibly less relevant to the children. The opportunities to maximise learning and increase motivation by making cross-curricular links are much reduced, and the need to move teachers around creates a much more rigid timetable, with much less opportunity for children to pursue an interesting idea or complete an investigation. Yet on the other side it is clear that a teacher who is interested in and knowledgeable about a subject can inspire interest and enthusiasm in pupils.

The importance of considering the interests of the children was underlined by research that suggests what happens to children's learning experiences when teachers with little confidence in this area have to cope with science. Harlen and Holroyd (1995) found that teachers adopt the following teaching strategies:

- compensating for doing less of a low-confidence aspect of science by doing more of a higher confidence aspect, which might mean stressing the process aims in science rather than the concept development aims, and doing more biology or nature study and less physical science;

- heavy reliance on kits, prescriptive texts and pupil workcards;

- emphasis on expository teaching and underplaying discussion;

- overdependence on standard responses to content-related questions.

The issue of teachers' subject knowledge cannot be neglected when it leads to the restriction of children's learning opportunities. However, there is also evidence that many teachers know more of what is really relevant to teaching primary science than they think they know. The point here is that a great deal of worry about 'not knowing enough' results from misunderstanding of what teaching primary science involves. If it is seen as the transmission of factual information (as experienced in their own schooling) then it is understandable that teachers feel very unprepared if they do not have the information to transmit. But the main message of our earlier chapters has been that teaching science to children means enabling them to engage in scientific exploration and through this to develop their understanding. There is no short cut to this understanding through a quick fix of facts.

At the same time this is not an argument for saying that teachers do not need understanding themselves; in fact quite the opposite, for without this they are not in a good position to guide children to materials and activities that develop their understanding. But the emphasis is not on facts but on the broad principles that, as adults with much existing relevant experience to bring together, teachers very quickly grasp, and, most importantly, on the understanding of what it is to be scientific. Research has confirmed that this does happen in relation to some (although not all) of the scientific ideas that teachers are expected to help children to develop. Teachers' understanding of various scientific ideas was revealed during individual interviews with researchers in which they collaborated in arriving at a satisfactory explanation of an event or phenomenon involving the ideas. The researchers reported:

One of the striking features of the interviews was that teachers who initially claimed not to know anything or who showed misunderstanding often came to understand the ideas involved by talking about how they made sense of what they observed and by recalling earlier, half-remembered learning or related events. But this was more common for some ideas than others. Indeed some ideas were already understood and others less often understood even after working with the interviewer.

(Holroyd and Harlen 1995: 24)

Thus, although more than a short discussion is needed for some more abstract concepts, given the opportunity teachers can come to a scientific view of many things by linking up their existing experience, using their common sense. Opportunity is the key point here. Steps have been taken to ensure that those entering the profession have a sound knowledge of science and of how to teach it. In England, the Teacher Training Agency has set out a national curriculum for initial teacher training in primary science (TTA 2001). For those already in service, schools are being encouraged to provide support for class teachers by appointing subject leaders to carry out the tasks indicated earlier (page 271). Support from outside the school is increasingly being offered through ICT, using the Internet or interactive CD-ROMs (see page 228).

These efforts are designed to enable primary teachers to continue to teach science to their own classes rather than separate it from other work by using specialist teachers. As the debate continues schools need to make decisions about how to support staff in developing their science knowledge and understanding and in how to deploy staff. The subject leader is crucial here in helping to identify the strengths and weaknesses of teachers and to develop staff while making maximum use of their expertise. One way of doing this and then providing the support that is needed is described in Box 25.2.

| Box 25.2 | The subject leader as subject knowledge support |

Caroline has a BEd science degree, she teaches seven- to eight-year-olds and has been, science coordinator for three years. There is no specialist science teaching in this two-form entry school, which is housed in a new building. The classrooms for each year group are semi open plan and linked by a shared work area. The year teachers develop their medium- and short-term plans together, with the member of the pair who is most confident in a subject taking the lead.

The school's long-term plan is based on, but is not the same as, the QCA scheme of work. Each section of the plan is supplemented by a series of notes developed over the years by Caroline. The notes focus on subject knowledge, with advice on additional sources, websites and books. Each year she makes a note of questions teachers ask her and the research she has done in order to answer the questions. In developing the long-term plan for the following year she reviews her file of notes and ideas and uses this to inform the development of the next plan. In this way she has built up a file of useful supplementary information and ideas for teachers that is organised in units according to the school plan. Teachers can then use this in their medium- and short-term planning.

The subject leader as resources manager

One of the roles that subject leaders have always recognised as important is that of resource manager. Primary science is demanding of resources. In Chapter 20 we discuss the issue of resources in some detail. However, it is important to note that the term resources can cover a multitude of things: practical equipment, storage space, the time to carry out science activities and the knowledgeable teachers to support it, the information technology, books and posters that can enhance subject teaching, as well as visitors to the school and places for the school to visit. How each of these is deployed depends on a great many decisions. Will teachers have their own resources or share them? Will there be specialist science teaching or not? What should any allocated money be spent on?

Time and timetabling

The timetabling of science activities is an issue confounded by topic work, the use or otherwise of subject specialist teachers and the setting of pupils for different subjects. Where broadly based topic work is the predominant way of working, the timetable usually allows this to take place for extended periods of time, interrupted only by the essential scheduling of activities for which space, staff or equipment have to be shared among all the classes. Thus there is time for children to carry out investigations that would not fit into small time slots. In theory this could still be the case when the school organises the curriculum on a subject basis, with the time for each area designated. However, in this case there is a greater likelihood of time being chopped up into portions that restrict opportunities for children to try things out, discuss them, try other ideas while things are fresh in their minds and so derive maximum learning from their activities.

Although the time to be spent on science is not prescribed, the general under-standing is that it should be at least one-tenth of lesson time for children aged eight to eleven or twelve and a little less for younger children. To make this the case means doubling the time provision that was the norm before the introduction of the National Curriculum. In Scotland the recommendation is that 'the minimum allocation of time for Environmental Studies (including science) is 25 per cent' (SOED 1993: 77), while a research study (McPake et al. 1999) found schools were spending about half that time on environmental studies in total. Although the quality of children's experience is clearly important to their learning, the quantity of learning time is also relevant. Science is often squeezed out in the implemention of planned activities for several reasons, including teachers' lack of confidence in teaching science or, as discussed in Chapter 19, the pressure to cover content knowledge needed for passing tests. A further factor is the special emphasis given to literacy and numeracy, noted in Murphy et al. (2000), and illustrated in the words of a teacher of seven- to eight-year-olds:

If I had science in the morning, pre literacy and numeracy strategies, I could start and let it run. I would have other topic work to feed in for children who had completed a task and I could keep working right down to the slowest. But now I've got to cut off. I find that very frustrating. The children find it frustrating.

It is clear that the precious resource, time, is one that the science subject leader needs to secure and, through negotiation, make the best use of.

The subject leader as monitor

The subject leader needs to know how science is developing in school. How satisfactory are the resources? Are they appropriate to our current needs? Is the intended curriculum being covered? Is the quality of learning and teaching being maintained and improving? The subject leader role in this respect has expanded dramatically over recent years. The subject leader should be given extra non-contact time to spend monitoring the curriculum, including observing other teachers teaching science. In addition, it is helpful to ask teachers to monitor their own science teaching, perhaps over a week, possibly using the criteria given on pp. 49–50 to help to structure teachers' reflections. Insights from these activities can then be used to support the development of robust discussions among staff about the best way to improve. Newton and Newton (1998) provide a model for monitoring and evaluating teaching and learning in science that is based on asking three questions: What do we want the children to learn? How do we want them to learn? How well do they learn? (see Figure 25.1).

In recent years the emphasis on raising standards (how well?), which has come to mean increasing scores of pupils on national tests, has rather overshadowed other elements of monitoring and evaluation. Children need to learn well what is worth learning. Thus, keeping the curriculum, how it is taught and what is taught in mind is a crucial part of ensuring that children develop positive attitudes to science, appropriate scientific attitudes and useful understanding of the nature of science. Subject leaders have a responsibility to nurture this debate and development.

The subject leader as staff developer

Subject leaders are often asked to provide support for classroom assistants, student teachers and newly qualified teachers. However, this tutor role should not stop there. All teachers in school should feel comfortable enough to ask for help when they feel they need it. No matter how experienced, we all need to keep updated, and to have the refreshment of learning new things. The science subject leader must not only monitor and evaluate the curriculum but also address weaknesses. Staff training in teaching methods, approaches to assessment and the integration of ICT in planning can be provided through regular after-school staff development sessions, through staff development days with outside trainers and through formal and informal courses out of school. In addition, a wider range of approaches to school development are now being adopted such as networked learning communities (groups of schools working together) and collaborative

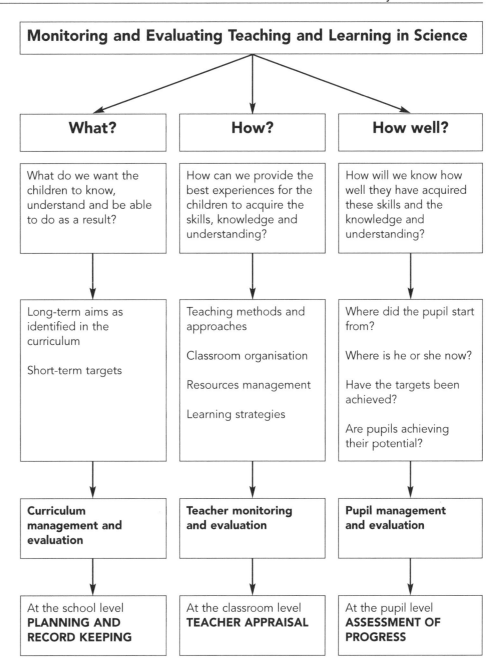

Figure 25.1 Model for monitoring and evaluating teaching and learning in science

research projects among staff in school, sometimes with staff from local higher education institutions. It is part of the job of the subject leader or coordinator to keep on top of his or her own professional development and to analyse the needs of colleagues so that their professional development requirements can be met.

Summary

■ The science subject leader role is a complex one designed to ensure that the quality of science learning in school is as high as possible.

■ The subject leader needs to meet exacting standards to ensure a strategic direction in science and consistently high quality learning and teaching, to support and lead other staff and to develop science in the school.

■ The coordinator needs to be a leader, advisor, resource manager, curriculum monitor and facilitator of teacher development.

■ It is the responsibility of the subject leader to keep up to date and refreshed in terms of teaching and to ensure that colleagues are also supported in their professional development.

References

American Association for Advancement of Science (1993) *Benchmarks for Scientific Literacy*. New York: Oxford University Press.

American Association for Advancement of Science (1989) *Science for All Americans. A Project 2061 Report on Literacy Goals in Science, Mathematics and Technology*. Washington, DC: AAAS.

Aldrich, F. and Sheppard, L. (2000) Graphicacy: the fourth 'R'? *Primary Science Review*, **64**, 8–11.

Assessment Reform Group (2002) *Testing, Motivation and Learning*. Cambridge: Faculty of Education.

Association for Science Education (1994) *Safety in School Science for Primary Schools*. Hatfield: ASE.

Association for Science Education (1998) *Primary Science*, Summer.

Association for Science Education (2001) *Be Safe*, 3rd edn. Hatfield: ASE.

Association for Science Education (2002a) *Be Safe! INSET Pack*, 2nd edn. Hatfield: ASE.

Association for Science Education (2002b) *Science Year Primary CD-ROM*. Hatfield: ASE.

Asoko, H. and de Boo, M. (2001) *Analogies and Illustrations. Representing Ideas in Primary Science*. Hatfield: ASE.

Ball, S. (2003) ICT that works. *Primary Science Review*, **76**, 11–13.

Barker, S. and Buckle, S. (2002) Bringing birds into the classroom. *Primary Science Review*, **75**, 8–10.

Barr, K. (2003) Managing science and technology. *Primary Science Review*, **79**, 4–6.

Barnes, D. (1976) *From Communication to Curriculum*. Harmondsworth: Penguin.

Black, P., Harrison, C., Lee, C., Marshall, B. and Wiliam, D. (2002) *Working inside the Black Box*. London: King's College London.

Black, P., Harrison, C., Lee, C., Marshall, B. and Wiliam, D. (2003) *Assessment for Learning: Putting it into Practice*. Maidenhead: Open University Press.

Black, P. (1993) Formative and summative assessment by teachers. *Studies in Science Education*, **21**, 49–97.

Black, P. and Wiliam, D. (1998a) Assessment and classroom learning. *Assessment in Education*, 5(1) 7–74.

Black, P. and Wiliam, D. (1998b) *Inside the Black Box*. London: School of Education, King's College London.

Bober, M. (1998) Online delivery: Is meaningful evaluation possible? *Distance Education Report*, 2(11) 2–7.

Boctor, S. and Rowell, P. (2004) Why do bees sting? Reflecting on talk in science lessons. *Primary Science Review*, 82, 15–17.

Braund, M. (2004) Bridging work in science: what's in it for primary schools? *Primary Science Review*, 82, 24–7.

Braund, M. and Driver, M. (2002) Moving to the big school: what do pupils think about science practical work pre- and post-transfer? Paper presented at the Annual Conference of the British Educational Research Association, University of Exeter, 12–14 September.

Budd-Rowe, M. (1974) Relation of wait-time and rewards to the development of language, logic and fate control: part II, *Journal of Research in Science Teaching*, 11(4), 291–308.

Butler, R. (1987) Task-involving and egoinvolving properties of evaluation: effects of different feedback conditions on motivational perceptions. *Journal of Educational Psychology*, 79(4), 474–82.

Burrows, P. (2003) Managing health and safety in primary science. *Primary Science Review*, 79, 18–20.

Butler, R. (1998) Enhancing and undermining intrinsic motivation: the effects of task-involving and ego-involving evaluation on interest and performance. *British Journal of Educational Psychology*, 58, 1–14.

Coates, D. and Eyre, D. (1999) Supporting highly able scientists at Key Stage 1. *Primary Science Review*, 60, 11–13.

Clarke, S. (1998) *Targeting Assessment in the Primary Classroom*. London: Hodder and Stoughton.

Conner, C. (1991) *Assessment and Testing in the Primary School*. Brighton: Falmer Press.

DES (1989) *Aspects of Primary Education: The Teaching and Learning of Science*. London: HMSO.

DES/WO (1983) *Science at Age 11: APU Science Report for Teachers No 1*. London: DES and Welsh Office.

DES/WO (1989) *A Report. National Curriculum Task Group on Assessment and Testing*. London: DES and Welsh Office.

DfEE (1998) *Science Teacher's Guide: A Scheme of Work for Key Stages 1 and 2*. London: DfEE.

DfEE (1999) *The National Curriculum. Handbook for Primary Schools*. London: DfEE.

DfEE/QCA (2000) *Curriculum Guidance for the Foundation Stage*. London: DfEE.

DFES (2003) *Excellence and Enjoyment: A Strategy for Primary Schools*. London: DFES (available at www.dfes.gov.uk/primarydocument).

Edmonds, J. (2002) Inclusive science: supporting the EAL child. *Primary Science Review*, 74, 4–6.

Elstgeest, J. (2001) The right question at the right time. In W. Harlen, (ed.), *Primary Science: Taking the Plunge*, 2nd edn Portsmouth, NH: Heinemann.

Evans, N. (2001) Thoughts on assessment and marking. *Primary Science Review*, **68**, 24–6.

Fairbrother, R. (1995) Pupils as learners. In R. Fairbrother, R. *et al.* (eds), *Teachers Assessing Pupils*. Hatfield: ASE.

Feasey, R. (1998) Scientific investigations in context. In R. Sherrington, (ed.), *ASE Guide to Primary Science Education*. Hatfield: ASE/Stanley Thornes.

Feasey, R. (1999) *Primary Science and Literacy*. Hatfield: ASE.

Feasey, R. (2003) Creative futures. *Primary Science Review*, **78**, 21–3.

Feasey, R. and Gallear, R. (2000) *Primary Science and Numeracy*. Hatfield: ASE.

Feasey, R. and Gallear, R. (2002) *Primary Science and Information and Communication Technology*. Hatfield: ASE.

Fletcher, L. (2000) Co-ordinating Subjects in the primary School: perceptions of subject leaders, their implementation of the role and the influence of external factors. PhD thesis, University of Liverpool.

Galton, M. (2002) Continuity and progression in science teaching at Key Stage 1 and 2. *Cambridge Journal of Education*, **32**(2), 249–66.

Galton, M., Gray, J. and Ruddock, J. (2003) *Transfer and Transitions in the Middle Years of Schooling (7–14): Continuities and Discontinuities in Learning*. DfES. Research Report RR443. London: DfES.

Gipps, C. (1994) *Beyond Testing? Towards a Theory of Educational Assessment*. Lewes: Falmer Press.

Goldsworthy, A. (1998) Learning to investigate. In R. Sherrington, (ed.), *ASE Guide to Primary Science Education*. Hatfield: ASE.

Goldsworthy, A. (2000) *Targeted Learning: Using Classroom Assessment for Learning*. Hatfield: ASE.

Goldsworthy, A., Watson, R. and Wood-Robinson, V. (2000) *Investigations: Developing Understanding*. Hatfield: ASE.

Guichard, J (1995) Designing tools to develop conceptions of learners, *International Journal of Science Education*, **17**(1), 243–53.

Harlen, W. (1999) *Effective Teaching of Science: A Review of Research*. Edinburgh: Scottish Council for Research in Education.

Harlen, W. (2000) *Teaching, Learning and Assessing Science 5–12, 3rd edn*. London: Paul Chapman Publishing.

Harlen, W. (ed.) (2001) *Primary Science: Taking the Plunge*, 2nd edn. Portsmouth, NH: Heinemann.

Harlen, W. and Altobello, C. (2003) *An Investigation of Try Science Studied On-line and Face-to-Face*. Cambridge, MA: TERC.

Harlen, W. *et al.* (1990) *Progress in Primary Science*. London: Routledge.

Harlen, W. and Deakin Crick, R. (2003) Testing and motivation for learning. *Assessment in Education*, **10**(2) 169–208.

Harlen, W. and Doubler, S. (2004) Can Teachers learn through enquiry on-line? Studying for professional development in science delivered on-line and on-campus. *International Journal of Science Education*, **26**(1), 1–21.

Harlen, W., Darwin, A. and Murphy, M. (1977) *Match and Mismatch: Raising Questions*. Edinburgh: Oliver & Boyd.

Harlen, W. and Holroyd, C. (1995) *Primary Teachers' Understanding of Concepts in Science and Technology*. Interchange No. 35. Edinburgh: SOED.

Harlen, W., Macro, C., Reed, K. and Schilling, M. (2003) *Making Progress in Primary Science Study Book*. London: RoutledgeFalmer.

Harrison, C., Coomber, C., Fischer, T., Haw, K., Lewin, K., Lunzer, E., McFarlane, A., Mavers, D., Scrimshaw., P., Somekh, B. and Watling, R. (2002) *Impact2: The Impact of Communication Technologies on Pupils Learning and Attainment*. A Report to the DES. Coventry: BECTA/HMSO (www.org.becta.uk/research/ Impact2).

Hart, G. (2003) Quality ICT resources to enhance science teaching. *Primary Science Review*, **76**, 6–8.

Hawkey, R. (1999) 'Exploring and investigating the natural world: Sc1 on line'. *Primary Science Review*, **60**, 4–6.

Hawking, S. W. (1988) *A Brief History of Time*. London: Bantam Press.

Hemsley, K. (1994) Using information technology in science. *Questions Magazine*, **6**(5) (available at www.connect.demon.co.uk/Questions).

Heslop, N. (2002) Science passport: a template for KS2/3 bridging projects. *Primary Science Review*, **73**, 24–6.

Hodson, D. (1993) Re-thinking old ways: towards a more critical approach to practical work in school science. *Studies in Science Education*, **22**, 85–142.

Hodson, D. (1998) *Teaching and Learning Science*. Buckingham: Open University Press.

Hollins, M. and Whitby, V. (2001) *Progression in Primary Science: A Guide to the Nature and Practice of Science in Key Stages 1 and 2*, 2nd edn. London: David Fulton.

Holroyd, C. and Harlen, W. (1995) Teachers' understanding of science: a cause for concern?', *Primary Science Review*, **39**, 23–5.

Howe, C. (1990) Grouping children for effective learning in science. *Primary Science Review*, **13**, 26–7.

Howe, A. (2004) Science is creative. *Primary Science Review*, **81**, 14–16.

Howe, C.J., Rodgers, C. and Tolmic, A. (1990) 'Physics in the Primary School: Peer interaction and the understanding of floating and sluicing'. European Journal of Psychology of Education, 4, 459–75.

Howe, C. J., Rodgers, C. and Tolmic, A. (1992) The acquisition of conceptual understanding of science in primary school children: group interaction and the understanding of motion down an incline. *British Journal of Developmental Psychology*, **10**, 113–30.

Isaacs, S. (1930) *Intellectual Growth of Young Children*. London: Routledge and Kegan Paul.

Jabin, Z. and Smith, R. (1994) Using analogies of electric flow in circuits to improve understanding. *Primary Science Review*, 35, 23–6.

Jannikos, M. (1995) Are the stereotyped views of scientists being brought into the 90s? *Primary Science Review*, **37**, 27–9.

Jarvis, T. and Pell, A. (2002) Changes in primary boys' and girls' attitudes to school and science during a two-year science in-service programme. *Curriculum Journal*, **13**(1), 43–69.

Jelly, S. J. (2001) Helping children to raise questions – and answering them. In W. Harlen, (ed.), *Primary Science: Taking the Plunge*, 2nd edn. Portsmouth, NH: Heinemann.

Jurd, E. (2004) Are children in my class thinking while taking part in science activities? *Primary Science Review*, **81**, 12–14.

Keogh, B. and Naylor, S. (1996) *Scientists and Primary Schools*. Sandbach: Milgate House Publishing.

Keogh, B. and Naylor, S. (1998) Teaching and learning science using Concept Cartoons. *Primary Science Review*, **51**, 14–16.

Keogh, B. and Naylor, S. (2004) Children's ideas, children's feeling. *Primary Science Review*, **82**, 18–20.

Kluger, A. N. and DeNisi, A. (1996) The effects of feedback interventions on performance: a historical review, a meta-analyis, and a preliminary intervention theory. *Psychological Bulletin*, **119**, 254–84.

Lawrence, E. (ed.) (1960) *Approaches to Science in the Primary School*. London: Educational Supply Association

Layton, D. (1990) Inarticulate Science. Occasional paper no. 17. Liverpool: Department of Education, University of Liverpool.

Layton, D. (1993) *Technology's Challenge to Science Education*. Buckingham: Open University Press.

Lias, S. and Thomas, C. (2003) Using digital photographs to improve learning in science. *Primary Science Review*, **76**, 17–19.

McFall, D. and Macro, C. (2004) Creativity and science in the nursery. *Primary Science Review*, **81**, 7–10.

McFarlane, A. and Sakellariou, S. (2002) The role of ICT in science education. *Cambridge Journal of Education*, **32**(2), 219–32.

McMahon, K. and Davies, D. (2003) Building bridges between primary and secondary science for children and teachers. *Primary Science Review*, **80**, 7–9.

McMeniman, M. (1989) Motivation to learn. In P. Langford (ed.), *Educational Psychology*: An Australian Perspective. Harlow: Longman.

McPake, J., Harlen, W., Powney, J. and Davidson, J. (1999) *Teachers' and Pupils' Days in the Primary Classroom*. Edinburgh: SCRE.

Millar, R. and Osborne, J. (1998) *Beyond 2000, Science Education for the Future*. London: King's College London, School of Education.

Miller, R. and Luben, F. (1996) Investigative work in science: the role of prior expectations and evidence in shaping conclusions. *Education, 3-13*, **24**(1), 28–34.

Monk, M. and Osborne, J. (eds) (2000) *Good Practice in Science Teaching: What Research Has to Say*. Buckingham: Open University Press.

Murphy, C. (2003) *Literature Review in Primary Science and ICT: A Report for NESTA Futurelab* (www.nestafurturelab.org/research/reviews/psi01.htm).

Murphy, C. and Beggs, J. (2001) Pupils' attitudes, perceptions and understanding of primary science: comparisons between Northern Irish and English schools. Paper presented at the annual conference of BERA University of Leeds September 13–15. (available at http://www.leeds.ac.uk/educol/)

Murphy, C. and Beggs, J. (2003) Children's perceptions of school science. *School Science Review*, **84**(308), 109–16.

Murphy, P., Davidson, M., Qualter, A., Simon, S. and Watt, D. (2000) *Effective Practice in Primary Science*. A report of an exploratory study funded by the Nuffield Curriculum Projects Centre.

NAIGS/ASE (1997) *ASE Primary Self-Review Document*. Hatfield: Association for Science Education.

National Advisory Committee on Creative and Cultural Education (1999) *All Our Futures: Creativity, Culture and Education* (available from www.artscampaigne.org.uk/campaigns/ education/report.html).

Naylor, S. and Keogh, B. (2000) *Concept Cartoons in Science Education*. Sandbach: Millgate House.

Naylor, S. and Keogh, B. (2003) Concept Cartoons in Science Education (CD-ROM). Sandbach: Millgate House.

New Standards (1997) *Performance Standards. Volume 1: Elementary School, English, Language Arts, Mathematics, Science, Applied Learning*. Pittsburgh, PA: National Centre on Education and the Economy.

Newton, L. and Newton, D. P (1998) *Coordinating Science Across the Primary School*. London: Falmer.

Newton, L., Newton, D. P., Blake, A. and Brown, K. (2002) Do primary school science books for children show a concern for explanatory understanding? *Research in Science and Technological Education*, **20**(2), 228–39.

Newton, L. and Rogers, L. (2001) *Teaching Science with ICT*. London: Continuum.

Nimmons, F. (2003a) Learning to lead the science curriculum. *Primary Science Review*, **79**,16–17.

Nimmons, F. (2003b) Tracking pupils' progress. *Primary Science Review*, **80**, 13–15.

OECD (2003) *The PISA 2003 Assessment Framework*. Paris: OECD.

Ofsted (1993) *Handbook for the Inspection of Schools*. London: HMSO.

Ofsted (1998) *Standards in Primary Science*. London: HMSO.

Ofsted (2004) *Ofsted Science Subject Reports 2002/3. Science in the Primary School*. London: DfEE

Osborne, R. J and Freyberg, P. (1985) *Learning in Science: The Implications of 'Children's Science'*. Auckland: Heinemann.

Osborne J. (2004) Clumsy tests dull passion for science. Times Educational Supplement, 2 January.

Parliamentary Office of Science and Technology (2003) Primary science. *Postnote*, 202.

Paterson, V. (1987) What might be learnt from children's writing in primary science? *Primary Science Review*, **4**, 17–20.

Peacock, A. and Weedon, H. (2002) Children working with text in science: disparities with 'literacy hour' practice. *Research in Science and Technological Education*, **20**(2), 185–97.

Peacock, G. (1999) Continuity and progression between Key Stages in science. Paper presented at the BERA Annual Conference. University of Sussex, Brighton, September (available at www.leeds.ac.uk/educol).

Piaget, J. (1929) *The Child's Construction of the World*. London: Routledge and Kegan Paul.

Piaget, J. (1955) *The Child's Construction of Reality*. London: Routledge and Kegan Paul.

Piaget, J. (1956) *The Child's Construction of Space*. London: Routledge and Kegan Paul.

Plowman, L., Leakey, A. and Harlen, W. (2000) *Using ICT to Support Teachers in Primary Schools: An Evaluation of the Science Online Support Network (SOLSN)*. SCRE Research Report 97. Edinburgh: Scottish Council for Research in Education (http://www.scre.ac.uk/resreport/rr97).

Poole, P. (2000) Information and communication technology in science education: a long gestation. In J. Sears and P. Sorensen (eds), *Issues in Science Teaching*. London: Falmer.

Popper, K. (1988) Science: conjectures and refutations. In E. D. Klemke, R. Hoblinger and A. D. Kline (eds), *Introductory Reading in the Philosophy of Science*. New York: Prometheus Books.

QCA (2004) *Key Stage 2, Years 3 to 6 Assessment and reporting Arrangements 2004*. London: Qualifications and Curriculum Authority.

Qualter, A. (1996) *Differentiated Primary Science*. Buckingham: Open University Press.

Ritchie, R. (1998) From Science coordinator to Science subject leader ' in Sherrington, R. (ed.) (1998) *ASE Guide to Primary Science Education*. Hatfield: ASE

Robertson, A. (2004) Let's think! Two years on! *Primary Science Review*, **82**, 4–7.

Roe, A. (1970) A psychologist examines sixty-four eminent scientists. In P. E. Vernon (ed.), *Creativity*. Harmondsworth: Penguin (1st published 1959).

Russell, T. and Harlen, W. (1990) *Assessing Science in the Primary Classroom: Practical Tasks*. London: Paul Chapman Publishing.

Russell, T., Longden, K. and McGuigan, L. (1991) Primary SPACE Project Report: Materials. Liverpool: Liverpool University Press.

Russell, T. and Watt, D. (1990) *Primary SPACE Project Report: Growth*. Liverpool: Liverpool University Press.

SCAA (1995) *Exemplification of Standards*. London: SCAA.

Schilling, M., Hargreaves, L., Harlen, W. and Russell, T. (1990) *Assessing Schools in the Primary Classroom: Written Tasks*. London: Paul Chapman Publishing.

Scottish CCC (1996) *Science Education in Scottish Schools: Looking to the Future*. Dundee: Scottish CCC.

Scottish Executive Education Department (1999) *Improving Science Education*

5–14. Edinburgh: SEED.

Scottish Office Education Department (1993) *The Structure and Balance of the Curriculum 5–14*. Edinburgh: SOED.

Scottish Office Education and Industry Department (1996) *How Good is our School? Self-evaluation using Performance Indicators*. Edinburgh: SOEID Audit Unit.

Serret, N. (2004) Leaping into the unknown: developing thinking in the primary science classroom. *Primary Science Review*, **82**, 8–11.

Shon, D. (1993) *The Reflective Practitioner: How Professionals Think in Action*. New York: Basic Books

Shulman, L. S. (1987) Knowledge and teaching: foundations of the new reform. *Harvard Educational Review*, **7**, 1–22.

Shulman, L. S. (1991) Pedagogical ways of knowing. In *Improving the Quality of the Teaching Profession. International Yearbook on Teacher Education, 1990*. Singapore: ICET.

Siraj-Blatchford, I., Sylva, K., Muttock, S., Gilden, R. and Bell, D. (2002) *Researching Effective Pedagogy in the Early Years*. DfES Report RR356 London: DfES.

Skinner, B. F. (1974) *About Behaviourism*. New York: Alfred A. Knopf.

SPACE (Science Processes and Concepts Exploration) Research Reports. *Evaporation and Condensation* (1990), *Growth* (1990a), *Light* (1990b), *Sound* (1990c), *Electricity* (1991a), *Materials* (1991b), *Processes of Life* (1992a), *Rocks, Soil and Weather* (1992b). Liverpool University Press.

Sutton, N. (2001) The literacy hour and science: towards a clearer picture. *Primary Science Review*, **69**, 28–9.

Teacher Training Agency (1998) *National Standards for Subject Leaders*. London: Teacher Training Agency.

Teacher Training Agency (2001) *Qualifying to Teach: Professional Standards for Qualified Teacher Status and Requirements for Initial Teacher Training*. London: TTA. (available at http://www.tta.gov.uk/php/read.php?sectionid=108).

Thornton, L. and Brunton, P. (2003) All about the Reggio approach. *Nursery World*, January 15.

Vygotsky, L. S. (1962) *Thought and Language*. Cambridge, MA: MIT Press.

Wardle, C. (2000) Literacy links to light and dark. *Primary Science Review*, **64**, 26–7.

Warwick, P. and McFarlane, A. (1995) IT in primary investigations. *Primary Science Review*, **36**, 26–7.

Watt, D. and Russell, T. (1990) *Primary SPACE Project Report: Sound*. Liverpool: Liverpool University Press.

Wenham, M. (1993) The nature and role of hypotheses in school science investigations. *International Journal of Science Education*, **15**(3), 231–40.

Willis, J. (1999) *National Curriculum Science: Walls*. Hatfield: ASE.

Woodford, G. (2000) Enriching food and farming with ICT. *Primary Science*, **62**, 23–4.

Index